D0064787

BILLY THE KID

MICHAEL WALLIS

BILLY THE KID

THE ENDLESS RIDE

W. W. NORTON & COMPANY

NEW YORK • LONDON

Frontispiece: Cooke's Canyon, New Mexico Territory, The Bob Boze Bell Collection. Pages xviii–xix: Billy the Kid Country, created by Gus Walker, *True West* mapinator.

For information about permission to reproduce selections from this book, write to Permissions, W. W. Norton & Company, Inc., 500 Fifth Avenue, New York, NY 10110

Manufacturing by The Haddon Craftsmen, Inc.
Book design by Judy Stagnitto Abbate
Production manager: Anna Oler

Library of Congress Cataloging-in-Publication Data

Wallis, Michael, 1945–
Billy the Kid : the endless ride / Michael Wallis.—1st ed
p. cm.
Includes bibliographical references and index.
ISBN-13: 978-0-393-06068-3 (hardcover)
ISBN-10: 0-393-06068-3 (hardcover)
1. Billy, the Kid. 2. Billy, the Kid—Pictorial works. 3. Outlaws—Southwest, New—Biography.
4. Southwest, New—Biography. 5. Frontier and pioneer life—Southwest, New. I. Title.
F786.B54W35 2007
364.15'52092—dc22
[B]   2006101364

W. W. Norton & Company, Inc.
500 Fifth Avenue, New York, N.Y. 10110
www.wwnorton.com

W. W. Norton & Company Ltd.
Castle House, 75/76 Wells Street, W1T 3QT

1 2 3 4 5 6 7 8 9 0

FOR SUZANNE, MY TRUE LOVE

AND

FOR JOHN, WHO FOUND ME

CONTENTS

PREFACE

THAT A YOUNG man known as Billy the Kid ever existed is an indisputable fact. His name is about all that anyone can ever agree upon when it comes to the telling of his story. It was not a name he sought for himself but one that was ascribed to him late in the final year of his brief twenty-one-year life by newspaper reporters and dime novelists. It also was the name that stuck. What were, in fact, his true given name and surname remain a mystery, like so much else about Billy.

What is astonishing for any potential biographer is to realize that there is no agreement about Billy's parentage and ancestry, his place of birth, and even the date and place of his death. No one can say with certainty when he came into this world, for his actual birth date remains open to debate. Although most historians concur that he was shot and killed by Pat Garrett in New Mexico Territory on July 14, 1881, there have always been those who cannot agree on the facts of his demise.

Since his death, which occurred just before President James Garfield succumbed to gunshot wounds inflicted by an assassin, hundreds of works have been written about Billy the Kid. Some are well researched and reliable, but far more are historically exaggerated or embroidered with sensational lies. This book, then, is an attempt to present a clear, concise, and truthful story of a young man who became a legend in his time. It is the story of Billy the Kid, one of the series of colorful bandits and outlaws, including Butch Cassidy and the Sundance Kid, Jesse James, and even Pancho Villa, who each in his own peculiar way captured the American imagination.

PERSONAL INTRODUCTION

DEEP IN NEW MEXICO's Billy the Kid country, my car broke down on Christmas Eve 1969. I left it on the shoulder of the highway and hitched a ride in a battle-worn pickup to Socorro, where I waited outside a garage while two diligent mechanics headed out to tow my car into town and fix it.

As I sat on a bench and sipped a cup of whiskey-laced thermos coffee, I spied an old man in the night shadows. He was bowlegged and scarred, with gunmetal hair that hung to his shoulders. He walked over, sat down next to me, and began talking just like we were everyday pals. He spoke about dust storms and blizzards, all "acts of God," but then he slipped into a reverie of what he knew best—those wild old days when he had been young and on the prowl.

The old man told me firsthand about range wars and shootings and jail breaks. Then he talked about Billy the Kid. He said it was hard to separate legend from truth when it came to the young man who died at the raw young age of twenty-one. "I knew the Kid," the old man soberly confided. "I knew the Kid as well as I knew my own brother."

Even then I knew that eighty-eight years had passed since Billy, as the history books said, died at Sheriff Pat Garrett's hand. But I chose not to challenge the claim of the wizened warhorse whose piercing eyes possessed a glint of truth. Maybe it was just the circumstances: the night before Christmas, the luminous desert moon, and just enough Jack Daniel's to tease my imagination.

Nine years later, as a reporter in Austin, I met Jarvis Garrett, the son of the legendary lawman who killed the Kid. Jarvis was only three years old in 1908, when his father himself was ambushed and shot dead while urinating alongside a road near Las Cruces, New Mexico, twenty-seven years after Billy the Kid's death. Thin and wiry, Jarvis said he had a faint memory of his father's wake. But with almost a judge's certainty, he told me that most of the books and movies about his father and Billy the Kid were worthless. "There are so many legends, so many falsehoods," Garrett said. "Writers let their imaginations work overtime." Then he let me hold the .44-caliber Colt revolver his father had used to write history.

I have often thought of this single meeting with Garrett and my own casual brush with western history. I have also recalled many times that mysterious old man whose improbable recollections on a cold midnight in Socorro have inspired my curiosity and sustained my passion for decades.

I actually knew, I suspect even then, that someday I would write a book about Billy. That time has come.

It was not, however, until 1992, just after I had finished writing *Pretty Boy: The Life and Times of Charles Arthur Floyd*, that I really began contemplating a book about Billy, the precursor of Pretty Boy, who, like Billy, was branded simultaneously as either a merciless killer or as a Robin Hood of the American landscape.

While examining the multiple legends about Pretty Boy Floyd, I had become more aware that many people have never accepted the fact of the Kid's death at the hand of Pat Garrett in 1881. Enough conspiracy theorists and naysayers abound to cause authorities in New Mexico to question Billy's demise. In 2004 investigators even wanted to exhume the remains of Catherine Antrim, Billy's mother, so her DNA could be tested and compared with DNA to be taken from the body buried under the Kid's gravestone. The case remained tied up in the courts, much to the delight of New Mexico Governor Bill Richardson, who knows all too well the value of Billy as a cultural icon and draw for tourists.

In preparing for the work involved in writing a biography of a small-time rustler whose short and violent life has inspired thousands of legends, I read as many books about Billy as I could find and spoke to people who I thought could shed a different and fresher light on the late nineteenth-century outlaw. My research and reportage helped me comprehend better the complex and shadowy incidents and circumstances that all added up to and created this indelible legend.

To understand his exceptional story, we must first place him in his times. Billy lived during the boom years of the American Industrial Revolution. America was rapidly shedding its agrarian past and becoming an urban behemoth. The devastation following the Civil War, particularly in the South, produced not only profound social dislocation but also a generation of desperate men, who, because of the war, were all too familiar with guns and death, men who were separated from their families and had become alienated. Not a few of them as a result came to be regarded as western outlaws. At the same time, the nation during these years of Reconstruction began a love affair with handguns. This interesting phenomenon created a culture of violence that has thrived to this day.

During this period sensationalism gripped the journalists of the land, and what emerged were newspapers labeled the yellow press, all too eager to create a pageant of instant celebrities to satisfy the burgeoning urban reading public. As a result of this latter-day "infotainment," a nation even more corrupt and violent than the Jacksonian mobs of a previous generation materialized in newspapers across the land, from the dusty southwestern mesas to Tammany Hall in New York City. Power and wealth were more than ever the signs of success.

This Gilded Age also marked the start of a pulp fiction industry that instantly realized its biggest bestsellers were often books that perpetuated the myths of the so-called Wild West. In times of economic trouble and despair it is often common for the poor and dispossessed to venerate outlaws who steal from the rich and stand up to the establishment. It has been noted, not infrequently, that native New Mexican villagers and the Hispanic herdsmen of the American West worshiped Billy in the same way that English peasants had venerated Robin Hood. For them and others, the Kid embodied youth, nobility, humanity, romance, and tragedy. With a blazing six-gun in hand, he symbolized the transition between the old and the new.

Dozens of dime novels and unreliable nonfiction accounts, including such titles as *The Cowboy's Career*, *The Daredevil Deeds of Billy the Kid*, and *Billy the "Kid" and His Girl*, sprang up less than a year after Billy died. This publishing explosion gave rise to Pat Garrett's book *The Authentic Life of Billy the Kid, the Noted Desperado of the Southwest, Whose Deeds of Daring and Blood Made His Name a Terror in New Mexico, Arizona and Northern Mexico*, which appeared shortly after Billy's death. The title suggests the windy yarns, misconceptions, and myths that were to follow. Ghostwritten by Connecticut-born Marshall Ashmun Upson, the book was commissioned by Garrett to help clear up and burnish his image. What was written became the reality that readers bought into, and the book established Billy both as hero and antihero.

Charles Arthur Floyd, whose colorful nickname, Pretty Boy, and story were tailor-made for newspaper headlines, came of age as a criminal in the 1920s, just at the time the American public was rediscovering Billy the Kid. Billy's dramatic reappearance in the culture of the 1920s seemed spawned by the disparity between the rich and poor of the time, and additional legends were propagated by Doubleday's 1926 publication of *The Saga of Billy the Kid*, written by Walter Noble Burns, a Chicago journalist. Thin on research but strong on fable, *The Saga* presents Billy as a Robin Hood figure, a "quixotic, romantic idealist who symbolized a lost pastoral world." The book sold well in stores and once selected and anointed by the

Book-of-the-Month Club, helped to reestablish Billy's enduring celebrity. The book as much as any work of its time confirmed the romanticized youth's status as a mainstay of popular culture in the 1920s, 1930s, and beyond to this very day.

Burns's book was quickly followed by the 1930 King Vidor movie *Billy the Kid*, in which Billy was depicted as a skinny kid from New York City who became an Old West icon. Johnny Mack Brown vigorously portrayed the Kid as a frontier superhero. Then, in 1936, Miguel Antonio Otero, a former governor of New Mexico Territory and an unabashed friend and admirer of Billy the Kid, wrote and published another biography, *The Real Billy the Kid*. Otero portrayed Billy as a tragic and misunderstood hero who dared take on a lawless and corrupt establishment.

Over the years motion-picture and television producers have continued to fuel Billy's legend. They more or less adapted the persona for the times. For example, whereas in the 1920s and 1930s Billy was a saintly figure who appealed to the masses, in the 1960s and 1970s, a time of protest and cynicism, he was cast, like Bonnie and Clyde, as a satanic and dark figure. Then, by 1988, the Reagan-Bush era, Billy was again regarded sympathetically, a martyred symbol of freedom and righteousness.

Many other writers and filmmakers, among them Zane Grey, Larry McMurtry, Gore Vidal, Howard Hughes, Sam Peckinpah, and Michael Ondaatje, followed suit with their versions of the Billy the Kid story. Aaron Copland memorialized Billy by composing the music for an eponymous ballet. Such popular singers and songwriters as Woody Guthrie, Billy Joel, Bob Dylan, and Jon Bon Jovi all have sung the Kid's praises. In movies and plays, Billy's portrayers have cast him alongside such diverse real and imagined characters as Jane Russell, Jean Harlow, Dracula, and Mickey Mouse.

In many of these books and films, Billy comes off not as a crazed killer but as a victim. They are a far cry from the equally flawed and overstated newspaper stories and dime novels published in the 1880s and the early 1900s that painted him as a bloodthirsty man-killer, a homicidal maniac, and a "young demon urged by a spirit hideous as hell." There has never been much middle ground when it comes to judging Billy the Kid, just black and white with scant gray to calm the palette.

Why and how Billy the Kid became such a cultural icon is as fascinating a story as the biography you are about to read. Indeed, we can understand his life only by considering the political context in which he played out his criminality. His powerful supporters and detractors, and the larger social audience that was open to the representation of criminal as hero, must be appreciated as part of a larger social pattern.

Billy continues to make news and, much like Elvis Presley, earns millions of dollars in memorabilia and collectibles for the tourist industry and the international western collectibles market. In many ways the mysterious young man's story may be as relevant today as it ever has been.

BILLY THE KID COUNTRY

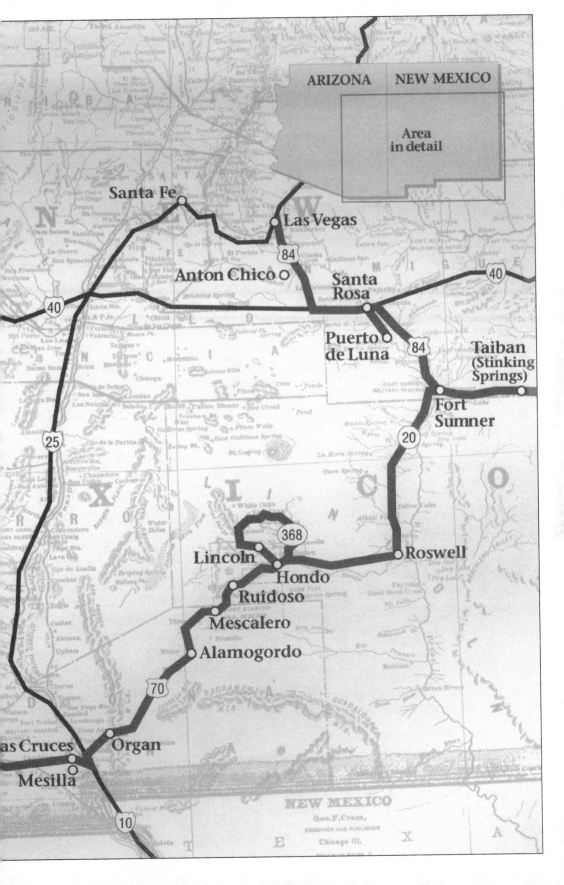

BILLY THE KID

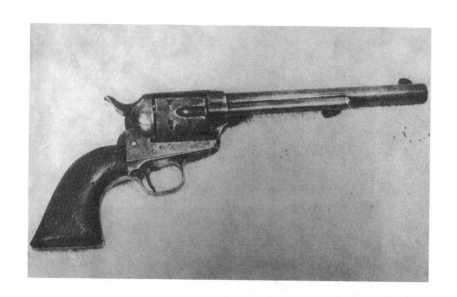

The gun that killed the Kid

THE ROBERT G. McCUBBIN COLLECTION

PROLOGUE

¿QUIÉN ES?

Wednesday, July 14, 1881, old Fort Stanton, New Mexico Territory

IT WAS FAST coming up on midnight, the witching hour. A full-blown moon worthy of a pack of wolves had emerged through the summer stars and would soon reach its highest elevation.

The Indians called this July full moon a buck moon since it coincided with the time when new antlers pushed out from the foreheads of buck deer. Other Indians, however, said it was a full thunder moon, because afternoon thunderstorms over the high desert plains were frequent at this time of year.

Folklore had it that full-moon nights brought out the worst in people and made for out-of-the-ordinary occurrences. Some folks reasoned that since a human body contained so much water, the moon surely could work its magic pull on people just as it did on the tides of the sea.

What is not folklore is that three armed men hunkered in the shadows of a big adobe house that had once lodged officer soldiers. Located on the Pecos River, this New Mexico Territory lodging had served as a government prison camp for tribal people forced from their homeland. But these men gave no thought to either lunar myths or Navajo and Apache ghosts lingering in their midst. This trio was man-hunting and paid no mind to anything but the business at hand. They listened to the liquid rustle of the cottonwood leaves down along the river, and they heard some muffled words in Spanish from dark figures sitting out in the nearby peach orchard bathed in summer moonlight.

In only minutes the end would come for the young prey the hunters sought. Billy would emerge before them through the shadows, fumbling with his trouser buttons, padding on stocking feet on his way to get some grub. A freshly butchered yearling was hanging from the portal, and he was carrying a kitchen knife to slice off some meat for a late-evening meal.

When two of the armed men first spotted him, he seemed a lunar mirage. But as he kept moving toward them, the two silhouettes on the porch stirred and spoke. The young man was startled. "*¿Quién es?* [Who is it?]" he hissed at them. He asked again, then a third time.

He backed away into the darkness and through a familiar door. The third manhunter had already gone inside and was sitting on the bed of the young man's friend, Pete Maxwell. "*¿Pedro, quiénes son esos hombres afuera?* [Peter, who are those men outside?]" Billy asked.

Then he sensed the presence of the other man in the room.

"*¿Quién es?*" he asked, and then in English: "Who is it?"

The only reply was the sudden explosion of a single-action .44 Colt pistol. It was quickly followed by a second blast.

The young man, best known as Billy the Kid, crashed to the floor. He gurgled his final breath and lay dead in the dark shadows of the adobe dwelling. He died hungry and without his boots on. He died not knowing who had taken his life.

His last spoken words had formed the question *¿Quién es?* How fitting that there was no response. There were even then so many unanswered questions about the young man who died in a shroud of darkness beneath a New Mexico moon full enough to burst.

Harper's *woodcut of New York City's Fourth Ward, 1860s*

inset: Catherine McCarty and infant son

ONE

ONCE UPON A TIME

*Few American lives have more successfully resisted research than
that of Billy the Kid.*[1]

•

—FREDERICK NOLAN

JUST BEFORE THE Civil War tore America asunder, a young boy
named Henry McCarty was born. During his short life he acquired other
monikers, including Henry Antrim, the Kid, Kid Antrim, the Wandering Kid,
William H. Bonney, Billy Bonney, and El Chivato. Just months before his death he
finally became known as Billy *the* Kid, really more of a title than a name and one
that would last for eternity.

As with other ordinary people from middling immigrant stock born in the
United States in the nineteenth century, few reliable records have been found confirming McCarty's origin. Conscientious historians and researchers have spent
their lives rummaging through legal documents, historical archives, period newspapers, marriage and baptismal registers, census records, city directories, and
every other imaginable source just to find a smidgen of truth about this young
man. Their Herculean efforts have yielded modest success.

Henry McCarty—Billy the Kid—remains "shrouded in mystery and buffeted by controversy," says Robert Utley, one of the historians of the West who have diligently followed the faint tracks McCarty left behind. "Discoveries have been tantalizingly suggestive but rarely conclusive."[2]

The identity of McCarty's biological father has always been shadowy, and not very much is known about his mother. Some people speculate that Henry was a bastard, while others claim he was not even a McCarty in the first place. They believe his last name was Bonney, a surname he assumed later in his life. Then there is also a question of the place of his nativity. Through the years stories have surfaced of his being born in New York, Indiana, Missouri, Ohio, Illinois, New Mexico, and even County Limerick, Ireland.[3]

The largest number of reliable authors and scholars of western history contend that Henry McCarty was born on the eve of the Civil War in the bowels of an Irish neighborhood in New York City. If, indeed, his birthplace was New York, no records that can prove beyond a reasonable doubt that he ever lived there have ever been uncovered.[4]

Although the identity of Henry's father remains total conjecture, those willing to hypothesize present us with some possibilities. On the basis of sketchy records, some theorize that Henry's father was named Patrick McCarty, while others hold out for Michael McCarty, William McCarty, or Edward McCarty.[5]

There is little argument, however, that Henry's mother was named Catherine McCarty although there have been continuing debates about whether McCarty was her maiden or married name. It is generally believed that Catherine was born in Ireland about 1829 (seemingly a reliable date since her obituary in 1874 gives her age as forty-five).[6] She had been one of the so-called famine Irish, coming in her teens to the United States during the potato famine that swept across the Emerald Isle in the 1840s and devastated an entire generation.

The anguish of that experience, when hunger and cholera stalked the Irish poor, must have left lasting scars on Catherine. The combination of famine and disease and the resulting immigration reduced Ireland's population from 8.1 million in 1840 to 6.5 million just a decade later.[7] Throughout Irish neighborhoods that swelled in large American cities, stories circulated for years about starving Irish children back on the old sod whose bones turned brittle as candy and whose mouths and lips were stained green from eating grass and leaves stripped from trees.

During the 1840s and 1850s, throngs of hollow-eyed Irish families huddled at the Irish port cities of Cork, Galway, and Dublin or on the Liverpool docks in England, waiting for passage to the United States and Canada. Families, aware that their departing kin would likely not be seen again, held "American wakes" to send them off, much as they waked the dead before burial. These destitute souls crowding the docks prompted Nathaniel Hawthorne to write with disgust: "The people [emigrants on the docks] are as numerous as maggots in cheese."[8]

Lucky ones, such as young Catherine, booked passage and were able to escape the suffering in their native land. One passenger list records a Catherine McCarty on board the ship *Devonshire*, departing Liverpool and arriving in New York on April 10, 1846.[9] Still, the sheer number of Catherine McCartys listed in New York records, including the 1850 federal census rolls, is staggering and fails to distinguish or single out anyone for Henry's mother.[10]

What is known is that once she was settled in America, Catherine gave birth to two sons, Henry and Joseph. It is uncertain if the two boys had the same father or were half brothers, and the circumstances of their births, including the precise dates, are unclear. It is widely believed, however, that Henry was born in 1859 on November 23, November 20, or September 17.[11]

"Everything about this young man is open to question including his date of birth," says Bob Boze Bell, author of *The Illustrated Life and Times of Billy the Kid*. "From birth to death, almost every facet of his life is completely undocumented."[12]

Whether Henry's brother, Joseph, was older or younger is also open to question. On the basis of available records, Joseph more than likely was the elder, born in 1854, 1855, or 1856.[13] Joseph himself confused the issue on several occasions. The year before Billy was killed, Joseph gave his age as seventeen in the 1880 federal census taken in Silverton, San Juan County, Colorado.[14] Then, in an 1885 census taken in Arapahoe County, Colorado, Joseph's age was listed as twenty-one. That would mean Joseph was born about 1863. Also noteworthy is that he stated his place of birth as New York, which was his father's listed birthplace, while his mother's birthplace was registered as England.

Thirty-five years later, however, in a 1920 federal census taken when Joseph was then living in California, he gave his age as sixty-four, making his birth year 1855 or 1856, and his birthplace is recorded as Indiana. Finally, in 1930, Joseph's death certificate declared his age seventy-six, which means he would have been born in 1854.[15] What is known for certain, though, is that no matter which was the elder or younger, Henry and Joseph were Catherine's only children.

Regardless of the lack of credible information about the adolescent Henry McCarty and other family members, it is necessary to consider some of the more feasible theories about their lives. With that in mind what is known is that if Henry and his mother and brother resided on the island of Manhattan at any time during the 1860s, they experienced a place that later was branded "the modern Gomorrah."[16] This most Irish of American cities, where in 1860 almost one-quarter of the city's 813,669 residents were Irish, was a veritable breeding ground for the criminal classes and wholesale corruption on all levels.[17] Like the burning soot from factory smokestacks, a pall of malevolence, while hardly limited to the Irish, hung over the city.

The Irish neighborhoods, especially the notorious downtown slum known as the Five Points, where thousands of people dwelled in rat-infested houses, were a case in point. Particularly dangerous and rampant with crime, alcoholism, opium addiction, and of course grinding poverty, the Five Points horrified even Charles Dickens, whose intimate familiarity with the slums of London is vividly evoked in many of his novels. "This is the place, these narrow ways, diverging to the right and left, and reeking everywhere with dirt and filth," Dickens writes in his *American Notes*. "Debauchery has made the very houses prematurely old . . . all that is loathsome, drooping, and decayed is here."[18]

The Five Points and Mulberry Bend districts serviced a great number of houses of ill fame, marked by gleaming red lanterns, as well as a host of notorious dives and dance halls, gambling dens, and concert saloons where eyecatching waitresses hustled drinks and prospective customers. These sordid enterprises were found throughout the Bowery and along the East River waterfront in the old Fourth Ward. To encourage a sense of family among the many fatherless boys, the Catholic Church in some instances encouraged the formation of Irish youth gangs. Rival gangs roamed the streets, controlled the neighborhoods, and had no option but to consider crime a suitable occupation.[19]

Many of these Irish ruffians participated in the bloody New York draft riots that broke out in the summer of 1863, after Congress passed the National Conscription Law, which established a draft of males between eighteen and forty-five. Much of the rage resulted from a provision in the law that allowed wealthy men to avoid the draft by paying three hundred dollars to hire substitutes. That was about the same amount of money the average manual worker in New York could earn in a year.[20]

With no other means of subsistence, impoverished men took the money from the rich and went off to battle, while those unable to buy their way out of the army had to face the random draft lottery. During that volatile summer of 1863 New

York laborers frequently were heard singing the "Song of the Conscripts," which included this revealing verse:

> We're coming, Father Abraham, three hundred thousand more
> We leave our homes and firesides with bleeding hearts and sore
> Since poverty has been our crime, we bow to thy decree;
> We are the poor and have no wealth to purchase liberty.[21]

At that point in the war, when the North's victory appeared in doubt, temperatures soared and tempers flared on New York streets. Armed mobs rampaged through the city during four long days and nights of unbridled violence and atrocity. The looting and burning, not to mention a spate of random murders, did not end until at last regiments of battle-hardened Union troops were rushed to the city.[22] Loss of life and property was substantial. Two thousand people were killed and eight thousand wounded during these melees, figures that matched the casualties in some Civil War battles. Citywide property loss was estimated at more than five million dollars.[23]

Out of the ashes of the riot rose more corruption in the form of William Tweed, better known as Boss Tweed, and his tight ring of corrupt city officials, Democratic Party workers, and private contractors.[24] Throughout Tweed's reign at Tammany Hall in the 1860s and early 1870s, he and his cronies are believed to have misappropriated at least two hundred million dollars from the city treasury by bribery, extortion, graft, and nepotism. The Tweed Ring openly bought votes of Irish immigrants to guarantee the election of its handpicked political candidates. Tweed also bought off judges and made sure lucrative construction contracts for city projects were awarded to those who carried out his orders.[25] Many among the city's impoverished Irish considered Tammany Hall a necessary evil and viewed Tweed and his gang as Robin Hood figures who essentially robbed the rich, inevitably helping themselves but at the same time aiding the poor with a bit of boodle, or bribe money, in order to keep their political power.[26]

Immediately after the Civil War and for decades to come, crime and corruption boiled over in New York, especially in the area dubbed Hell's Kitchen on the west side as well as in the Tenderloin, which lay at the northwestern fringe of developed Manhattan at this time. That notorious district reportedly supported more crime, saloons, and whorehouses than any other place in America.[27]

During this postwar period thousands of homeless boys, often known as street arabs, evolved into ethnic neighborhood gangs. For many years an unending parade of killers and thieves emerged from the dispossessed in the squalid tenements. Some of them took on colorful names. Among them were Worcester Sam Perris, Banjo Pete Emerson, Red Rocks Farrell, Baboon Connelly, Piker Ryan, Big Josh Hines, Dandy Johnny Dolan, Bull Hurley, and a thief and bank sneak named William Burke, known to police and pals alike by his alias of Billy the Kid.[28]

If Catherine McCarty and her two young sons were indeed living in New York in this atmosphere, it should come as no surprise that she would have sought to leave and move west. Even if the family had departed New York before the draft riots, the crowded conditions and crime alone would have been cause enough to strike out.

None of these scenarios can be confirmed, although many earlier chronicles treat them as fact. Still, the lands to the west offered hope for a single woman trying to care for a pair of unruly growing boys. Perhaps the time had come for a fresh beginning and a chance to concoct new lives.

Nineteenth-century rural Indiana road

The Wallis Collection

Two

ON THE TRAIL

From the beginning it is clear that the spaces west of where you are always
seem to contain the essence of America . . . the West has always been
something that receded before Americans—that wherever they were, that
was the West, that was the frontier.[1]

•

—Frederick W. Turner

New York City might have been the birthplace and home of the
boy who became known as Billy the Kid, but there is also evidence that other
locales ought to be considered. Some historians and researchers theorize that Indiana is another credible site for Henry McCarty's birth. New York became the city
of preference as a result of newspaper reports about Billy's death filed by eastern
journalists eager to lure readers and build circulation by giving the story an East
Coast twist.[2]

"There are no absolutes. He just may have been born in Indiana," says Nora
Henn, a respected historian and authority on all things Billy. "Although New York
might very well be the correct place after all, I believe that particular story angle
was cooked up by writers and the press after Billy was killed. Then, like so much
else about him, once New York became the chosen birthplace, many people felt it

was set in stone. We have all learned that is something that's never wise to do when pursuing this young man."[3]

Whether or not Henry McCarty was born in New York or Indiana or any other place, it is known that he and his mother, Catherine, and brother, Joseph, called Josie when a boy, resided in Marion County, Indiana, not long after the Civil War. One of the family's first recorded addresses was 385 North New Jersey in Indianapolis.[4]

When the McCarty family arrived, the city of Indianapolis was in large part a prison camp housing Confederate soldiers. More than five thousand incarcerated men suffered through the long winter of 1864–1865 in less than salubrious conditions, but when the war was declared over, the detention center, Camp Morton, was disbanded.

By 1868 Catherine McCarty has shown up in the Indianapolis City Directory, but neither boy's name appears since minor children usually were not listed. By then the family's home address was given as 199 North East Street.[5]

Another key piece of information also was revealed at that time. Catherine reportedly told the compilers of the directory that she was the widow of one Michael McCarty. She seems to have provided no further details.[6] "Appearing in such terse simplicity, that single clue to the elusive identity of the legendary Kid's sire has a singularly anti-climactic aspect in the face of the years of effort which has gone into its search," writes Waldo Koop in *Billy the Kid: The Trail of a Kansas Legend.* "There is not much room for doubt that Michael McCarty, wherever he may have lived and died, was the father of Billy the Kid."[7]

But which Michael McCarty? Was he from the ranks of the famine Irish? Was he a New Yorker? Was he a proud Hoosier? Or none of these? In New York State alone, more than two dozen men named Michael McCarty served in the military during the Civil War, but the bits of evidence they left behind are inconclusive.[8] After eliminating several possible candidates, some researchers reasoned that no matter where he came from, the Michael McCarty they sought was a soldier killed in the Civil War, leaving a widow and two sons who moved to Indianapolis.[9]

Catherine's deceased soldier husband may have been a certain Michael McCarty, a native of County Cork, Ireland, who enlisted as a private in the Union army from Whitley County, in northeastern Indiana, in 1861.[10] This particular McCarty died two years later at age twenty-seven of a wound received during the Battle of Chickamauga. Considered the bloodiest two-day battle of the Civil War, Chickamauga, in northern Georgia, took place on September 19–20, 1863.

McCarty's outfit, the Fifth Independent Battery Light Artillery, took part in the horrific clash, and the young Irishman was badly wounded in the legs. He lingered for more than two months and died in the Fifth Battery General Field Hospital on November 30, 1863, five days after his unit participated in the Battle of Chattanooga in Tennessee.[11] His death is documented in official service records signed by his commanding officer. It reads in part:

> I certify, on honor, that Michael McCarty, a private of Captain Simonson's 5th battery of Artillery Volunteers, of the State of Indiana, born in Cork County of Ireland, aged of 27 years; 5 feet 6 inches high; fair complexion, blue eyes, brown hair, and by occupation a laborer, having joined the company on its original organization in Indianapolis, Indiana on the 22nd day of September 1861, to serve in the Regiment for the term of three years and having served honestly and faithfully with the 5th Ind. Battery to Nov. 30, 1863, is now entitled to a discharge by reason of death in General Field Hospital at Chickamauga Nov. 30th, 1863 of gun shot wound received at Battle of Chickamauga, Georgia.[12]

A letter from the army surgeon in charge to McCarty's commander explained that the soldier died from a gunshot wound to the knee joint. The only personal effects he left behind were a pocket wallet containing fifty cents and a three-cent postage stamp, a hat, a blouse, a pair of pants, and a smoking pipe.[13] Records concerning compensation to surviving relatives of the pay and allowances due the dead soldier have not been found, nor is there any reference to a wife or dependents.

This lack of critical information casts serious doubt on whether this Michael McCarty had any relationship at all with Catherine and her sons. The exact identity of Henry McCarty's biological father remains unknown. However, the man who became his stepfather entered the McCarty family circle in Indianapolis.

William Henry Harrison Antrim was born in 1842 at Huntsville, Indiana, a year after the death of an apparent namesake, the general turned Whig politician, President William Henry Harrison. His father, Levi Antrim, was a merchant and the proprietor of the Railroad House, a hotel in nearby Anderson, the seat of Madison County. While attending country school, Billy Antrim and his siblings washed dishes, hauled wood, and waited tables at the hotel.[14]

In June 1862 twenty-year-old William Antrim enlisted for a three-month hitch in the Union army. He mustered in as a private with the Fifty-fourth Regiment of the Indiana Volunteer Infantry and was assigned to I Company, commanded by Captain John V. Bowman. After organizing the company at Cambridge City, Bowman marched his fresh troops sixty miles to Indianapolis.[15]

Following a hasty training period, the Fifty-fourth Regiment did not stray far from the city. The unit's soldiers served as guards for almost two months at Camp Morton, site of the state fairgrounds, which had been converted to a camp for captured Confederates. From there elements of the regiment were stationed in Kentucky again to serve as guards, this time for a railroad bridge near the town of Shepherdsville. During that month of guard duty troops from C Company took part in a brief skirmish when the Confederates invaded Kentucky.[16]

At the end of the three months of guard duty, men of the Fifty-fourth mustered out of service in October 1862. Only two of their ranks had died from disease. None had been killed or wounded in battle.[17]

Honorably discharged from service in Indianapolis after his short and undistinguished tour of duty, Antrim remained in the city and readjusted to civilian life. He took up residence at 58 Cherry Street and found employment as a driver and clerk at the Merchants Union Express Company, located within a few blocks of the McCartys' residence on North East Street.[18]

Exactly how Antrim made the acquaintance of Catherine McCarty is unknown. In a sworn statement he signed in Kansas in 1871, he simply stated, "I have known Catherine Antrim for 6 years last past,"[19] confirming that the two first met in Indianapolis in 1865. Fifty years later in El Paso, Texas, when he was an old man, Antrim applied to the U.S. Bureau of Pensions for an annuity based on his brief service in the Civil War.[20] At the time, although he said he knew very little about Catherine's life before they met in Indianapolis. Antrim claimed that she had been married to a man named McCarty who had died in New York and had had no military service.[21]

Some people believe the initial meeting between Antrim and Catherine might have taken place when Antrim delivered an express parcel to the widow McCarty's residence.[22] Whatever the circumstances of their first encounter and despite the fact that Catherine was twelve years Antrim's senior, the couple soon started a lengthy courtship, but not one limited to Indiana.

Just before the dawn of a new decade, as Ulysses Grant presided over the war-torn nation, Catherine and Antrim decided to pull up stakes. Indianapolis, where clouds of coal smoke filled the air, was bustling and showed some commercial promise. As a crossroads, Indianapolis was perfectly poised to house the steam locomotives that not only brought goods but people to and from the West. Yet despite the new commercial promise posed by the city, Catherine and her boys and "Uncle Billy" Antrim were no longer willing to be part of that process.

By the summer of 1870 the foursome turned up in Wichita, Kansas, a raw town struggling to life near the junction of two rivers, the Arkansas and Little Arkansas.[23] Now Henry McCarty, on the brink of adolescence, and his family really did live on the authentic frontier. There would be no turning back.

First church in Wichita, circa 1873
WICHITA STATE UNIVERSITY LIBRARIES,
DEPARTMENT OF SPECIAL COLLECTIONS

THREE

WICHITA

The streets clanged with the noisy spurs of Texas cow boys and Mexican
ranchmen, while the crowds that marched along the resounding sidewalks,
were as motley as could be seen at any one spot in America. Texan
sombreros and leather leggins; brigandish-looking velvet jackets, with
bright buttons, close together, of the Mexicans, buckskin garments of the
frontiersmen, and the highly-colored blanket; representatives from a half
dozen different tribes of Indians, were familiar sights on the streets.[1]

•

—WILLIAM G. CUTLER

ATHERINE MCCARTY, HER two sons, and William Antrim, most
likely carrying all they owned in a horse-drawn wagon, arrived in Kansas in the
summer of 1870. They settled about two hundred miles east of Kansas City in
Wichita, an infant prairie village named for an Indian tribe. The federal census
recorded in late June of that year showed 607 people living in newly formed Sedgwick County, but the newcomers from Indiana did not surface in time to be
counted.[2] Wichita clearly was growing, a railroad town through which millions of
cattle passed as they were transported north for butchering. Here Billy first saw
both the commerce and carnage involved in the cattle business. It was to be the
backdrop of his life in the years to come.

Until they could secure permanent quarters, odds are the foursome, like many new settlers, found provisional digs in the two-story frame Empire House, at the time Wichita's lone hotel.[3] As soon as they shook off the trail dust, the family surely realized that they were a long way from Indiana in more ways than distance.

Wichita was a rough-and-tumble place surrounded by an endless sea of grass that had long been the domain of Indians, buffalo hunters, and fur traders. It was not a milieu for the faint of heart. Folks in Wichita enjoyed pointing out to greenhorns that back in the bygone times of 1860, a mere ten or so years before, Osage tribesmen on a hunting expedition had murdered one of the first white residents in the area. A search party of twenty resolute horsemen scoured the prairie, but all they ever found of the missing man was a booted human leg and a severed head for his widow to bury.[4]

During the Civil War a trading post was established near the future site of Wichita. A few years later Jesse Chisholm, a half-breed Cherokee and an adopted member of the Wichita tribe, settled in the area for a time and marked a path that turned into a choice route for cattle drivers bringing up great herds of longhorns from Texas to the Kansas beef markets. It soon became known first as Chisholm's trail and later as *the* Chisholm Trail.[5] In fact, newspapers of the 1870s abounded with tales of the crusty Chisholm, but young Henry McCarty did not get a chance to meet him. The pioneer trailblazer had died on the North Fork of the Canadian River in Indian Territory in 1868 after eating bear grease contaminated by a melted brass kettle.[6]

Still, there were plenty of other colorful characters and nomads congregated in Wichita. A boy could take his pick from an assortment of soldiers, bullwhackers, sodbusters, renegades, Indians, wolf and buffalo hunters, misfits, scouts, and some of the rowdiest drovers ever to mount a pony. Retribution for wrongdoing was swift, brutal, and often dispensed by persons other than law officers. Just a few weeks before Henry and his family arrived in Sedgwick County, a vigilante posse chased down a pair of hapless horse thieves and straightaway lynched them from a cottonwood limb.[7]

There were few amenities in the settlement. For a dime fee, foot passengers boarded a glorified raft to cross the Arkansas. Indians ferried their families on tub-shaped bullboats, each made from a single buffalo hide.[8] Crude boardwalks flanked streets thick with mud or layers of dust depending on the weather. Water for drinking and cooking or the occasional bath was hauled from springs, shallow wells, and cisterns.

William "Dutch Bill" Greiffenstein, a pioneer Indian trader who later served as mayor for a couple of terms, built the town's first two-story house on South Water Street near the river crossing, while most citizens lived in dugouts or crude wooden cabins.[9] Because of the scarcity of wood and the cost of coal, dried buffalo and cattle manure known as chips served as fuel. Cottonwood sprouts pulled from the riverbanks were planted to replace trees destroyed by the many prairie fires. Rattlesnakes and wolves were common. Winters were brutal, and summer temperatures ungodly. Come springtime, tornadoes were a constant threat.

At the time Catherine McCarty and her boys moved to Kansas, the extermination of the great herds of bison in the surrounding prairies and across the high plains was at its height. Catfish and carp from the rivers, prairie chickens, venison, rabbits, and buffalo hump, at four cents per pound, were customary fare at Wichita supper tables. Buffalo hides were pegged out to dry all over town, penetrating the air with their feral odor. Bits of putrid meat clinging to the shaggy skins and great piles of horse dung attracted enormous swarms of pesky bluebottle flies.[10]

The town had more grime than grace although a few attempts were made to tend to practical matters such as education. Wichita's first school, an abandoned army dugout made of cottonwood logs and sod, opened in the winter of 1869–1870. Indian lodges could be seen in the distance. William Finn, who arrived in Wichita just as the Civil War was ending, was the first schoolmaster hired for a salary of forty-five dollars a month. Finn had to get his pupils' books from distant Topeka, and he paid for them from his own pocket. At the close of the first term he was in so much debt that he quit teaching and became a surveyor.[11]

There is no record of the McCarty brothers attending school in Wichita, but it would seem they became streetwise, for better or for worse, during the fourteen months they roamed the town's dirt avenues.[12] In an 1881 column, Colonel Marshall M. Murdock, founding editor of the *Wichita Weekly Eagle*, briefly recalled the former resident who became the Kid. Murdock wrote that "many of the early settlers remember him as a street gamin in the days of longhorns."[13]

While her sons grew accustomed to life on the frontier, Catherine McCarty, with ample help from her friend William Antrim, set out to make a go of it in her adopted hometown. Jobs for women, even for schoolmarms and domestics, were especially scarce in small towns. Unless a woman was wealthy, in which case she did not need to work, or had a working husband, she had few choices. Even respectable women, unable to support themselves and their families through other means, often ended up taking employment at dance halls or brothels. That was not the case, however, with the self-reliant widow McCarty, who had grand plans for her family's future. "This was, remember, at a time when the women in Wichita came in one of two varieties: either the settlers' wives and merchants' ladies who lived east of the river, or the buffalo girls who danced by the light of the moon to the west of it," writes historian Frederick Nolan. "She [Catherine] clearly intended to be something more than just another farmer's wife."[14]

Catherine, who probably had little formal schooling, promptly made her presence known in town. On July 21, 1870, less than a month after arriving in Wichita, she was one of 124 citizens who signed a petition that was presented to Probate Judge Reuben Riggs calling for the incorporation of the town.[15] Catherine was the only woman to sign the document that helped make Wichita an official municipality. She is believed to have attended the first meeting of the city board of trustees in McAdams Hall the following day right along with the menfolks.[16]

However she had earned a living back East, Catherine's entrepreneurial bent blossomed in frontier Wichita. She quickly opened a hand laundry service in a two-story building on North Main Street with enough room upstairs to house herself and her two boys comfortably. Mindful of the perceived impropriety of a couple's living together out of wedlock, Antrim filed on a quarter section of land just six miles northeast of Wichita. On August 1, 1870, he moved into a snug frame house he had built and began cultivation of a five-acre plot.[17]

As they watched the laundry business take off, both Catherine and Antrim snapped up parcels of real estate. Numerous entries in Sedgwick County records of property purchases made by Catherine include the purchase of a vacant lot on Chisholm (later Market) Street. At the same time, Antrim obtained title to neighboring lots as well as to the property on which the laundry was located, a tract that he later deeded over to Catherine.[18] "All of these entries, indicating modestly extensive holdings in what was then the very hub and center of the village's business district," observes author Waldo Koop, "give an entirely different view of the legendary picture of an impoverished widow barely able to make ends meet for a family of two growing boys."[19]

Located in the heart of Wichita's up-and-coming business district, Catherine's City Laundry attracted a steady stream of customers from the start. The laundry did well enough to merit mention in the March 15, 1871, inaugural edition of the *Wichita Tribune*:

The City laundry is kept by Mrs. McCarty,
To whom we recommend those
Who wish to have their linen made clean[20]

Only ten days after the plug for her laundry business appeared in the newspaper, Catherine traveled to nearby Augusta, the seat of Butler County. She presented herself at the United States Land Office and filed claim on a quarter section in Sedgwick County adjoining Antrim's land.[21] In support of her claim, Antrim submitted a sworn statement attesting to Catherine's qualifications. The document reads in part: "I have known Catherine McCarty for 6 years last past; that she is a single woman over the age of twenty-one years, the head of a family consisting of two children, a citizen of the United States, and a bona fide settler upon the foregoing described land, which she seeks to purchase. . . ."[22]

The deposition also reveals that the McCarty family had moved out of the city and had been living on the claim since March 4, three weeks before the filing date.[23] Antrim, with some help from the boys, had built the family a cabin that was "12 by 14 feet, 1 story high, board roof, 1 door and 2 windows." The sale of the quarter section was approved, and Catherine paid $1.25 per acre or a total of $200 cash for her land.[24]

She and the boys cultivated seven acres and set out fifty-seven fruit trees. They took comfort knowing they had a decent water well and an outdoor cellar covered with earth and timbers that could be used for storage and for protection from sudden storms and killer twisters. They enclosed the large plot of land with split rails and also put in long rows of bois d'arc trees.[25] Better known as osage oranges, the spiny hedges served as a windbreak and were commonly used as fencing before the advent of barbed wire. In late summer Henry and Josie could pick juicy sand plums along the creek and riverbanks while Catherine and Antrim enjoyed sips of sweet wine made from wild elderberries.

By moving her young boys to a rural setting, Catherine no doubt hoped to shield them from the sordidness that proliferated in the more woolly center of the city. Indeed, the settlement was fast becoming a haven for the lawless elements, an unending procession of gamblers, painted prostitutes, con artists, bushwhackers, and man-killers who flocked to Kansas cow towns.

High crimes and misdemeanors had become commonplace in the town. This was particularly true at Main and Douglas, not far from Catherine's laundry. Law-abiding folks considered Keno Corner, named after the popular game of chance, the wildest spot in Wichita. There large numbers of Texas drovers, taking a break from the rigors of the cattle trail, congregated to gamble, carouse, and swill hard liquor from sunrise to midnight.[26] To attract customers to the gambling dens, a brass band on a two-story platform serenaded visitors from morning until far into the night. Chaos and violence inevitably erupted.

"It was a seething humanity that has never been paralleled to the present day," according to a historical vignette in the *Wichita Eagle* in 2004. "Day and night this sweltering corner was lined on either side by unbroken rows of cow ponies tethered to the hitching rails. Horse corrals were filled to overflowing. Flimsy hotels were sleeping six and eight cattlemen to the room. Along the old board walks from saloon to gambling house, to dance hall, to stores and back to saloons again, roamed hundreds of Texas men, in sombreros, chap and high-heeled boots, looking for recreation and excitement."[27]

It was a setting that caused any mother worthy of the name concern for the welfare of her children. That would have had to include Catherine McCarty, who, after only a year of living on the frontier, might have asked herself if she had made the right decision.

*Wichita's Main Street in 1870, looking north
from Douglas Avenue*

FOUR

BROTHERHOOD
OF THE GUN

Perhaps the real violence of the frontier was related more to anxiety, tension, frustration, and prejudice than to any action by outlaws, Indian fighters, and assorted vigilante groups. Even so, our folklore tends to support the image of Americans as tough, aggressive, and unafraid—real go-getters who tamed the wild frontier and never lost a war.[1]

•

—W. EUGENE HOLLON

CATHERINE MCCARTY HAD every reason to be apprehensive about her family's well-being in Wichita. It was as rough and raw a place as any frontier town in the making and prone to growing pains as it wrestled with all the temptations of the cattle trail. Her concerns, especially about the outbursts of random lawlessness, began shortly after their arrival.

On July 27, 1870, only six days after Catherine had signed the petition seeking Wichita's incorporation, the dramatic news of a cold-blooded murder spread throughout town. On that day, Jesse Vandervoort, a saloonkeeper who had moved to Sedgwick County from New York, was slain by George P. Murray over a land claim dispute. The murder dominated the talk of the town, especially on the following day, when Allison J. Pliley, an associate of the dead man, captured the fleeing Murray and dragged him back to Wichita.[2]

A native of Ohio who moved to Kansas as a lad, Pliley was well known on the plains. During the Civil War he enlisted as a private in the Union forces of the Fifteenth Kansas Volunteer Cavalry and fought in several battles while rising through the ranks to become a commissioned officer. After the war, when outraged Indians increased their raids on the waves of white homesteaders pouring into Kansas, Pliley again answered the call for volunteers as a civilian scout and Indian fighter.[3] It came as no surprise to anyone that he rode off in pursuit of his friend's killer and captured him so quickly.

Captain Pliley, with a stylish drooping mustache, cut a dashing figure astride his horse with the trussed-up culprit in custody. Youngsters like Henry McCarty would never have missed such an event. The excitement only mounted when just after the end of Murray's preliminary hearing he easily escaped from the town's flimsy makeshift jail.[4]

Pliley immediately saddled up again and went in pursuit of the fugitive. He caught up with Murray two months later down in the Creek Nation in Indian Territory (now Oklahoma), shot him dead, then buried him on the prairie. Upon his return to Wichita, Pliley made sure that the slain man's horse and handgun were put on prominent public display for all to see.[5] It is easy to imagine that among the gawking crowds was a towheaded boy who had heard the accounts of Pliley seeking revenge. "It must have been a wide-eyed Henry McCarty who heard the tale of Pliley's vengeance for the murder of his friend," writes Waldo E. Koop. "Perhaps this was Henry's first lesson concerning the frontier code placed on the remaining friends of a murder victim."[6]

Just after Pliley came back to Wichita with his trophies for exhibit, disturbing news came from neighboring Butler County. Weary of an epidemic of horse stealing, a large band of citizen vigilantes shot and killed four suspected thieves. For good measure, a few days later the vigilante committee tracked down four more men and straightaway hanged them from a tree along the Walnut River. In the aftermath of the executions, warrants were sworn out, charging nearly a hundred settlers with the murders of the eight men, but in the end, not one of the accused killers ever went to trial.[7]

Law-abiding folks, such as Catherine McCarty and William Antrim, learned to keep an ear cocked for danger and instinctively knew that innocent bystanders stood a good chance of getting caught in someone else's crossfire. Everyday life on the frontier was difficult enough, and contrary to later accounts, there was nothing romantic about it. Danger in the form of a rabid skunk, tick fever, or an armed drunk was always close at hand. Gunplay, whether celebratory or malicious, could explode on the town streets at any time of the day or night.

That was the case on February 28, 1871, when a fierce gun battle erupted just down the street from Catherine's laundry, leaving a man dead. The victim of "lead poisoning" was hotelier John Ledford, known around town as Handsome Jack, the proprietor of the Harris House. A notorious character with a reputation for being "wild and reckless," Ledford at one time was reportedly the chief of a band of counterfeiters, horse thieves, and desperadoes that operated throughout Kansas and Indian Territory.[8]

After settling in Wichita, Ledford supposedly quit his lawless ways. Although he had recently married a respectable local woman and seemed to have settled down, he still faced serious legal problems. An arrest warrant implicated him in the plundering of a government wagon train and the deaths of several teamsters.[9]

At high noon on February 28 a detachment of soldiers, accompanied by the army scout Lee Stewart and the deputy U.S. marshal Jack Bridges, with a warrant for Ledford tucked in his pocket, rode into town from the north. Newspaper reports later revealed that there may not have been any valid grounds for seeking Ledford's arrest. There had been bad blood between Ledford and Bridges since earlier in the year, when an argument resulted in Ledford beating Bridges soundly and Bridges vowing that one day he would shoot Ledford.[10] That time seemed to have come.

Once in town, the combined civilian and military posse questioned Ledford's wife and searched the family home on North Main before surrounding the hotel. The lawmen and soldiers finally determined that Ledford was hiding in a privy behind a nearby saloon, and they ordered him to surrender.[11] Ledford did not comply. In response to the demand that he give himself up, he threw open the outhouse door and sprang forward with a pair of blazing guns. Ledford was a pistol expert who could fire with either hand or both hands simultaneously and with deadly precision. The odds this day, however, were against his escape. In the melee a bullet through the arm wounded Deputy Marshal Bridges. Badly wounded himself, Ledford was taken prisoner after Lee Stewart shot him in the back. Some soldiers carried Ledford up Main Street to his residence, where a doctor tended to him until he died a half hour later.[12]

With the reek of gun smoke still hanging in the air, a warrant for the arrest of Bridges, Stewart, and "another whose name is unknown," on a charge of first-degree murder, was issued that same afternoon by a Wichita justice of the peace.[13] At the time, however, the posse was already headed back to Fort Harker, on the north bank of the Smoky Hill River, where Bridges recovered from his gunshot wound. He eventually resumed his career in law enforcement despite vigorous attacks on his character in some Kansas newspapers.[14]

Years later, when Bridges was appointed marshal of Dodge City, an editorial in the Caldwell Commercial noted: "Jack [Bridges], like Wild Bill [Hickok] and Bat Masterson, belongs to the killer-class and it is only a question of time when he will lay [sic] down with his boots on."[15] It is not known if this prediction about Bridges came true. What is known is that none of those named for Ledford's murder ever answered to the charge and stood trial.

"If little Henry McCarty was not an eyewitness, one can be reasonably sure that the sound of gunfire brought him to the scene before Ledford expired," writes Waldo Koop. "Possibly this outbreak of six-shooter promiscuity so close to the McCarty home was the occasion that brought about his mother's decision to remove Henry from the ranks of the street gamins[,] for within four days she had packed up her belongings and moved into the outlying claim cabin which Antrim had erected for her."[16]

What Catherine McCarty could not have known is that no matter where she moved her family in the West, the violence and hazards of daily life in that tumultuous time were unavoidable. American culture in the decades after the Civil War was based on the gun. The national murder weapon of choice prior to the war had been a knife or bludgeon.[17] That had drastically changed by the end of hostilities, largely owing to the huge surplus of firearms and the technological improvements that made them both cheaper and easier to use. All firearms to this point had been single-shot, requiring the shooter to reload continually. In 1866 Winchester developed and sold the first commercially available repeating firearms, both rifles and handguns. The new technology enabled gunmen to have far more flexibility and power.

At the beginning of the Civil War, shoulder arms and handguns were in short supply even though gun manufacturers, mainly Colt and Remington, had been gearing up for the conflict for several years. Soon large quantities of weapons that proved to be accurate and lethal were being manufactured.[18] They altered the very nature of traditional warfare and resulted in staggering numbers of casualties on both sides. Perhaps as many as 620,000 Americans perished from disease or in battle, and another 50,000 returned home as amputees. Union troops alone counted more than 236,000 cases of gunshot wounds.[19] Veterans returned to loved ones and hometown parades, but many of them bore bodily wounds as well as deep and lasting psychological scars.

"More terrible than the number of casualties was how they were inflicted—not by foreign enemies, but by fellow citizens," explains historian Geoffrey C. Ward. "After it was all over and the fury and fever had died away, survivors of the Civil War were still haunted by the horror and madness of what had happened in the last few years."[20]

This was the legacy of the horrendous conflict as violence spilled into civilian life in the postwar period. Many veterans, trained to kill and hardened by acts of cruelty they had witnessed or committed, came home with their guns along with their nightmares. Some Union soldiers were permitted to keep their firearms; others kept them illegally. Although the articles of surrender stipulated that the Confederates give up all their weapons, there was little, if any, enforcement.[21]

Crime rates skyrocketed, particularly in large eastern cities. New York City police commissioners blamed the rise in felonies on the Civil War and said it was "a school for violence and crime."[22] Homicide and suicide rates, especially among veterans, soared across the nation. During Reconstruction, as many as two-thirds of the inmates entering prisons in northern states were veterans. Paranoia gripped many of these men. There were reports of veterans, forever terrified of being killed, constantly carrying handguns and even keeping weapons at their sides when they slept.[23]

The atmosphere in the South was even more debilitating. The war resulted in a deep poverty that scarred the region for generations. Violence broke out repeatedly across the Reconstruction South. Bands of former Confederate soldiers with no jobs and few families to return to turned into vicious thugs and went on crime sprees across the bloodstained landscape. The outlaw gangs were challenged by vigilante posses that were no less vile. These included the newly created Ku Klux Klan, an organized rabble of reprobate bigots and hatemongers who attempted to regulate the moral conduct of the public and were responsible for much racial strife and violence.[24]

"In every state in the Union, the number of cases of manslaughter and assault with the intent to kill increased ten to twenty fold over that in prewar years," writes W. Eugene Hollon. "In most of the crimes of blood, whether on the raw frontier or in the crowded city slums, the revolver was the weapon of death."[25]

By the 1870s the gun had suddenly become central to America's identity. In fact, guns had become so popular that in 1871 two Union army veterans from New York, George W. Wingate and William Conant Church, founded the National Rifle Association (NRA) to make available firearms training and improve marksmanship and shooting skills. The organization promoted weapons expertise, sponsored marksmanship contests, and distributed literature about developments in the gun industry.[26]

The weapon that became the symbol of American individuality, especially in the West, was not the rifle but the pistol. On the 1870s frontier the six-shooter helped create some of the most lasting myths of the West. In reality, most people using guns for hunting or personal defense turned to a rifle, carbine, or shotgun. Long guns were more accurate at great distances and easier to control than the six-shooter, which was effective but only at close range.[27]

As Garry Wills notes in his book A Necessary Evil, "the gun is credited with a leading role in the 'taming' of the West. . . . It was the main tool by which men held their own against nature, Indians, and other frontiersmen. The rifle was the most effective, reliable, and used weapon of the time. One would never guess that from the myths of the West, especially as they have been embroidered in the twentieth century. These focus almost entirely on the handgun, the 'six-shooter.' "[28]

The steady rise of the gun culture, or six-shooter mystique, throughout the American West coined catchy expressions, such as "There's more law in a Colt Six Gun than in all the law books," and "God created men; Colonel Colt made them equal." The six-shooter became known as "Judge Colt and his jury of six" and "the great equalizer."[29]

The revolving pistol, as the inventive Samuel Colt called it, allowed a man to keep his hands free while he drank or tended to chores. More important, the development of the six-shooter meant that for the first time in history man could kill critters or his fellowman in rapid succession.[30] The fame of Colt's revolver spread, and it became the most popular handgun for both the military and civilians in the West. One of the most favored models was the 1873 army model, ironically dubbed the Peacemaker. It was possibly the most famous firearm ever made and certainly one of those mythologized in those annals of western history.[31]

In the Wichita, Kansas, of 1871, however, as some writers of western history point out, the title of gunfighter belonged to no man. The term "gunfighter" did not become common until much later. Even so, the gunmen of that day, mostly called shootists or man-killers, were already renowned.[32]

Texas cattle fording the Arkansas River at Wichita, Kansas,
July 1869

FIVE

CONTAGIOUS WAR

*It would be hard to overestimate the impact of the Civil War on late
19th-century American culture. . . . As veterans returned home at war's end
and people began to reconstruct their lives, disease and war were
irrevocably linked in the popular imagination.[1]*

•

—DALE KEIGER

LIFE IN WICHITA may have seemed sweet as huckleberry pie for
Catherine McCarty, at least on the surface. Her steamy City Laundry did a brisk
trade thanks to the bundles of soiled hotel and whorehouse linens left at the door
and the piles of grimy clothing regularly deposited by working stiffs and cattle
drovers. In the evenings at the homestead, she could see to it that her sons learned
their letters and numbers after they tended the farm chores. Henry and Josie toiled
alongside Antrim, who earned fair to middling wages from part-time bartending
and carpentry work.[2]

Yet Catherine remained uneasy. Moving her family to the piece of land just
outside town did little to dispel her concerns for her boys' welfare on the unruly
Kansas frontier. Her anxiety for both herself and her family, amid the dangers of
the prairies and the disorder on the streets of Wichita, was fed by a new factor in

her life. By the beginning of 1871 she had become mindful that she was not physically well. Because of the lack of public health precautions and the prevalence of unsanitary conditions, from raw sewage in the streets to polluted drinking water, disease like typhoid, cholera, diphtheria, pneumonia, pleurisy, and smallpox beset frontier communities. Wichita was no exception.[3] "Pedestrians on Main, Market and Water Streets, anywhere north of Douglas Avenue, were regaled with quintessence of putrefaction," reported the *Wichita Eagle* at the time. "All agree that some sanitary measures are needed, and heavy fines should be imposed on those who will throw slops, old meats and decaying vegetable matter at their doors or on the street."[4]

Catherine's illness may have started earlier than the move to Kansas. She might have realized for a long time that something was wrong before she sought help. She may have experienced constant fatigue, loss of appetite, and night sweats, some of the symptoms associated with tuberculosis. To confirm her fears, especially if she had begun to run sharp fevers or coughed up blood, she could have consulted one of the local physicians, Dr. Edwin Allen or his partner, Dr. Andrew Fabrique.[5] In the 1870s contracting tuberculosis anywhere in the world was practically the same as a death sentence. Called consumption, lung sickness, the long sickness, "captain of the men of death," and the "white plague," this chronic infection, caused by airborne bacteria, typically attacked the lungs. Spread by coughing or sneezing, it was the nation's greatest killer at that time and for many years to come.[6]

The druggist on Wichita's Main Street would have offered Catherine an array of balms, powders, herbal nostrums, and patent medicines heavily laced with alcohol, but affording little relief. The few doctors available would not have been much more helpful. Most physicians believed consumption could not be cured.

Difficult to diagnose, tuberculosis in the mid-nineteenth century was often confused with other diseases. Doctors prescribed all manner of cures and concoctions, including worthless "snake oil" medicines. Some doctors believed opium could cure tuberculosis. Others said the most effective remedies were vigorous horseback riding and adherence to an all-meat diet. Folk medicine called for a sick person to pack a pipe with dried cow dung and inhale the fumes. The worst of the charlatans prescribed eating mice boiled in oil and salt or using butter made from the cream of cows that only grazed in churchyards.[7] Most sufferers became desperate enough to try any cure. Some of them believed that the disease was a punishment from God.

A German doctor developed turtle serum as a healing treatment and sold the bottling rights to an American syndicate. In Denver, patients often took the "slaughterhouse cure," gulping down tumblers brimming with the blood of freshly killed animals. Some physicians treated their patients with so-called heroic therapies: sweating, purging, vomiting, and bleeding. One medical practitioner promoted men growing beards, a sure way, he claimed, to ward off consumption since facial hair protected the throat and lungs from infection.[8]

Tuberculosis claimed lives at all ages and at every level of society. Some famous victims from history include John Calvin, Wolfgang Mozart, Frédéric Chopin, John Keats, Percy Shelley, Edgar Allan Poe, Washington Irving, Robert Louis Stevenson, Simón Bolívar, Ralph Waldo Emerson, Henry David Thoreau, the Brontë sisters, Stephen Foster, Florence Nightingale, Jay Gould, and Stephen Crane. For the most part, however, consumption was considered a disease of the urban poor because they were the most affected social class, the inevitable result of the unsanitary conditions and overcrowding in the teeming slums of large cities.

Tuberculosis could lie dormant for many years before becoming full blown. Caring physicians believed the highly contagious disease was best treated by the patient's eating plenty of wholesome food and getting as much exercise and fresh air as possible to clear the lungs of harmful pollutants. Those afflicted who had a modicum of horse sense knew they had to cover their mouths when coughing and as much as possible avoid physical contact with loved ones.[9]

As with other diseases, the contagious sick in large towns and cities were sent to community pesthouses. Those deemed incurable entered almshouses to await slow but certain death. On the frontier, however, there were hardly any hospitals and certainly no pesthouses. Sick folks, even those carrying tuberculosis, had few options but to rest at home as much as possible. Those who could manage to leave sought a cure elsewhere instead of slowly wasting away. That was Catherine McCarty's choice. Restless and in all probability motivated by the quest for a better clime, Catherine opted to leave the prairie and move to a healthier locale. Tuberculosis was a disease of time, as anyone with this long-term illness knew full well.

A stifling hot laundry was far from the ideal place for someone battling a chronic respiratory illness. In leaving Wichita, Catherine was leaving behind tubs filled with dirty clothing to be scrubbed with brushes and bars of strong yellow soap on metal washboards, linens boiling in soapy water with a tub of cold water nearby into which she could plunge her hands and prevent scalded flesh. Gone also would be the wet sheets and clothing that she had to lug outside to hang on backyard lines or drag to the attic to dry when the weather was bad. In short her never-ending arduous life in Wichita would be over.

Apparently William Antrim was also ready to leave Kansas with Catherine and her sons. His decision to uproot came even though some of his family had moved from Indiana to Wichita in the spring of 1871. After incorporation as a city in 1870, Wichita experienced an immigration boom that ballooned its numbers up to make it the third-largest city in Kansas within a couple of years. Among those who came were Antrim's parents, a sister, and his brother James, who became a well-respected citizen and a popular law officer.[10]

Although blood family may have been important to Antrim, by this time he was fully committed to Catherine and her boys. "Of more concern to Billy Antrim and her two sons was Catherine's deteriorating health," writes Frederick Nolan. "Whether she already had tuberculosis before she arrived in Wichita or whether, as seems likelier, she contracted it there, it can only have been exacerbated by the constant heat and damp of the laundry in which she spent her every waking day. Her condition must have been serious enough for her doctor to recommend, as was the custom then, a higher, drier climate: Colorado, perhaps, or New Mexico."[11]

Catherine began to sell off her properties on June 16, 1871, when county records show she sold her improved quarter section. Although he was ready to leave with Catherine and the boys, Antrim filed on yet another unimproved claim directly northeast of Catherine's land the very next day. Some historians theorize that possibly Antrim acquired the land because he hoped that someday Catherine's health would be restored and they could return to Kansas. That was not to be.[12]

In a flurry of activity that summer, Catherine and Antrim disposed of their properties in town. By late summer the foursome was ready to depart. After August 25, 1871, there is no further record of any of them residing in Wichita.[13] Catherine, her pubescent sons, and Antrim vanished, at least from a trail of later historians, for more than a year and a half.

Larimer Street looking West, Denver, Colorado, 1870

Six

PULP FICTION

The Far Western frontier of the nineteenth century still exists—in the American imagination. And it is the hero of that frontier, the trapper, outlaw, soldier, and gunfighter, who personifies the period and the place. In his biography Americans have found all the action and color needed for a great national myth.[1]

•

—KENT LADD STECKMESSER

FROM THE LATE summer of 1871 and for the next eighteen months, it is not known where Catherine McCarty, her two boys, and William Antrim were. A few places, mostly in the West, have been suggested. Some people claim the four of them, or at least Catherine, went south and resided for a time in New Orleans, but that theory is not very likely.[2]

Many reliable researchers believe that Denver, the largest city in Colorado Territory, is probably where the McCarty-Antrim party landed after they departed the Kansas frontier.[3] Denver was certainly not the worst place to go; it really was an extension of Kansas Territory and people whispered that there was gold in the mountains. This conjecture gained credence in 1928, when Catherine's son Joseph, by then a penniless old man back in Denver and the lone survivor of the foursome, told a newspaper reporter that in 1871 he arrived in Denver "with his father [William Antrim], a Wells-Fargo Express agent."[4] Unfortunately Joseph said little else that shed any light on either his brother or his family history, and the reporter doing the interview did not press the old man for details.

Henry McCarty himself spoke of living in Denver, according to an old pal. In March 1927, Frank Coe, one of McCarty's closest friends in New Mexico Territory, spoke to the historian J. Evetts Haley of the young man who became known as Billy the Kid. Although some of the information from the interview is inconsistent with substantiated facts, Coe stated McCarty told him that as a youth he and his family had lived in Denver for a short time.[5]

Considering Antrim's past experience as a teamster in Indiana, taking a position with the American Express Company (the eastern counterpart to Wells, Fargo & Company), as Josie recalled, would have been reasonable. After all, as many have speculated, Antrim perhaps first encountered Catherine McCarty when he delivered an express package to her Indianapolis residence.[6]

Wells Fargo offered plenty of opportunity for anyone not allergic to hard work. Its headquarters, a two-story stone building in Denver, was a beehive of activity as dusty Concord coaches, overland stages, and horse-drawn wagons came and went, hauling oysters, eggs, and other coveted provisions into mining camps and returning with shipments of gold dust and silver bars.[7] Possibly this is where Antrim first became interested in the lucrative field of mining, a profession he soon took up and stuck with for the rest of his working life.

Following a trail due west to Colorado Territory also makes the most sense in light of Catherine's poor health. Denver had become a thriving commercial hub sparked by a mass migration ever since 1858 when a party of prospectors discovered gold at the confluence of Cherry Creek and the South Platte River.[8]

Certainly by the early 1870s not everyone who moved to Denver had come to seek out the mineral wealth that had attracted so many newcomers to the "Mile High City" for the preceding twenty years. There was another lure. Thousands of ill people, most of them stricken with tuberculosis, came to the Rocky Mountains in quest of comfort and, they hoped, a cure in the dry mountain air.

Wealthy "lungers," as tuberculars were known, took up residence at one of the first-rate health resorts that popped up throughout the region. As more consumptives poured into Colorado, the state became known far and wide as the Switzerland of America and the World's Sanatorium.[9] Even less affluent consumptives, however, such as Catherine McCarty and others who could not afford residency at a resort, took comfort from the dry, sunny climate and the fresh, invigorating mountain air.

"Colorado is the most remarkable sanatorium in the world," wrote Isabella Lucy Bird, a celebrated British adventurer who in 1873 climbed Long's Peak, at 14,255 feet the monarch of the Rockies. "The climate is considered the finest in North America . . . consumptives, asthmatics, dyspeptics, and sufferers of nervous diseases are here in the hundreds of thousands."[10]

Others who agreed with Bird's assessment of Colorado's healing powers included the flamboyant showman P. T. Barnum. "People come here to die and they can't do it," wisecracked Barnum about the city where he purchased 760 acres to winter his famous circus.[11] Barnum became one of Colorado's biggest promoters. In 1873, three years before Colorado Territory joined the Union, he published *A Paradise for Dyspeptics and Consumptives*, a treatise extolling Colorado's value as a sanctuary for lungers.[12]

"I am in love with Colorado," Barnum writes in the brief introduction. "Believing that I may thereby save many lives, and add to the happiness of thousands of my fellow-beings, I requested an eminent physician in Denver to write a careful description of the climate and its effects upon invalids. That description I have published for the benefit of mankind. It fully coincides with my own personal observation."[13]

In the text that followed, Dr. William Harmon Buchtel, the physician-author lauded by Barnum, paid his own tribute to Colorado, which he described as "one of the most favored spots on the face of the globe for a consumptive's refuge."[14] As it turned out, Buchtel was Barnum's son-in-law. He had married Barnum's daughter Helen, a young woman who earlier had scandalized Victorian America as well as her father by abandoning her husband and children to live openly as the mistress of a man in Connecticut. In 1871 she married Buchtel, a native Ohioan who had served in the Civil War. Shortly after the wedding the couple moved to Denver, where Buchtel became a medical school professor and later a university president.[15]

Barnum and his daughter continued to stay at odds, and eventually he removed her name from his will and left her only a tract of land near Denver. "Barnum privately considered the so-called 'valuable property' he had conveyed to

Helen as 'worthless,'" writes Irving Wallace. "He justified his deceit as punishment for the disgrace she had brought upon the family. But the last laugh was Helen's own. For, ironically, after Barnum's death [1891] the 'worthless' property was discovered to be rich in mineral deposits, and it made Helen more prosperous than all the other Barnum heirs combined."[16]

Barnum may have guessed wrong when it came to the land he left for Helen, but it was one of the few times his instincts failed him. A consummate huckster and charlatan, Barnum generally guessed right when it came to making money. During his lifetime the incorrigible showman introduced the American public to an array of shocking and amusing freaks, curiosities, hoaxes, and spectacles. Among the many unusual attractions he unveiled was a dead monkey that he claimed was the "Fejee Mermaid," the original Siamese twins Eng and Chang, a popular dwarf he named General Tom Thumb, and Jo-Jo the Dog-faced Russian Boy.[17]

It was Barnum, forever captivated by the Wild West, who in 1843 had staged the "Great Buffalo Hunt" in Hoboken, New Jersey. His free exhibition of supposedly ferocious bison, captured near Santa Fe, attracted more than twenty-four thousand people to Hoboken. Barnum promised that "every man, woman, and child can here witness *the wild sports of the Western Prairies*."[18]

The crowd, mostly New Yorkers who paid six and a quarter cents each way to ride to Hoboken on the crowded ferries, watched as a mounted rider, costumed and painted like an Indian, prodded and poked emaciated beasts into a trot around an arena. Eventually the noise of the screaming patrons so terrified the bison that they fled to the sanctuary of a nearby swamp. While the forlorn rider hired by Barnum rounded up the wayward animals, a spectator died when he fell from a tree.[19] Considering there was no charge for the exciting show, the crowd more than got its money's worth of thrills.

Moreover, by day's end Barnum had pocketed a hefty thirty-five hundred dollars. Unbeknownst to the public the shrewd impresario had purchased the rights to the receipts of all who paid to ride the ferryboats back and forth between New York and Hoboken. He also controlled all the food and drink concessions.[20]

Three decades later, by the 1870s, when Barnum was busy establishing what became known as the Greatest Show on Earth, he remained fascinated with the culture and life of the American West. For a time he even became a gentleman rancher of sorts when he purchased the Dipper Ranch on the Huerfano River about forty miles from Pueblo, Colorado. He later sold an interest in the ranch to

Robert Moody, a former Santa Fe Trail freighter who went on to become a prominent rancher and banker in Texas and Oklahoma.[21]

In 1870 Barnum visited Hays, Kansas, one of many rough-and-tough frontier towns.[22] Not a large town, Hays nonetheless sported almost forty drinking establishments and following the Civil War had been the home of such notables as William F. "Buffalo Bill" Cody, James Butler "Wild Bill" Hickok, and Generals Nelson Miles, Phil Sheridan, and George Armstrong Custer.

"P. T. Barnum, wishing to satisfy his taste for curiosities, stopped off at Hays City to see 'man-eaters' of that town 'eat,'" reported the *Daily Kansas State Record* of Topeka. "He fell in with several of the more carnal-minded youth of the place, who invited him to be sociable and take a hand at poker. The cards that were dealt to his companions literally 'knocked the spots off' anything Mr. Barnum ever 'held' in his life, and when the exercises of the solemn occasion were ended, Phineas mourned the departure of $150 that he will never see, not any more."[23]

When Barnum joined a group of men for a Kansas buffalo hunt, his friend George Custer, commanding officer at Fort Hays, warmly received him.[24] The army post had been established to protect railroad workers and travelers on the Smoky Hill Trail from Cheyenne and Arapaho warriors trying in vain to halt Indian genocide on the plains. To prevent Barnum and the others from losing their scalps, Custer provided the hunting party with horses, weapons, and an escort of fifty cavalrymen. Barnum and his companions quickly encountered a herd of grazing buffalo and killed twenty. The slaughter continued unabated until it was mercifully halted because of what was described as "wanton butchery."[25]

Such experiences clearly influenced Barnum, who early in life grasped the marketability of the vast American West. Throughout a long and colorful career he sponsored Wild West extravaganzas featuring a crusty mountain man and his grizzly bear, Indian warriors fresh from the warpath, and a peculiar woolly horse supposedly captured in the wilds by the intrepid pathfinder John C. Frémont.[26]

Barnum tapped into the public's imagination and gave them the American West as entertainment long before Buffalo Bill Cody and others got into the act with productions of their own.

If there ever was a patron saint for the many purveyors of bunkum, con artists, pulp writers, frauds, and fantasizers who helped create and perpetuate the many myths of the American West, a case could be made for Phineas Taylor Barnum. The self-described "Prince of Humbugs" is one of the most charismatic figures in the history of popular entertainment. His talent at using exaggeration to his benefit allowed him to turn fraud into an art while holding the rapt attention of the American public. Barnum and other self-promoters and hustlers realized the powerful influence of hype and the media.

Unwittingly they served as masterful propagandists for the forces engaged in the so-called Western Civil War of Incorporation and thereby both popularized and romanticized the largely mythical Wild West. Barnum's illustrated newspapers were designed to intrigue the public and pique its curiosity before his traveling show appeared in its towns. He also pushed his autobiography and sold thousands upon thousands of copies through subscriptions and use of a sales force that trudged door to door across the country. At one time the less than critically acclaimed book sold so well that it rivaled works by Dickens and Thoreau as a bestseller.[27]

Interestingly enough, the creation of this western myth that Barnum had so well established contributed to both the celebrity and exploitation of Henry McCarty as Billy the Kid. While new subways and instant skyscrapers were rapidly transforming the East Coast, the West remained a wide-open arena populated with gunfighters, Indians, miners, and outlaws whose existence became mythologized by the writers of the day and the press.

Like Barnum, the clever Edward Zane Carroll Judson also realized the persuasive power of the written word. Best known by his pen name, Ned Buntline, the native New Yorker knocked out four novels about Cody, including *Buffalo Bill, King of the Border Men*, serialized by the *New York Weekly* in 1869. Buntline also developed a play, *The Scouts of the Prairie*, which brought Cody to New York for the first time in 1872.[28] Buntline followed that with more melodramas and sensational writing about Cody, who also appeared onstage with Wild Bill Hickok, another western character whose deeds of daring were vastly exaggerated.[29]

Cody was touted as the quintessential westerner. Others compared the flashy frontiersman with P. T. Barnum. While Buntline, the father of the frontier romance story, convinced the nation that the American West was a wild place, he invented Buffalo Bill and made him one of the most mythologized figures in American history.

"William F. Cody's 'invention,' begun with a nudge from Ned Buntline and developed with the help of his long-suffering assistants Ned Salsbury and John Burke," Larry McMurtry writes, "was to take the kind of pageants current in Barnum and others and focus them on the West, the winning of which thus came to seem a triumphant *national* venture."[30] The audiences not only loved these shows but received a heady dose of patriotism at the same time.

The proliferation of these shows gave rise to a profoundly American, if not raucous, new entertainment industry. Leisure time was becoming something that Americans, who had suffered through the Civil War and the bitter days of Reconstruction, were only now learning to deal with. What better than to take something a little familiar, make sure it was American, exaggerate it, and the masses would eat it up. Those who found the formula—the Barnums, the Codys, the Buntlines—loaded their guns with myth and shot away at the ever-hungry American public.

Both Barnum and Buntline realized they would reap the spoils if they properly promoted the American West to the general public. The advent of the dime novel in the middle of the nineteenth century advanced their promotional efforts, and as McMurtry notes, "what they needed next was the movie camera, so that all that pulp fiction could be changed into pulp film."

In the 1870s the advent of film remained in the distant future, but as McMurtry points out, the mythmakers and pulp writers of that era were creating a distinct American consciousness, a form that the nascent film industry borrowed decades later. Mainstream newspapers and magazines of the time also contributed to the sensationalizing of news in general and coverage of the western frontier in particular.

In the years after the Civil War and throughout the Gilded Age, the profane pictorial press and such newspaper publishers as Joseph Pulitzer battled fiercely for market share. All these publications found ample readership for gossip and scandalous stories. They also relied on exaggeration and especially lush prose when reporting on the West and the flamboyant figures who dwelled there.

"There is progress everywhere, and the van-guard [sic]—the pioneers of civilization—are actuated and inspired by the principles which have made America free and glorious,"[31] said *Harper's Weekly* in an 1868 story about life on the Great Plains.

An article in 1871 from the same periodical describing opportunities in the American West notes: "People who have never visited the great West, and in whose eyes a farm of two or three hundred acres is large, have little conception of the magnificent scale on which farming operations are carried on in the regions of prairie country."[32] These magazine and newspaper articles may have caught the attention of Catherine McCarty and William Antrim and convinced them that their future would be best served on the new frontier.

Beyond daily newspapers and shocking periodicals such as the *National Police Gazette*, dime novels and pulps became the real mainstay of a public anxious to learn more about the Wild West. The dime novels published by the brothers Erastus and Irwin Beadle of the mass-market publisher the House of Beadle and Adams were some of the most popular of that era, starting in June 1860 with *Malaeska: The Indian Wife of the White Hunter*.[33] Considered the first dime novel, *Malaeska* tells the tragic tale of an Indian maiden married to a white settler. It proved a romantic sensation and sold more than sixty-five thousand copies within the first few months.

Nathaniel Hawthorne complained bitterly about what he perceived as a gaggle of female romance writers, whom he called "this damned mob of scribbling women," who clogged the bestseller lists and prevented his own literary works from being read and discussed. Churned out by a new breed of prolific writers, the books were printed on cheap paper made from pulpwood and commanded considerable popular appeal by promoting the traditional American values of patriotism and moral behavior. With the appearance of the typewriter in the 1870s imaginative authors could earn good wages at a penny a word. Many of them could knock out a thousand words an hour for hours on end.[34] It also helped that more public schools were being built, resulting in a dramatic increase in literacy and an ever-expanding reading public.

"Very soon, the dime-novel Western showed certain consistent, indeed programmatic, elements: a hero who represented a synthesis of civilization and wilderness; an affirmative finding with regard to progress; an emphasis on action; and a setting of epical import—usually vast, wild, open spaces," writes Thomas Lyon in an essay about the literary West. "By his actions in the plot, the typical hero supported civilization, dramatizing a faith in progress (this despite any and all contemporary evidence of corruption, uncertainty of economic opportunity, unfairness in distribution of wealth, or environmental degradation) thus lending overall reality to the developing formula."[35]

According to mass-market publishers, the idea for their popular western pulps sprang from the romantic tales of James Fenimore Cooper. When they first appeared on the scene, most dime novels and penny dreadfuls extolled the virtues of rugged individualism as found in such larger-than-life characters as Daniel Boone, Davy Crockett, Kit Carson, Buffalo Bill Cody, Wild Bill Hickok, George Custer, and other manufactured heroes. Publishers found they also had to include villains in the distinctive fantasy genre. No matter if the evil element was human, beast, or the land itself, it became a necessary foil for the western protagonists to battle and conquer.

Dime novels especially appealed to working-class men and boys, such as the McCarty brothers, eager to read about the perils of frontier life and the adventures of their favorite western heroes. In the early 1870s, however, as Henry McCarty's family grew restless and considered moving yet again, the pulp westerns that the youngster reportedly loved to read were about to change. Many of the tales of the Wild West were about to present a new kind of hero. Soon the pulps featured brigands, renegades, and rogues and transformed them into heroic criminals, driven to their lawless ways by social injustice and the need to defy an oppressive and corrupt establishment. On the pages of pulp novels, at least, outlaws openly defied the law and got away with it.[36]

There would have been little time for Henry McCarty to be reading much pulp fiction in early 1873, as he and his family made their way south to New Mexico Territory. Not a soul who met him along the way would have ever guessed that within a decade the gangly kid barely in his teens would be a mainstay in countless western pulp novels and the most mythical desperado hero of the American West.

Presbyterian Church, Santa Fe, New Mexico Territory, circa 1880

COURTESY PALACE OF THE GOVERNORS

(MNM/DCA, NEG. NO. 15855)

SEVEN

SILVER THREADS AMONG THE GOLD

. . . if we believe in that mysterious wind that blows our lives, like tumbling
tumbleweeds, into new shapes, we must ride blind with it.[1]

•

—CAROL MUSKE-DUKES

ESTERN HISTORIANS ARE certain that Catherine McCarty, her sons, and the dutiful William Antrim quietly slipped into New Mexico Territory in early 1873.[2] At about the same time, a newcomer of an altogether different species also took up residence there: the soon-to-be ubiquitous Russian thistle, better known as the tumbleweed.

Tumbleweeds had first appeared in the American West a few years earlier, when some seeds were accidentally imported with shipments of flaxseed from the Russian steppe.[3] The tenacious shrubs with no natural enemies gained a foothold on the range and quickly spread across the Southwest, particularly in the decades following the Civil War. Every autumn, as the prickly bushes died and turned rigid, they snapped off at the roots, and the thorny skeletons rolled in the wind, often for miles, scattering more seed. Tumbleweeds arrived in New Mexico Territory in 1873 and 1874 when fertile seeds clinging to the hooves of longhorns trailed in from Texas.[4]

The tumbleweed, regarded as a nuisance by some and a picturesque symbol of the West by others, shared a kinship with the footloose, such as consumptives like Catherine McCarty and those with gypsy hearts who never stayed in any one place too long. The tumbleweed stood for the sturdy individuals. "I wouldn't have my New Mexico without its brave pioneers, its rugged individualism, and its tumbleweeds," writes Robert Leonard Reid. "Like all myths they began in truth. Examined with sympathy and care, they provide important clues to our past and valuable starting points for judging and interpreting history."[5]

Like the tumbleweed, Henry McCarty's nomadic life, also destined to become part and parcel of the West of imagination and myth, truly began in New Mexico Territory. At least the young man's public existence started there. For it was in the historic city of Santa Fe, snug against the Sangre de Cristo Mountains, that the first indisputable documentation of Henry McCarty's existence was recorded.

The precise date was March 1, 1873, when, after eight years of courtship and frequent cohabitation, William H. Antrim and the ailing Catherine McCarty at last wed.[6] The bride was forty-four, and the groom thirty-one. It was probably a clear, chilly late-winter day, with the air scented by the aroma of piñon and juniper fires warming the adobe houses of the area. The simple marriage ceremony took place in the First Presbyterian Church of Santa Fe, constructed of adobe bricks at the corner of Grant and Griffin streets in 1854. Originally a Baptist mission, it was the first Protestant church in the territory but was eventually abandoned and stood empty until 1867, when the Presbyterians bought it and added a square tower and Gothic windows.[7] Officiating at the Antrim-McCarty wedding was the Reverend David F. McFarland, who would be forced to retire in ill health before the end of that same year.[8]

According to both church and Santa Fe County records for the date, there were five witnesses to the nuptials that changed Catherine's surname from McCarty to Antrim. The witnesses included Amanda R. McFarland, the minister's wife; Katie McFarland, the couple's daughter; and Harvey Edmonds, a local citizen who frequently acted as a backup witness to marriages. The fourth and fifth witness names scrawled in the ledger in Dr. McFarland's hand were brothers Josie and Henry McCarty.[9]

Since a couple had to show proof of three weeks' local residency prior to taking the marriage vows, Antrim and the McCartys must have been in Santa Fe for at least a month before the wedding. They may have temporarily lived with Antrim's sister, Mary Ann Hollinger, believed to be residing in the city at that time, or taken rooms at the Exchange Hotel, perched on the corner of the Plaza, the termination point of the busy Santa Fe Trail.[10] For many years tales persisted of the boy who became Billy the Kid washing dishes in the hotel kitchen and banging away on a lobby piano in his free time.[11]

No records indicate Henry McCarty ever learned to play the piano, but his appreciation of music was well documented by many of his friends and others who crossed his trail in the Southwest. It was said that his love of song and dance came from his Irish mother.[12]

In 1873, the year Henry and his family showed up in New Mexico Territory, a song entitled "Silver Threads Among the Gold" made its debut and soon became the most popular tune in the nation. Henry McCarty was taken with the song the first time he heard it played. From then on he declared it was his favorite, right up there with "Turkey in the Straw," the old fiddle tune derived from an even older Irish ballad.[13]

Some music critics later said that "Silver Threads" was clichéd and ordinary, but Henry was drawn to the sentimental lyrics that told the story of two people facing fear and denial while growing old together.[14] For the rest of his life he reportedly often whistled the song as he rode horseback across the high plains and ranchlands.

Besides the popular mainstream melodies of that time, Henry seemed captivated by the homegrown music of New Mexico Territory. For unlike other Anglo newcomers, who found the territory a foreign and peculiar land mostly populated by Hispanics and Indians, Henry quickly adjusted to his new surroundings.

Passages about a fictional Catholic cleric written more than fifty years later in *Death Comes for the Archbishop*, Willa Cather's novel set on the nineteenth-century frontier, could also describe young McCarty's attachment to New Mexico: "In New Mexico he always awoke a young man. . . . He had noticed that this peculiar quality in the air of new countries vanished after they were tamed by man and made to bear harvests . . . that lightness, that dry aromatic odor . . . one could breathe that only on the bright edges of the world, on the great grass plains or the sagebrush desert. . . . Something soft and wild and free; something that whispered to the ear on the pillow, lightened the heart, softly, softly picked the lock, slid the bolts, and released the prisoned spirit of man into the wind, into the blue and gold, into the morning. . . ."[15]

Instead of experiencing culture shock, Henry embraced the strange and foreign New Mexico Territory lifestyle, so different from the other places he had lived in for his first thirteen years. He soon adopted many of the manners, habits, and customs of the local populace. Henry found that the savory native cuisine featured all sorts of new delights seasoned with piquant chile peppers and perfected through the years by both the Indians native to the land and their Spanish conquerors. The aroma of simmering frijoles, tamales, posole, and piping hot tortillas wafted down the narrow streets of Santa Fe. Chocolate was customarily served along with delicious cakes after meals, and the *ricos* (the wealthy) sipped aguardiente, a domestic brandy that the Anglos commonly called pass whiskey because it was shipped from El Paso del Norte.[16]

Anglo observers were impressed by the suave Hispanics and noted that their manners were not confined to the higher classes since "the humblest beggars often exhibited an address and air of refinement that a prince of blood might envy." Both sexes of native New Mexicans smoked fine-cut tobacco, and it was said that a gentleman never lit his cigarito in the presence of another without saying, "*Con su licencia, señor* [with your permission, sir]."[17]

Gambling was a vice common to all classes of society, and gambling houses were frequented by rich and poor. Cockfighting was another accepted amusement, but by far the most popular leisure activities were the many bailes, balls, and the colorful fandangos.[18] "From the gravest to the buffoon—from the richest nabob to the beggar—from the governor to the ranchero—from the soberest matron to the flippant belle—from the grandest señora to the *cocinera* [female cook]—all partake of this exhilarating amusement," wrote Josiah Gregg, chronicler of the Santa Fe Trail. "To judge from the quantity of tuned instruments which salute the ear almost every night in the week, one would suppose that a perpetual carnival prevailed everywhere."[19]

Still, there was more to Santa Fe than music and dance, gambling dens, engaging señoritas, and zesty gastronomical fare. On the dusty and teeming Plaza the local merchants mingled with both traders from El Camino Real, the trail winding northward from the old colonial capital of Mexico City, and freighters who traversed the Santa Fe Trail. The townspeople shared stories of highwaymen and marauding bands of Plains Indians who preyed on the Pueblo Indian people and the trade caravans journeying across the plains.

A steady flow of newcomers had been coming to the territory ever since the

Santa Fe Trail opened in 1821. Many went back and forth on the trade route between the ancient city and Missouri, but others stayed. They made themselves at home in a land that in some ways had changed little since the arrival of the conquistadors. The Spaniards came with a cross in one hand and a sword in the other and forced both on the tribal people living along the Rio Grande.

A wealth of stories sprang up about the Plaza being the site for bullfights, public floggings and executions, gun battles, political rallies, and fiestas. Running the full length of the Plaza's north side was the Palacio, the Palace of the Governors, a simple adobe structure built in 1609–1610 and used continuously as a seat of government. By the time Henry McCarty and his family reached Santa Fe, four different flags had flown over the Plaza and El Palacio: Spanish, Mexican, Confederate, and United States.[20]

Undoubtedly Henry and his brother, Josie, like other youngsters who passed through the city, heard the tales of how justice was meted out in the old adobe palace. It was known to be one of the first in the territory to have windows with glass, and, in the not-too-distant past, the ears severed from slain Indians had adorned the outside walls. "The festoons of Indian ears were made up of several strings of dried ears of Indians killed by parties sent out by the government against the savages, who were paid a certain sum for each head," writes R. E. Twitchell in his history of New Mexico. "In Chihuahua, a great exhibition was made with the entire scalps of Indians which they had killed by proxy. At Santa Fe only the ears were exhibited or retained."[21] Although the Anglo and Hispanic citizens of New Mexico Territory were still in conflict with several Indian tribes, especially assorted bands of Apaches, the macabre custom of hanging human ears for public viewing had thankfully ended and remained only in accounts told to recent arrivals and visiting Yankee traders.

William Antrim, his alert ears secured in place, surely heard such grisly tales, but he also heard the stories of mineral riches in the territory and was anxious to try his hand in the mines well to the south of Santa Fe. The high desert of mountainous New Mexico Territory also made sense for the family's new home since much like Colorado, it was a haven for people stricken with consumption like Catherine Antrim.

Antrim grew increasingly anxious to find his sickly wife a comfortable home. He also wanted to get the two boys into school, and there was no public education in Santa Fe at the time.[22] Moreover, and probably most important, Antrim was eager to try his hand in the silver mines.

Late that spring, after no more than two months in Santa Fe, the Antrim family—for by then Henry and Josie had dropped the name McCarty and assumed the surname of the man who married their mother—left the city. Railroads were still years away from the territory, so the Antrims undoubtedly took a stagecoach to Albuquerque. From there they would have turned south and followed El Camino Real flanking the Rio Grande through the center of New Mexico Territory. After long days traversing desolate country frequented by bandits and renegade Apaches, they reached La Mesilla, so named because the settlement was on a small tableland rising above the Rio Grande floodplain. The Antrims then turned west and headed for Grant County, formed in 1868 and named for Ulysses S. Grant, the Union general credited with winning the Civil War and by 1873 into his second term as president.[23]

Once in the county, they reportedly paused in the mining camp of Georgetown, site of the first important silver strike in the territory. Catherine immediately disliked what she saw in the makeshift settlement of prospectors and miners. She had hoped for a more suitable town with other youngsters and the potential of opportunity for her sons. Much to Antrim's chagrin, they hastily departed Georgetown.[24]

They traveled a short distance to a town that appeared to be booming and was situated in the foothills of the Pinos Altos Mountains. Catherine and the two boys liked what they saw there. The name of the place alone appealed to Antrim. It told him all he needed to know: Silver City.

Main Street, Silver City, New Mexico Territory, 1870s

The Robert G. McCubbin Collection

EIGHT

LAND OF LITTLE TIME

New Mexico answers no questions. It is as impersonal as an equation, as unpersonified as a law of physics, and more immutable. Yet not immutable at all, but ever-changing; set solid as a boulder, yet changing with the sun. The land itself sings no songs, tells no tales, will not be romanticized into prettiness. It does not give, nor does it ask.[1]

•

—JOHN DeWITT McKEE

WHEN THE ANTRIMS appeared in Silver City in the early summer of 1873, they settled right into the little silver-mining town. While waiting for a chance to purchase a plot of land for a residence, the family moved into a rented log and frame cabin, thirty-feet-square with a stone fireplace, gables, and a few promising shade trees.[2]

An early prospector had built the simple residence on the east side of Main Street just north of Broadway. It was a small dwelling for four people, but the Antrims felt fortunate to get it. The influx of miners and settlers to the boomtown meant many people had to live in tents. One such campground was set up in the fenced yard of the local barber who because of the shortage of freshwater had stopped selling baths to grimy miners.[3]

Silver City was only about two years old when the Antrims arrived. Native tribes had hunted and farmed this land for many centuries before the coming of first the Spanish and much later the Anglos. By A.D. 900–1000 Mogollon Indians were living where one day Silver City would be built, near a large ciénega, a marsh, that provided life-sustaining water. In the 1870s daring town boys, on alert for marauding Indians, dug up ancient potsherds, flint, and bits of bone from the earth outside town. The treasures were remnants of an Indian people who had mysteriously vanished long ago. Many years later other tribes moved into the region. They included nomadic warriors and gatherers from the Great Plains who eventually were called Apaches, the name derived most likely from a Zuni word meaning "enemies."[4]

Not until the arrival of the Spanish adventurers, priests, and colonists who advanced north from New Spain (later known as Mexico) did the Apaches acquire horses. The new rapid mode of transportation proved most useful for raids on other tribes. By the 1700s, and for many years to come, Apaches were assaulting the Spanish settlements along the Rio Grande and sparring with the iron-clad soldiers.[5] Spanish miners, however, when negotiating with the Apaches to mine copper in the area, wisely agreed not to settle permanently in the Apaches' valley, which the Spaniards called La Ciénega de San Vicente, in honor of St. Vincent, the earliest of Spanish martyrs, who died in Valencia in 304.[6]

Hostilities with the Apaches increased in the 1860s and continued over the next twenty years. Resentful of the intrusion of more and more white settlers, bands of Apaches roamed the hills and countryside around the mining camps, attacking travelers and harassing and robbing supply caravans. The settlers and mining interests wanted the soldiers to incarcerate all the Indians in reservations. Other white settlers believed that the best solution to the "Indian problem" was total extermination.

The army troops assigned to the area found that their heavy cavalry mounts, used to being fed on grain, were not accustomed to grass diets and climbing steep, rocky mountainsides. The cavalry steeds were simply no match for fleet Apache ponies. Consequently, the army hired some "good Indians" as scouts and mercenaries. Now and then those Apaches experienced a change of heart, however, and used their government-issued arms and munitions to attack the soldiers.[7] Despite tales of a trail of fire and blood left by raiding Apaches, both sides in this vicious clash of cultures commonly practiced atrocities and acts of cruelty. There was little middle ground. From the outset of the conflict, mercy and understanding throughout the territory were in short supply. "When we came to the Ciénega, the present Silver City, there were a few Mexican people scattered around," recalled Robert Golden, an elderly Grant County pioneer, in a 1938 interview. "A large spring was where the Big Ditch is today, and where Main Street was in the '70's. At the east end of Broadway, where the armory now stands, the Indians would creep up and try to kill the people that camped at the spring. There was a standing reward that every time anyone brought in the head of an Indian or other evidence that he had killed an Apache he would get ten dollars. The Indians caused a great deal of trouble during the early days, but we early settlers caused them quite a lot of worry after we became used to their customs."[8]

In 1870, Apaches killed twenty-four-year-old John Bullard, considered a founding father of the fledgling settlement. Nonetheless, the Anglo immigrants, eager to tap into the rich silver ore deposits, decided to stay and build a permanent town. They changed the Spanish name for the mining camp to Silver City. By 1871 it had become the seat of Grant County.[9]

From the beginning the town's founders tried to create an American-looking city by using lumber whenever possible and fired red bricks instead of the more practical and comfortable adobes. Even when they used adobe bricks, the builders incorporated gabled roofs, wooden trim, and frame porches into the structures. Ever mindful of Apache warriors, crews of men harvested ponderosa pines and oaks from the Pinos Altos Mountains.[10] After milling, a good deal of the lumber was also used in the mines and at nearby Fort Bayard, built after the Civil War to protect settlers from the wrath of the Warm Springs Apaches.

"Like much of the frontier, Silver City—despite a strong regional pride—continued for many years to look, not South or West, but East for its inspiration," write historians Susan Berry and Sharman Apt Russell. "The psychological importance of the red brick cannot be overstated, for to the settlers it gave the town an air of permanence and civilization. Brick was the material that had built the architectural backbone of America and to many of these displaced settlers, a reminder of home—of St. Louis, Detroit, Chicago, New York . . . a confirmation of 'American' values, which some Eastern settlers may have felt needed shoring up against the centuries of Hispanic influence."[11]

By March 1871, just ten months after the discovery of silver in the area, Silver

City had mushroomed from a camp with just three houses "to a town of over eighty nice shingle eastern-looking buildings," noted the *Las Cruces Borderer*.[12] The article failed to report that the growth was so unending that many new residents had to live in tents or boardinghouses until they could provide proper dwellings for themselves. Instead, the reporter sang the praises of the town: "Silver City is essentially an eastern town, full of live energetic and intelligent men who have come there to stay. There is no jumping of claims, no quarreling. The town already contains three stores, a boarding house, livery stable, two blacksmith shops, one shoe shop and a paint shop; and situated as it is, in the beautiful Ciénega surrounded by rolling and picturesque hills covered with pine, cedar and oak, must in time become the most beautiful town in southern New Mexico."

Two years later, when the Antrim family became residents, Silver City had grown even larger. By 1873, besides the Star Hotel and three dance halls, the town supported fifteen busy saloons, including one operated by Bill McGary. His saloon served as the setting for the first session of district court as well as for the first church meeting.[13]

While the town appeared to be occupied mostly by virile white men, that was definitely not the case. A good many women, some respectable and others clearly not, and their children also lived there. Despite published reports to the contrary, the census for 1873 revealed Silver City's population to be just 350 Anglos, compared with 700 Hispanic citizens, many of them descendants of early pioneers.[14] Although Hispanics lived throughout the town, a number of them resided in a predominantly Spanish-speaking neighborhood on a rocky slope that became known as Chihuahua Hill.

No matter the ethnic ratio of the citizenry, town boosters pointed with pride to the building boom and the large amount of silver bullion flowing from the area mines. A chauvinistic editorial in the *Silver City Mining Life* referred to the territorial capital of Santa Fe as "insufferably dull." It went on to note smugly that just a few days spent in the ancient city "serves to make one anxious to be back again among the silver hills of our own, favored county of Grant."[15]

Silver City was no frontier utopia. Far from it. Warring Apaches posed a threat for several more years, and until railroads came to New Mexico Territory in the early 1880s, the remote location remained an annoyance. Violence in the streets and saloons erupted sporadically. Gussied-up sporting women paraded through the streets and haunted gambling dens and saloons. They plied their trade with Welsh and Cornish miners and with soldiers, while tinhorn gamblers tried their luck at what was said to be the world's second-oldest profession.

"When the Antrims arrived in the early summer of 1873, Silver City was a town with all its hair on, its population a mixture of the most fearless and the most desperate men on the frontier," writes Frederick Nolan. "It was a town where three shifts of bartenders were needed to cope with the round-the-clock thirst of the patrons of saloons like the Blue Goose and the Red Onion or more elegant places like Joseph D. Dyer's recently opened Orleans Club on Main Street, where high rollers sat all night with their gold and silver stacked in front of them, betting into pots running to thousands of dollars."[16]

Besides the boast of continuous gambling, the Orleans offered elegantly appointed private rooms for preferred male patrons. In newspaper advertisements, Joe Dyer, who called himself "the eminent mixologist," bragged that his establishment was the ideal haunt for "all those who hanker after the good things of this life (in the fluid line) and he is prepared to 'set them up' (for a consideration) at any or all times, day or night, and that the belligerent portion of the community can find a particularly rampant specimen of the Feline species, usually denominated the 'TIGER,' ready to engage them at all times."[17]

Greeners, also called greenhorns or tenderfoots, and others unschooled in the gambling arts may have thought the "TIGER" of Dyer's newspaper advertisement was a blatant tribute to the female companions provided for the high rollers, but not so. It was actually a reference to faro, a popular card game in the West of the nineteenth century that derived its name from the Egyptian pharaohs depicted on the cards and was often called Tiger because of the image of a tiger painted on the dealer's faro box. Someone playing this game of chance was said to "buck" or "twist the tiger."[18]

Bridegroom William Antrim was in no position to fool with tigers of any stripe, either the high-stakes wagerers or the two-legged, painted prowlers at the Orleans Club. Although notoriously frugal, Antrim thoroughly enjoyed gambling and always found a way to come up with enough money to stake him at the gambling tables around town. To fund his favorite pastime and still support his family, he did some carpentry and other odd jobs. For a time he worked as a butcher in Richard Knight's meat market. There customers selected their suppers from a medley of wild game, bacon, beefsteak, mutton, pork, and delectable animal innards, much of which came from Knight's ranch near the southern end of the Burro Mountains, southeast of town. Whenever possible, Antrim also learned all he could about mining, and he tried his hand at prospecting at Pinos Altos, Chloride Flat, and other working mines near the Arizona border.[19]

As she had done in the past, Catherine Antrim ignored her poor health and pitched right in to earn money for the family. She washed clothing and bedding for bachelors, and she baked and sold pies, bread, and sweetcakes that were regarded as the best in town. Despite cramped quarters in the family's cabin, Catherine supposedly even took in the occasional boarder, although in later years some people who lived in Silver City at the same time as the Antrims, including a good pal of Henry Antrim's, could not recall Catherine's ever running a boardinghouse. As one writer put it, the frame cabin was so small "the boys could not swing a cat in it."[20]

Most of those acquainted with Catherine Antrim in Silver City had fond memories of her. Such was the case with Louis Abraham, who came to Silver City in 1870, when he was seven years old. According to Louis, his friend Henry Antrim was from "an ordinary good American home. Good parents and good environment in the home."[21] Especially memorable for Louis, whose family were prominent Jewish merchants, was Catherine's considerable talent at cooking and baking. "There were very few American [white] boys in Silver City when the Antrims lived here, therefore the few American boys that were here all ran together all of the time," said Louis, sixty-seven years later.[22]

Besides Louis and his brother, Hyman, four other sets of brothers befriended the Antrim boys: Gideon and Chauncey Truesdell, John and Vincent Mays, Albert and Charley Stevens, and their cousins Harry and Wayne Whitehill, sons of Harvey Howard Whitehill, who served as coroner and later three terms as sheriff. Others in the boys' circle were Anthony Connor, Jr., and Cortie Bennett. By 1875 Thomas and Daniel Rose had joined the fold.[23] In the parlance of the time, the band of boys was "as happy as a preacher in a saloon away from home." They shot agate marbles in the dust, played at being landlocked pirates, and ran races on Market Street.

"Mrs. Antrim always welcomed the boys with a smile and a joke," recalled Louis Abraham. "The cookie jar was never empty to the boys. From school each afternoon we made straight for the Antrim home to play. My mother was dead, and my father had a Spanish woman for a cook, her food never tasted as good as the meals that Mrs. Antrim cooked."[24]

Henry was about thirteen or fourteen when he came to Silver City, making his brother, Joseph, still called Josie or Joey, either a few years older or younger, depending on which of the boys' various birth dates one believes. "The question of whether Joey was the older or younger brother has never been satisfactorily resolved," writes Frederick Nolan. "The testimony of his Silver City contemporaries on the subject is conflicting. Compared to his 'mild-mannered, flaxen-haired, blue-eyed' brother he was 'larger and very husky,' Chauncey Truesdell said. 'He looked to be a year and a half or two years older than Henry.' Anthony Connor also believed that Joe was the older, as did Harvey Whitehill's daughter. But was he?"[25]

This and many other questions about Henry and his family remain unanswered. No matter whichever was the elder or the larger, both finally attended school in Silver City. Whether the boys ever went to school in the other locales where the family lived or were home-schooled is unclear, but both lads, albeit briefly, received some academic instruction in Silver City.

In the years immediately after the Civil War, teaching became a more respected occupation, and by the 1870s public schools had been established throughout the United States. Territorial public schools were another matter. Since the days of Spanish colonization and later under Mexican rule, education in New Mexico had been largely left up to religious orders, resulting in the mission schools in remote Spanish villages and Indian pueblos and the parochial schools founded by the Christian Brothers and the Sisters of Loretto. Although a royal decree called for a public education system in 1721, the few schools that were established had quickly closed for lack of funds.

Not until 1850, when New Mexico became a U.S. territory, was the question of public schools addressed. Progress was slow, and funding remained a key issue. That same year the territorial legislature provided for a school in each settlement to be supported by a tax of fifty cents per child. This tax was unpopular. Because of debt, many laborers, known as peons, were in servitude, and the wealthy resented being taxed for their education.[26]

Hence education did not become a priority. According to New Mexico Territorial Governor Marsh Giddings in 1871, "New Mexico with a population of 113,000 and yet not a single common school of the character found in every other state and territory of the Republic of America. . . . New Mexico claiming to be a civilized people exhibits the mournful fact outside of Santa Fe there is scarcely a school of any kind whatever. . . ."[27]

The deficiency was made even more apparent in an article on the state of education published in 1872 in *Scribner's Monthly*: "The illiteracy in the different States and Territories varied, in 1860, from two or three per cent in Utah and some of the eastern states, to eighty-four per cent in New Mexico, where it is not probably any less today, as there has not been a public school, or even a school-house, in the entire territory in the last twenty-five years. In this same territory a recent vote on establishing free schools stood 37 *for*, 5,016 *against*."[28]

All attempts to establish a public school system either failed to pass the territorial legislature or were regularly defeated at the polls for almost twenty years after the Antrims moved to Silver City.[29] Private and subscription schools came and went, but recruiting good teachers was a challenge, and because of notoriously low pay and spotty enrollment, keeping them was even more difficult. Any school that managed to stay open for more than a few months was a rarity.

"The great want of this community is a public school," lamented the local newspaper in 1873. "There is now, in the hands of the county officials nearly $1,400 in school funds and there are enough in the town of Silver City alone, at least 50 children who are large enough to attend school. So far, in the history of the town, there has [*sic*] been two private schools taught for a time; but for want of support they both failed. The last one had a teacher, Mr. P. J. Ott, a gentleman who has devoted his life to the pursuit of school teaching and who gave entire satisfaction, but on account of the want of interest manifested by parents he was forced to close."[30]

In the fall of 1873 one Jessie Anderson started yet another private school in the residence of Robert Black. The five-dollars-per-month tuition for each scholar was far too much for most families, and after just two months low attendance forced the school to close. The town's priorities were obvious. As the school board struggled to raise funds to build a proper schoolhouse, stone work began on a new jail for lawbreakers, who, unlike pupils or teachers, were never in short supply.

On January 5, 1874, during what was remembered as a particularly hard winter, Dr. J. Webster finally opened the first public school in Silver City, with fifth grade the highest level.[31] Webster acted as principal and teacher and announced in the newspaper that all children between the ages of five and fifteen years would be admitted to classes free of charge. Because the school still had no money for a building of its own, it rented McGary's Hall on Main Street. A head count showed that there were 30 Anglo and 119 Hispanic youngsters eligible to enroll as students.[32] Among the Anglo boys and girls to attend classes that first semester, which stretched only from January 5 to March 28, were the Antrim boys and many of their friends, such as the Truesdells, Bennetts, and Whitehills.

Previous histories of the Southwest during this period of time rarely, if ever, examined the role of schools in integrating Hispanics with the Anglo population. In fact, Hispanic children stayed away from the school because their parents thought they would have to pay Dr. Webster for his services. Once they found that it was a free public school, Hispanic attendance significantly increased. "I have never seen learners more interested in their studies than those attending this school," Webster wrote in a progress report seven weeks into the semester. "Most of the older pupils seem determined to do all in their power to progress in their studies. And the Mexicans show no less energy in advancing their studies than their American fellow pupils."[33] Although Hispanic students were in the majority and appeared eager to learn English, there was criticism around town charging Anglo bias. Less than two weeks after classes started, a contributor to the *Mining Life* newspaper, who signed his name only as Justice, lambasted local officials for not ensuring that the teacher they hired was proficient in both English and Spanish:

> To teach a public school in Silver City it is necessary that the teacher should be proficient in Spanish and English. The law requires that both languages shall be taught; but apart from the law, common sense should dictate to our "city fathers" that a child who has no more knowledge of the English language than it has of Spanish without a teacher to expound every word and sentence in that mother tongue, can make no progress toward enlightenment.
>
> And the American pupil will, also, be benefited by this mode of teaching, for he will acquire a knowledge of one of the most fluent and expressive languages in the world without any effort, more than attention to the elucidation of the teacher.[34]

"Justice" was correct in his criticism of the curriculum deficiency. Any "English only" rule was in direct noncompliance with the terms of the Treaty of Guadalupe Hidalgo, signed in 1848, which ended the war with Mexico. The treaty guaranteed citizenship rights for all inhabitants of a vast portion of the Southwest that now belonged to the United States and included protection of the residents' Spanish language, although it had already become an all-too-regular pattern in the West that expedience, if not outright greed, might result in abrogation of such a treaty.

Many Anglos disagreed with the language provision of the historic treaty and believed it was an impediment to progress in New Mexico Territory. Just a week after "Justice" published his commentary, the newspaper editor made a case in opposition to bilingual education. "Justice [in his article] demands that the school be taught in Spanish as well as English, forgetting that, according to all recognized authority, a pupil to learn any language will progress much faster if he is thrown entirely among persons who speak that language."[35]

Apparently, Henry Antrim was of a different mind. The schoolboy, who immediately took to the New Mexican lifestyle and culture, instinctively knew that the mysterious writer who called himself Justice was correct: Spanish was an expressive and fluid language. Anglos often learned at least a modicum of Spanish to get along and communicate with the majority of the population. Henry must have spent considerable time with Hispanics in the community, for although the young man was pure gringo, he soon picked up Spanish and spoke it almost like a native.[36] Within a short time, that natural linguistic gift would serve young Henry well and, at least for a while, help keep him from harm's way.

*Hudson's Hot Springs, New Mexico Territory, spring 1888, Mary
and Richard Hudson, second and third from the left*
PHOTO COURTESY OF THE SILVER CITY MUSEUM,
HARLAN COLLECTION

NINE

ONE STEP OVER THE LINE

[Henry] was a good boy, maybe a little [more] mischievous at times than the rest of us with a little more nerve.[1]

•

—LOUIS ABRAHAM

FTER A YEAR in Silver City, everything for the Antrim family seemed to be "ace high," as a stud poker player on a lucky streak at the Orleans Club would have put it. They were a long way from wallowing in silver dollars, but at least they had a roof over their heads, some wages coming in, and Catherine's tuberculosis appeared at this high, dry altitude to have stabilized for the time being.

Best of all, as far as Catherine was concerned, both her boys, far away from the outlaws and juvenile delinquents in Wichita, were in school studying arithmetic, geography, grammar, and penmanship under the tutelage of Dr. Webster. She also had to be proud of Henry's evident aptitude for learning a foreign language and peppering his conversation with Spanish words and phrases. Unlike other Anglos who referred to all Hispanics as greasers, a derogatory label that had originated in Texas, Henry was drawn to the Hispanic culture and people. He fancied their spicy food, their style of dress, and especially their music.[2]

It did not take long before townfolk took notice of Henry Antrim. In later years, when asked what they remembered about the boy, most of those acquainted with him seemed to appreciate his better qualities rather than dwell on any deficiency of character. On the basis of a composite description of Henry from several of his boyhood friends, historian Jerry Weddle wrote:

> He was unfailingly courteous, especially to the ladies. Like his mother, he was a spirited singer and dancer. He had an alert mind and could come up with a snappy proverb for every occasion. He read well and wrote better than most adults. A taste for sweets resulted in bad teeth, and two of his upper incisors protruded slightly. His rambunctious sense of humor always got a laugh, whether it be about himself or someone else. Because of his small stature, he took a lot of ribbing from those bigger and stronger, but what he lacked in size he made up [for] with tremendous energy and quick reflexes. Anxious to please, willing to take extraordinary risks, Billy [Henry] would dare anything to prove his worth. The other school kids soon realized that he had genuine courage.[3]

Long after Henry had become forever known as Billy the Kid and Josie was living out his life in obscurity, some of those classmates recalled the Antrim brothers with affection. "I know he [Henry] was a better boy than I was," Anthony Connor recollected. "He was very slender. He was undersized and really girlish looking. I don't think he weighed over 75 pounds."[4] Another boyhood chum, Chauncey Truesdell, said that neither Antrim brother was very big but that "Henry was only a small boy, small for his age." Chauncey recalled that of the pair, Joe was "larger and very husky" and "looked to be a year and half or two older than Henry," and that was why Joe sat at the back of the classroom with the older, more advanced pupils, while Henry "sat near the front with us younger ones."[5] Even the children of the local sheriff remembered Henry favorably. "My sister and I went to school with Billy the Kid," reminisced Harry Whitehill when he was elderly. "He wasn't a bad fellow."[6]

On the whole, the town's lads were routinely mischievous but no more troublesome than other boys in similar circumstances. Of course not everyone agreed. Among those who kept a wary eye on local youths and carefully monitored their deportment was the newspaper editor Owen L. Scott. In his early thirties about the time Henry and his friends were prowling the streets, the Virginia native had only recently become the editor of *Mining Life*. He and his young wife moved to Silver City from Fort Selden, a territorial army post on the Rio Grande, built to protect settlers and travelers of the Mesilla Valley and San Augustin Pass from outlaws and marauding Gila and Mescalero Apaches. Scott was working as a government clerk at Fort Selden when he decided to try his hand at journalism.[7]

In Silver City, Scott soon earned a reputation for churning out persuasive yet often cantankerous editorials about various aspects of town life, in particular the lack of good public education and the need for a proper public school to corral the local kids. He dubbed them village arabs, a term much like street arabs, which was used in cities back East for vagabond children or homeless urchins who lived by their wits on the streets.[8] Disparaging names were nothing new to Henry. A few years earlier the newspaper editor in Wichita had called Henry a street gamin when the family resided there.[9]

"In the race of life, we know of a few boys in town who would benefit by coming in on the home stretch across the maternal knee," Scott wrote in one of his officious editorials. In an earlier column he stressed the need for the children to receive what he called "a real American education" because they were growing up "in idleness without an opportunity to improve their minds."[10]

Scott never published names of any specific village arabs, but he began associating the need for a public school with the need for a more substantial jail. When a sneak thief made off with thirty-five dollars from the cash drawer at Richard Knight's butcher shop, the newspaper advised: "It will pay to keep a good look out for these petty thieves now, as there are a number of them in town and they don't let any chance slip." On the same page another story noted that "the good attendance of children has been secured" for the Sunday school, perhaps a subtle hint for recalcitrant arabs.[11]

On March 28, 1874, when Dr. Webster dismissed classes and the school term ended, *Mining Life* recommended staging a series of amateur theatricals instead of allowing the students to grow idle and get into more trouble. According to the newspaper, the children could participate in the dramas and at the same time help raise funds to construct a schoolhouse. It was thought that morality plays would be the most appropriate fare for the village arabs.

One of the suggested plays was *Uncle Tom's Cabin*, based on Harriet Beecher Stowe's novel, already regarded as the most influential novel of the nineteenth century. Another was *Ten Nights in a Barroom*, a tearjerker temperance melodrama that gave audiences a vicarious glimpse of alcohol-induced wickedness.[12] Apparently no one raised the point that it really was not necessary to stage a play to reveal the adverse impact of liquor on the population. All anyone had to do was stroll past the saloons and whiskey mills lining the streets and witness up close the abysmal results of too much potent red-eye or mescal.

The reality of life in the mining town aside, other responsible parties must have agreed with the newspaper's proposal, for minstrel shows and sentimental melodramas were soon being staged at dance halls and meeting rooms around Silver City. Several of the arabs participated, and one of the most enthusiastic of them was Henry Antrim. No reviews of his performances survived, but fortunately his cohort Harry Whitehill furnished a glimpse of the troupe's shenanigans. In an interview, Whitehill described an episode that transpired just after runoff from torrential rains and snowmelt tore down the hillsides into arroyos, causing one of the town's periodic floods:

> I was what you call the property man. Well, some of us boys were walking down to Bailey's Drug Store on the other side of the old saloon. Billy the Kid was right behind me. He gave me a shove and I turned around and cussed him; and Billy gave me another shove and I went down in the flood. Well, I would have been drowned right there if two men hadn't come out of the Post Office just then and saved me.
>
> That night we went over there to give the minstrel. Billy was the Head Man in the show. When he came around to me I said, "I want you to pay me what you owe me." And Billy said he wasn't going to. "Well, if you don't I am going to tear this show up," I said. But Billy wouldn't give me a thing, so I went through a curtain and pulled it after me, you know. Later I happened to meet him but [Charley] Stevens kept him from beating me up.[13]

It was well known that Henry enjoyed singing. Perhaps one of his favorite songs, "Silver Threads Among the Gold," was included in the boy minstrel's repertoire. The popular tune had long become a standard of the minstrel form, especially among the professional companies touring the West as well as with amateurs attempting to entertain the hometown folks.

Henry's appreciation of song and dance came from his mother, and when her health allowed it, Catherine and her spirited son regularly attended the bailes. Public dances were held several nights each week at halls that usually adjoined saloons such as the social hops at McGary's Hall, the establishment that had served as the town's first courtroom and church on North Main. At Ward's Hall, only men were permitted to use the front door for easy access to gaming tables and the bar. Respectable ladies, such as Catherine Antrim, who had a hankering to dance had to go to the alley at the rear of the building and enter through double barn doors that opened onto a spacious dance floor, two hundred feet long and fifty feet wide.[14] Many townspeople turned out for the dances, some of which lasted until the wee hours.

Public bailes were also held in the Hispanic neighborhoods of Silver City, just as they were in villages throughout New Mexico Territory. Often these balls took place in a large sala, a reception room, where several cotillions—elaborate ballroom dances with frequent changing of partners—occurred at the same time.[15] Other popular dances included the vals (waltz), chotiz (schottische), polca (polka), and an assortment of regional dances found only in Nuevo México.

Musicians with violins, harps, guitars, horns, and sometimes an Indian tombe, or drum, played from a raised platform, and spectators took seats on both sides of the sala. Without fail, mothers or older female relatives accompanied young señoritas who came to the dances, hoping to enchant their dance partners. The chaperones quietly visited with one another on the sidelines, but their sharp eyes never left their charges twirling on the crowded floor.[16]

For amusement, some dancers still observed an old custom of filling hollowed eggshells with cologne water, which they broke over the heads of their friends as a matter of sport.[17] If Catherine and her musical son ever made it to one of the bailes on Chihuahua Hill—and given his love of the Hispanic culture, those chances are quite good—perhaps the young man with agile dancing feet experienced a burst of sweet liquid streaming down his smooth cheeks.

Back at the Americano shindigs, couples danced to some of Henry's favorite tunes such as "The Arkansas Traveler," "Fisher's Hornpipe," and "The Irish Washerwoman." Still, the dance tune that he loved the best remained "Turkey in the Straw," and he frequently requested it whether he was doing the jig with a young lady or his mama. "Mrs. Bill Antrim was a jolly Irish lady, full of life, and her fun and mischief," recalled Louis Abraham. "Mrs. Antrim could dance the Highland Fling as well as the best of dancers."[18]

Unfortunately Catherine's dancing days were drawing to a close. By the spring of 1874 the tuberculosis that seemed to be under control had resurfaced with a fury. Acrid fumes pouring from the smelter furnaces formed a canopy over the town. Every day Catherine's hacking, dry cough grew worse as she inhaled more of the smoky poison into her failing lungs. In a desperate effort to ward off the inevitable, Catherine made the journey to a lush high-desert oasis just twenty-six miles southeast of Silver City.[19]

For centuries the natural hot springs there had lured various Indian tribes, Spanish explorers, stagecoach travelers, soldiers, miners, and others seeking relief in the miraculous healing waters. Through the years the site had had many names such as Ojo Toro, or bull spring, because large numbers of wild bulls came there to drink daily; Ojo Caliente, or hot spring; and by the 1870s Mimbres Hot Springs, from the Spanish word for willows. Only in 1878–1879, after Colonel Richard Hudson acquired the property, did it become Hudson's Hot Springs.[20]

Besides their therapeutic qualities, those who camped there found other uses for the hot springs. Cooking fires were not necessary since a dressed rabbit, stuffed with bacon and seasoned with salt, could be submerged for a short time and cooked to perfection. Some said the water was hot enough to brew coffee and tea. There was even a cockeyed commercial scheme that was likely inspired by whiskey and not a soak in the sulfur waters. The fellow who thought it up suggested the organizing of the Toro Soup Company, arguing that "it would be such an easy matter to throw in some cattle and pipe the soup out over the plains." Alas, just days later the hapless gent was found dead of thirst on the southern plains.[21]

Richard Hudson first visited the hot springs in 1870 to seek relief from gout. His recovery was so remarkable he decided to purchase the property and open it to others suffering from various ailments, including consumption. His wife, Mary Stevens Hudson, became one of Catherine's friends and took a personal interest in her treatment.[22] "She [Catherine] was a sweet gentle little lady," recalled Mary Hudson, "as fond of her boys as any mother should be."[23]

Regrettably the baths could not restore Catherine's lungs. By May 1874 she was confined to her bed in the small cabin on Main Street in Silver City. At least she had some peace of mind as she took to her sickbed, knowing that her sons were back in the classroom. On May 18 a new teacher took the teaching reins from

Dr. Webster. Known to history only as Mrs. Pratt, the schoolmarm began a summer school session after some of the pupils, including Henry and Josie, had helped repair the adobe building's roof and whitewashed the walls. Unfortunately the school term was cut short when the annual deluge of August rains reduced the layer of dirt on the flat roof to a pool of mud and the weight caused the ceiling to come tumbling down on the students. School was promptly dismissed, and Mrs. Pratt left town never to return.[24]

It was apparent to Catherine's family and friends by then that she was in the final stages of her battle with consumption. Remarkably, it was at that critical juncture that William Antrim began spending even more time away from home on his prospecting trips. With their mother incapacitated and their stepfather gone most of the time, the Antrim brothers had little means of support. They also had no real adult supervision.

Right about this time Henry Antrim, dancing on the boundary that separates the lawful and the lawless, took his first step just over that very thin line. "Well, the first thing he [Henry] done, he tried to get an uncle of mine named Charlie Stevens to go in with him and rob a little peanut and candy stand an old fellow named Matt Devershire [Derbyshire] had," said Wayne Whitehill.[25]

The loot Henry sought was a display of costume jewelry in Derbyshire's store window that was to be raffled off by a Mexican circus passing through town. According to Wayne Whitehill, Henry and Charlie Stevens planned to break into the store, swipe the jewelry, and then hightail it to Mexico and dispose of their ill-gotten booty. On the eve of the burglary Charlie got cold feet and told his father, Isaac Stevens, about the plot. The angry father marched the boy directly to Derbyshire, and Charlie told the men that Henry "had me hypnotized."[26]

Stevens and Derbyshire tracked down Henry and gave both boys a thorough scolding. So that Charlie would not be labeled a squealer and become a target for Henry's revenge, the men said they learned about the burglary scheme from an old drunk who overheard the boys talking about their nefarious plans and reported it.[27] Following the thwarted burglary, a chastised and supposedly contrite Henry stayed on the straight and narrow for a while and tried to behave himself. Still, his mother grew more worried as well as angry. Perhaps this was the incident she found so disturbing she warned her son that if he took up a life of crime, "You'll hang before you're 21."[28]

Catherine's health quickly deteriorated. The disease consumed her lungs, and her body wasted away as she continually hacked up bloody sputum and bravely endured excruciating pain. With Bill Antrim mostly away, the two boys needed help in caring for their mother and themselves. Luckily for the family, Clara Louisa Truesdell, the mother of Henry's pal Chauncey, had graduated from nursing school in Chicago. She dutifully came to the Antrim cabin and tended to Catherine's needs for several months.[29] "When Mrs. Antrim was sick, she was worried about Joe and Henry, and she made my mother promise to look out for them if anything should happen to her," recalled Chauncey.[30]

Near the end, Catherine made another plea for Clara Truesdell's help. "When she was dying she said she was leaving two boys in a wild country and asked my mother if she would try to help them," said Chauncey. Clara promised Catherine that she would do her best to see after the boys. On Wednesday, September 16, 1874, Catherine Antrim took her last gasping breath, and her fevered life ended. She had lived to be forty-five years of age. She died in her own bed surrounded by her sons, Henry and Joseph, and Clara Truesdell. William Antrim was still gone, searching for riches that he never did find. He was not back in time for his wife's funeral, which took place the next afternoon at two at the family cabin.[31]

Clara Truesdell prepared Catherine for the ceremony. She washed the body, combed the hair, and dressed the dead woman in the best gown she owned. Besides Catherine's sons, members of the Truesdell, Stevens, and Whitehill families attended the simple service. Young Louis Abraham helped Henry and Josie dig their mother's grave in the town's burying ground. A coffin was built, and they made a wooden headboard to mark the place. "There was not a hearse in Silver City then so my father's Surry [sic] was used to carry the body to the cemetery," said Louis. "Billie [sic] and I as well, soon learned we had lost a dear ally and friend, as well as his mother. I have often been thankful that she never had to know of the trouble Billie [sic] became involved in for it would have broken her heart. How thankful I am to know that that good woman never had to face that heartache."[32]

On September 19 a notice of Catherine's death appeared in the newspaper. Of the three obituaries posted for that week, Catherine, at age forty-five, was the eldest. The other two, a miner and a married woman, were thirty-five.

Henry was just fourteen when his mother died. After she passed away, the two boys undoubtedly felt alienated and alone. For Henry, this loss was especially devastating. Without the parent he most loved and respected, Henry soon returned to his dance on that invisible line between the lawful and the lawless. It was a dance that proved to be a complete tragedy.

Darling, I am growing old,
Silver Threads Among the Gold,
Shine upon my brow today,
Life is fading fast away;

But my darling you will be, will be,
Always young and fair to me,
Yes, my darling you will be,
Always young and fair to me.[33]

Sheriff Harvey Whitehill, Silver City, New Mexico Territory,
date unknown
Photo Courtesy of the Silver City Museum,
Harlan Collection

TEN

GONE ON THE SCOUT

*As Henry grew into adolescence . . . he also grew increasingly free willed
and independent. Now on his own, with a mixture of anxiety and resolve
that may be imagined, he fixed a westward course into the unknown.*[1]

—ROBERT UTLEY

ENRY ANTRIM REMAINED in Silver City for almost a year follow-
ing the death of his mother. He did not always manage, however, to stay clear of
trouble. Far from it. Try as he might to keep on the straight and narrow, trouble had
a way of finding Henry and turning him upside down. Silver City was wide open
now with midwestern migrants filing in on their way to California, and Mexican
emigrants passing through on their way to Albuquerque and Denver. Without his
mother's guidance, not even the boldest gambler would have risked taking odds on
Henry ever becoming a productive citizen. In some ways, the Antrim brothers
might as well have been orphans. Although stories alleging that Bill Antrim was an
abusive stepfather are without merit, he appeared to be a man who not only did not

want the burden of looking after Catherine's sons but really did not know how to do it. As one writer cleverly puts it, Antrim seems to have done little for Henry "other than to lend him the second of three last names he used interchangeably."[2]

Other historians are kinder to William Antrim. They place most of the blame for Henry's problems squarely at his own diminutive boots, or more accurately his moccasins, since that was the footwear he and his chums preferred to wear.[3] Despite the less than ideal circumstances of Henry's upbringing and the dysfunctional aspects of his early life, many other children from similar backgrounds became productive members of society. Indeed, much of the nineteenth century was not ideal for a child growing up in the East or West.

There was little or no time for grieving over the loss of Catherine. When Antrim finally came home, he quickly farmed out his stepsons to obliging families while he sold the cabin on Main Street. Then he lit out again to prospect new mineral strikes in nearby Arizona Territory.

There is conjecture about the sequence of households that accommodated the Antrim brothers from early autumn of 1874 until the next year. For a brief period Henry and Joe may have stayed at the residence of Richard and Mary Hudson. The Hudsons owned the Legal Tender Livery and Feed Stable in Silver City. They later bought what became Hudson's Hot Springs, the place where Catherine had tried without success to regain her health. Mary had been one of Catherine's caregivers during her final months, so it makes sense that Antrim might have prevailed on the couple to take in his stepsons for a short time.[4] Others who knew Catherine also helped out, including the Knight family and, of course, Clara Truesdell, who later in the year gave Henry a place to live in her family home.

After a brief period of mourning, both Henry and Joe returned to school. On September 14, 1874, only two days before Catherine's death, public school classes started once more in Silver City, this time with Mary Phillipa Richards as the teacher. Described as "a willowy twenty-eight-year-old English gentlewoman," she supposedly was fluent in French, Italian, German, and Portuguese (no mention of Spanish) and claimed to be related to Alfred Lord Tennyson, Benjamin Disraeli, and John Ruskin. She had been schooled in England, Germany, and Paris. Her fancy pedigree aside, Mary Richards had also lived along the Texas-Mexico border as a young girl and moved to Silver City from a ranch in south-central Texas.[5]

When the Antrim brothers resumed book learning, their compadres quickly recognized that Henry was smitten with Miss Richards. A picture of refinement in her long bustled gowns, the stylish teacher parted her dark hair in the center and pulled her rolled tresses back smoothly into a chignon of braids, most likely made from someone else's hair, as was the mode in the mid-1870s.[6] Perhaps Henry developed a close attachment to his teacher because of the void left by the very recent loss of his mother. According to some sources, he was so taken with Miss Richards that he even fantasized that they were blood kin.

"He thought this because they were both ambidextrous," the teacher's daughter, Patience Glennon, said in later years. "My mother could write equally well with either hand, and so could Billy [Henry]. He noticed this and he used to say to my mother that he was sure they were related because she was the only other person he had ever seen, besides himself, who could do things equally well with either hand."[7]

Miss Richards proved to be a capable teacher. For the most part, Owen Scott, the crusading newspaper editor who considered taming the village arabs his personal crusade, frequently applauded her. While he praised her for transforming unruly youngsters into conscientious scholars, he also doled out criticism, including a critique of the students' poor posture. Following one of his periodic visits to the school, Scott wrote: "The larger boys, we are sorry to see, were inattentive. It is a shame for the big lubberly boys to lean against each other, or hang their bodies while in recitation class."[8]

Miss Richards taught in Silver City until October 5, 1875, when she wed Daniel Charles Casey, a carpenter from Wisconsin. The couple moved to Georgetown, New Mexico Territory, where they raised six children and where Mary died on the first day of January 1900.[9] Before her death the former teacher of the Antrim brothers recalled the few months they were in her charge. She said that the student Henry Antrim was "a scrawny little fellow with delicate hands and an artistic nature ... always quite willing to help with the chores around the school-house. He was no more of a problem than any other boy growing up in a mining camp."[10]

In 1937, Augusta Levy Abraham, wife of Louis Abraham, shared more memories of those school days as told to her by her husband. "I didn't know Billie [sic] the Kid, but my husband went to school with him. The boys and girls that knew him never thought of him as a criminal, but a boy that was full of fun and mischief. He like all boys liked to put a snake on the teacher's desk or chase a girl with a mouse, and the other hundreds of things that fun loving mischief boys like to do. His eyes were always dancing and full of mischievous fun."[11]

Henry's eyes left an impression on other folks as well. "His eyes were full of fun," remembered Silver City resident Dick Clark. "He was generous and kind to everyone until someone did him dirt then he would seek revenge, which was his beginning on the road to crime."[12]

Sheriff Harvey Whitehill had a different opinion about Henry Antrim's eyes. Whitehill thought the young man's eyes may have danced but that only meant they were shifty and indicated Henry had larceny in his heart. "There was one peculiar facial characteristic that to an experienced manhunter, would have marked him immediately as a bad man and that was his dancing eyes," Whitehill told a reporter in 1902. "They never were at rest but continually shifted and roved, much like his own rebellious nature."[13]

Whitehill, whose children ran with Henry, was not yet an established man-hunter when he first became acquainted with the Antrim family. He had served as the county coroner until 1874, when Sheriff Charles McIntosh suddenly vanished. It turned out that McIntosh, recovering from wounds received in the line of duty and weary of low pay, absconded with three thousand dollars in county funds and took out for Mexico. In April 1875 the voters gave the job to Whitehill.[14]

By then William Antrim had decided his obligations as stepfather were coming to an end. It was high time for Joseph and Henry to make their own way in the world. After the brief stint living with the Hudsons following Catherine's death, the boys joined Antrim as boarders in the home of Richard and Sara Knight. Henry worked part-time at Knight's butcher shop, as did William Antrim when he was not off somewhere prospecting.

By the end of 1874 the brothers were split up. Joseph Antrim moved in with Joe Dyer and his family and earned his keep by working at Dyer's infamous Orleans Club. Under Dyer's tutelage Joseph learned all about gambling, taking bets, running numbers, and serving hard liquor to thirsty men.

"We used to have a pretty good sized Chinatown in Silver City and there were several opium dens running then," recalled Olive Whitehill, daughter of the sheriff. "Wayne [Olive's brother] said he and some other boys used to go there and peek through the cracks in the windows and doors to see who was smoking opium. Wayne told me that they saw Billy the Kid's brother, Joe, down there smoking opium, along with the Chinamen. At least I never heard tell of Billy doing that."[15]

Gerald and Clara Truesdell, pillars of the community and the parents of Chauncey, took in Henry. Clara had established a millinery shop on Hudson Street in late 1874, and a few months later her husband purchased and renovated the Star Hotel, which he renamed the Exchange.[16] "When Henry was living with us after his mother died, he earned his room and board by waiting on tables and helping with the dishes," said Chauncey Truesdell. "After he was gone, my father said Henry was the only kid who ever worked there who never stole anything. Other fellows used to steal the silverware. No, I don't know if it was real silver but they stole it because that kind of stuff was scarce in camp in those days."[17]

When he was not working at the hotel or going to school, Henry spent most of his time with his fellow village arabs. By now the boys' favorite diversion was tormenting Charlie Sun, a Chinese immigrant who had come to Silver City from Albuquerque and opened a hand laundry on Bullard Street. Sun's presence so threatened Nellie Johnson, a town laundress, that she placed an advertisement in *Mining Life* that warned, "Boys, that Chinaman can't do as well for you as I can. Bring your washing to Texas Street."[18]

Charlie Sun did not necessarily endear himself to the white citizens already prone to racial prejudice when it came to the growing number of Chinese moving into Silver City and other mining towns throughout the West. According to Wayne Whitehill, when Sun's Mexican wife became pregnant, "he was around celebrating around the saloon, treatin' everybody on account of this baby. And when that baby was born it was a nigger. And so he had an old sow out in the backyard and he took that baby and threw it in there and the sow killed it. No, there wasn't anything done about it."[19]

Even after Sam Chung, who, like Charlie Sun, did not subscribe to all the traditions of ancient Chinese culture such as wearing the distinctive pigtail, became a partner in the laundry, most white citizens still had little respect for the Chinese. "In fact," writes Frederick Nolan, "the residents of Silver City looked on their presence and their opium dens in Hop Town with undisguised disfavor. It didn't take the 'arabs' long to learn that nobody cared what pranks got played on the Asians."[20]

In interviews Wayne Whitehill later granted, he recounted tales of the local boys bullying the Chinese after unnamed adults "gave us orders to chase all the Chinamen out of town, they didn't want Chinamen there."[21] From then on the boys openly mocked the singsong cadence of the Chinese laundrymen's speech and even pelted them with rocks. Wayne recalled that one boy threw a rock that found its mark, and as a result, "this Chinamen was floppin' around like a chicken with his head cut off. . . . We all took to our heels. God, I was home in no time under the bed. . . . We knew damn well that Chinamen was killed all right. Well, there was never a thing said about it at all."[22] According to Wayne, among the boys present when the man was stoned to death was Henry Antrim.

The stoning death described by Wayne Whitehill remains in doubt since no record of it has ever been found, at least from the time Henry Antrim was part of the village arabs, 1873 to 1875. If such a crime did take place, it must have been several years later, when Henry was long gone from Silver City. Still, many journalists and dime novelists who heard the story, eager to ascribe as many savage murders as possible to the young man, actually attributed the brutal slaying to Henry as a lone operative. Some claimed he killed the man with a rock; others said that he used a knife to cut the man's throat.

Over the years more exaggerated stories and outright lies about other crimes and killings supposedly carried out by young Henry also surfaced. One tall tale that made the rounds claimed Henry used a jackknife given to him as a gift by his stepfather to behead a neighbor's kitten.[23] Another falsehood popped up in Pat Garrett's ghostwritten book. It alleged that the first murder the young man committed was the stabbing death of a blacksmith in Silver City. Henry supposedly knifed the man, after he insulted Catherine Antrim and then later attacked Ed Moulton, a sawmill owner and friend of the Antrim family's, who came to Catherine's defense.[24]

"Billie [sic] the Kid never did kill anyone in Silver City," Jim Blair, Moulton's son-in-law, told a researcher in the late 1930s.[25] "That story is all false. The story of him killing a man over Ed Moulton is positively not true. Mr. Moulton never would read an article about Billie [sic] because he would become angry for he said 'They write so many lies about that boy, and I know the ones are false about his killings in Grant County.'"

Several of Henry Antrim's boyhood friends backed up Moulton's denial of Henry's supposed revenge killing. They insisted on the record that he never killed anyone in the town. Wayne Whitehill branded such stories "poppycock," and Louis Abraham and Chauncey Truesdell agreed. "The story about him killing a man here in Silver City is all foolishness," said Anthony Connor, recalling the days Antrim and his stepsons boarded at the Knight home. "We were just boys together. I never remember him doing anything out of the way, any more than the rest of us. We had our chores to do, like washing the dishes and other duties about the house." Connor believed that Henry's problems with the law came from his choice of reading material. "Billy got to be quite a reader. He would scarcely have the dishes washed, until he would be sprawled out somewhere reading a book. It was the same down at the butcher shop, if he was helping around there. The first thing you know, he would be reading. Finally, he took to reading the *Police Gazette* and dime novels."[26] Given the vast number of boys and men who faithfully devoured the pulps and dime novels of that time and did *not* end up criminals, it is unlikely that reading such lurid stories was a major contributor to Henry Antrim's youthful behavioral problems.

Antrim's earliest biographers sought excuses for the youngster's descent into the world of crime and placed much of the blame on his reading the *Police Gazette* and dime novels. A more likely factor, however, was Henry's slight physique, which placed him in precarious situations with bigger and stronger boys.

Whatever caused Henry's decent into a life of crime, he was fifteen years old when a transgression finally brought him to the attention of the law. Larceny of fresh butter from an unattended buckboard may not have been cold-blooded murder, but it was enough to earn the young man a stern scolding and a spanking from the sheriff himself. "I believe I was the first officer who ever arrested him," remembered Harvey Whitehill twenty-seven years later. "The lad early developed a proclivity for breaking the eighth commandment. His first offense was the theft of several pounds of butter from a ranchman by the name of [Abel] Webb, living near Silver City, and which he disposed of to one of the local merchants. His guilt was easily established, but upon promise of good behavior, he was released."[27]

Henry wasted no time in getting into more trouble. By July 1875, because of what have been described as domestic problems in the Truesdell home, Henry was forced to seek other lodging and moved into a boardinghouse maintained by Sarah Brown.[28] With school out of session, Henry worked at various odd jobs and hung out with his "opium-smoking" brother, Joe, at the Orleans Club. This experience convinced Henry that gambling might be more profitable than peddling stolen butter.

Gambling was looked upon as a legitimate way to make a living in most frontier settlements. Silver City was no exception, where it was said folks gambled on everything from dogfights to the weather. Taking a cue from his brother and stepfather, Billy became a diligent cardplayer. At the Orleans Club and the other saloons around town the youngster soon realized that his youthful appearance made older men think of him as an easy mark as he dealt monte and poker.

Meanwhile Henry had mistakenly placed his trust in a rascal named George Schaefer, a young stonemason and fellow boarder at Mrs. Brown's. Nicknamed Sombrero Jack because of his love of the distinctive Mexican headwear, Schaefer had a penchant for strong drink and property theft.[29] He was not the ideal companion for a youngster susceptible to recklessness like Henry Antrim. "Every Saturday night, George would get drunk," said Sheriff Whitehill. "But he thought a lot of Billy and Billy used to follow him around. The fellow George liked to steal. He had a mania to steal and he was always stealing."[30]

On Saturday, September 4, 1875, his usual night for binge drinking, Sombrero Jack broke into the residence of Charlie Sun, the Chinese laundry operator often besieged by the village arabs. He made off with a pair of revolvers and a large bundle of blankets and clothing that belonged to several customers. The total worth of the loot came to between $150 and $200.[31] The thief stashed the booty in a pit at Crawford's Mill in nearby Georgetown and offered Henry a share if he would smuggle the bundle back to Silver City. Henry jumped at the chance to get some fresh clothing and accepted.

Some days later, when cleaning his room, Mrs. Brown discovered the contraband stashed in a trunk. She hurried straight to Sheriff Whitehill and told him that Henry was wearing stolen clothing and hiding more of the ill-gotten property at her boardinghouse. The sheriff, not knowing anything about Sombrero Jack's role in the crime, collared Henry on September 23. By then the real culprit was long gone. Ironically, in his later years George Schaefer rehabilitated himself enough to become a justice of the peace in Georgetown.[32]

"I did all I could for the orphaned boy," Whitehill later said of Henry Antrim. "After all, he was somebody's son and a boy who didn't need to go wrong."[33] Despite Whitehill's sentiment, Henry was hauled before Justice of the Peace Isaac Givens, who listened to Whitehill's recital of the known facts of the case. Even after learning that Sombrero Jack was the actual perpetrator of the burglary, both Givens and Whitehill could not ignore Henry's involvement. To teach the delinquent a lesson, Henry was charged with larceny and ordered bound over to the county jail to await the next session of the grand jury.[34]

For the first time in his life Henry Antrim found himself incarcerated. The sheriff placed him in a cell in the new jailhouse, which was highly touted as the best prison in the area with the possible exception of the Fort Bayard guardhouse.[35] The sheriff later admitted that he had not intended to keep Henry jailed too long, just long enough to give the youngster a jolt as well as a taste of life as an inmate. At home the sheriff faced what was described as a "storm of protest" from the rest of the Whitehill family for jailing Henry. Even the sheriff's wife, Harriet, beseeched him to bring Henry home for a proper breakfast.[36]

"It [Henry's crime] did not amount to anything, and Mr. Whitehill only wished to scare him," said Anthony Connor. "I think he planned on releasing him after allowing him to think it over for a short time. He did not pay much attention to him. I believe the sheriff merely wanted to leave him there alone for awhile so that Billy [Henry] could realize what such acts could lead to."[37] Sheriff Whitehill did not get the opportunity to offer the youngster the hospitality of his family's home. On September 25, after only two days in jail, Henry, as anxious as a whore in church, made his escape. Whitehill later described it:

> One day the "Kid" complained to me that the jailer was treating him roughly and kept him in solitary confinement in his cell without any exercise. So I ordered that he be allowed to remain in the corridor for a limited time each morning. He was only a boy, you must remember, scarcely over 15 years of age. Yet we made the mistake of leaving him alone in the corridor for a short half hour. When we returned and unlocked the heavy oaken [sic] doors of the jail, the "Kid" was nowhere to be seen. I ran outside around the jail and a Mexican standing on a ridge at the rear asked whom I was hunting. I replied in Spanish "a prisoner." "He came out of the chimney," answered the Mexican. I ran back into the jail, looked up the big old fashioned chimney and sure enough could see where in an effort to obtain a hold his hands had clawed into the thick layer of soot which lined the side of the flue. The chimney hole itself did not appear as large as my arm and yet the lad squeezed his frail slender body through it and gained his liberty. Then commenced his career of lawlessness in earnest.[38]

The next morning the story of Henry's daring escape appeared in the *Silver City Herald*: "Henry McCarty, who was arrested on Thursday and committed to jail to await the action of the grand jury, upon charge of stealing clothes from Charley [sic] Sun and Sam Chung, celestials sans cue [queue], sans joss sticks, escaped from prison yesterday through the chimney. It is believed that Henry was simply the tool of 'Sombrero Jack,' who done the stealing whilst Henry done the hiding. Jack has skinned out."[39] It was the first story ever published about Henry (McCarty) Antrim. It was far from being the last.

Like his criminal mentor Sombrero Jack, Henry had dodged the consequences. He was now a fugitive running from the law, or in the lingo of that time and place, he was "among the willows, on the dodge, gone on the scout."[40] Henry had danced well over that thin line separating the lawful and lawless, and he never quite found his way back to the other side.

Old overland stage

ELEVEN

SADDLE TRAMP

*New Mexico Territory was a harsh and uncertain world for a youngster
to face, but it didn't seem to have caused the boy much concern.
Self-confident and fearless, if he ever looked back, except to miss his
mother's love, it was not recorded.*[1]

•

—LEE PRIESTLEY WITH MARQUITA PETERSON

COVERED FROM HEAD to toe in soot and looking like a minstrel in
blackface, Henry Antrim knew of few places to flee to after squirreling up the Silver City jail chimney and making good his bold high noon escape.

Over the years, as with so many incidents in his life, several people later
claimed that they had provided Henry safe haven from the long arm of the law in
Silver City. Among the claimants was Manuel Taylor, one of Henry's older pals.[2]
He said that when the fugitive showed up at the Taylor residence, he gave the
youngster an old shotgun and that Henry took off for Camp Thomas, an army
post in Arizona Territory. There Henry supposedly shot and killed a buffalo soldier, stole his horse, and hightailed it back to southern New Mexico Territory. This
scenario is entirely fictitious. Camp Thomas did not even exist until August 1876,
almost a year later.[3]

Sarah Brown, the landlady who had turned in Henry to Sheriff Whitehill in the first place, said the boy came to her and that she and another woman put him on a stagecoach bound for Arizona Territory. It is also unlikely that this occurred since Henry would have known better than to seek help from the person responsible for his arrest.

The Knight family maintained that Henry trudged the fifteen miles from town to their ranch and stayed there for a few days before moving to Arizona Territory. Mary Richards Casey, the ambidextrous schoolmarm who had won Henry's heart, backed up the story.[4] Years later she related the details to her daughter, Patience Glennon.

"She and Mrs. Knight put him up in the barn and brought him food for a couple of days and they tried to reason with him," said Patience. "They advised him to go back to Silver City and give himself up, that the penalty for what he had done was in no way as harsh as would be the life he would live in hiding. He agreed to go back to Silver City and they loaned him a horse to go back on. But he was afraid to be put back into jail and he went in the opposite direction as soon as he was out of their sight. He went to Arizona, my mother learned later."[5] As believable as it sounds, the main problem with Richards's account is that she and her husband, Daniel Casey, did not wed until ten days after Henry's escape and several months before the couple moved to the ranch. The teacher, someone not given to tall tales, may have confused the incident with another time when she assisted Henry.

Of all the people Henry might have turned to, the most plausible candidate was Clara Truesdell. Chances are good that after he made his escape he went straight to the Truesdell home. Almost his surrogate mother, Clara disposed of his soiled garments and gave him some of Chauncey's clothing to wear. At nightfall she sent Henry up to Ed Moulton's sawmill on Bear Mountain, where Joe Dyer's wife cooked for all the working hands. Clara figured Henry would be safe there until she could reason with Sheriff Whitehill about giving him still another chance.[6]

That was not to be. She failed to sway the lawman, who was determined to apprehend Henry and return him to the hoosegow, the anglicized word for the Spanish term for "jail."[7] Once he got a bead on the runaway, Sheriff Whitehill and his tenacious deputy, the five-foot-seven-inch-tall Dan Tucker, mounted up and made tracks to Moulton's place. They were too late. Henry Antrim had been tipped off. He was long gone.

"He had a mind whose ingenuity we knew not of at the time," said Sheriff Whitehill, reflecting on Henry's last days in Silver City.[8] "He [Henry] managed to get away and come to us," said Chauncey Truesdell. "My mother washed Henry's clothes and dried them by the stove. My brother Gideon, Henry and I slept on the floor that night. The next morning mother stopped the stage as it passed our door and asked the driver to take Henry to Globe City [Arizona Territory]. Mother gave Henry all the money she had and a little lunch to eat."[9]

Although the stage he took from Silver City went to the mining camp of Clifton, not to Globe City, Henry spent most of the next two years, if not all of his time, on the scout in Arizona Territory.[10] Nonetheless, future chroniclers of his life would have their readers believe that travels of the young desperado spanned the nation and that he even journeyed beyond, committing outrageous acts of violence. Many of those stories were published and widely accepted as the truth, adding fuel to the myth that would one day become Billy the Kid. Jerry Weddle writes:

> Later, when dime novelists wrote up the adventures of Billy the Kid, they imaginatively filled in the next two years with border raids into old Mexico, a jail break at San Elizaro [*sic*], and the mass slaughter of Indians, Mexicans, and Chinese, all in the flowery and racist dime-novel tradition. But the most fanciful tale came from the pages of a New York City newspaper. In a ludicrous case of mistaken identity, the *Sun* reported that Billy the Kid had stabbed a drunk to death in a street brawl—in the Fourth Ward ghetto of New York City. Writers ignored the more pragmatic testimony of Billy's contemporaries amidst all this imaginary blood-letting. They agreed on his destination if not his mode of transport. Billy headed west, not east.[11]

Travelers from Silver City to the mining camps in Arizona Territory still made their way in the mid-1870s by stagecoach, freight wagon, buckboard, and army ambulance over barely passable roads twisting through mountainous country. The notion of Henry's taking a stage flagged down at the Truesdell residence makes sense inasmuch as that mode of travel was the most common. It also was uncomfortable, with often as many as nine or ten passengers crammed into one coach.[12]

Besides a harrowing ride that promised plenty of steep paths, hairpin turns, and deep gorges, there remained the threat of Indian attack or armed robbery.

"A rifle at your head and a six-shooter at your breast are terrible persuaders," explained an Arizona Territory stage passenger who in 1877 had been left penniless and terrified by outlaws demanding, "Your money or your life!"[13]

For travelers stage-station food, "notoriously hard on the digestive tract," was almost as much to be feared as Apaches and highwaymen. Most meals lasted only as long as it took to change the teams of horses. Standard fare consisted of salt pork or greasy beef as tough as boot leather, mesquite beans, coarse bread, and chicory coffee sweetened with molasses. Sometimes wild game, such as venison or antelope, was served, and it was not uncommon to dine on mule flesh.[14] Fortunately on his stage ride to the mining camp of Clifton in southeastern Arizona Territory, Henry had the lunch Clara Truesdell had made for him.

When his jolting coach ride came to a halt in Clifton, the terminus for the westbound stage, Henry had to be thankful. Nestled in a narrow, cliff-lined gorge carved by the San Francisco River and its main tributary, Chase Creek, Clifton was one of the oldest and richest copper camps in the Southwest.[15] It had in fact become a center for mining starting in the 1860s, when army scouts found copper outcroppings just north of the confluence of the Gila and San Francisco rivers. After 1870, as the demand for copper grew, so did Clifton, and within a few more years so did nearby Joy's Camp, later named Morenci.[16] Mine workers and prospectors poured into the region, filing claims and erecting tents and ramshackle cabins across the hillsides.

Hoping to get rich in a hurry, they came from across the nation and around the world. There were Mexicans from Sonora, New Mexicans from the mining country to the east, gringos out of the copper mines of Michigan, ex-Confederate soldiers, and contingents from Spain, Scotland, Wales, and China. When the day's work was done, everyone flocked to Chase Creek Street to fight roosters or watch dogs and badgers go at it.[17] There were gambling and drinking establishments galore and enough soiled doves to help the most stiffly crippled miner forget his aches and pains for a few minutes.

Henry Antrim did not stop in Clifton to mine copper for four dollars a day in wages. He went to find his stepfather.[18] While some historians argue William Antrim was residing at Chloride Flat, a mining camp just west of Silver City, other authorities contend that Clifton is where Henry sought out his stepfather. There is no record of exactly where Henry stopped first after entering Arizona Territory, but it was likely he knew his stepfather had relocated to Clifton to work the mines.

Henry tracked down his stepfather but received a far from cordial reception.

After explaining his plight and sharing details of the Silver City caper and subsequent escape, Henry asked his stepfather for help, but William Antrim replied that he would no longer support his stepson. According to Harry Whitehill, an angry Antrim told Henry: "If that's the kind of boy you are, get out."[19] Whitehill added that if Antrim "had taken him in then Billy [Henry] would have been all right. But he didn't and the kid turned bad. The boy didn't know what to do, so he went up into the old man's room, stole his six-shooter and some clothes, and beat it." It was the last time Henry ever saw William Antrim.

Abandoned, destitute, and with no prospects apparent in Clifton, Henry took to the open road once more. He stayed in Arizona Territory for two years. He was out of the reach of authorities back in Silver City, and for a short time his record was clean. But what he found in Arizona Territory was a conflict among Anglos, Indians, and Mexican laborers. Large companies from back East had moved into the ore business and employed inexperienced Mexican laborers to work their mines. Their presence, combined with that of the "free-lance" prospectors who only picked away for riches, then moved on, made Arizona Territory even more dangerous than Silver City.

Some of Henry's friends claimed he went to work for cattle rancher Peter Eldridge Slaughter, a native Texan and former Confederate soldier who grazed sizable herds across Texas and in Arizona Territory as far north as the high-country ranges of the White Mountains.[20] Slaughter's rough trail hands worked livestock in the thin mountain air, shot meddlesome bears, and bunked in log huts with dirt floors.

Slaughter hailed from a well-known family of Texas cattle barons who included his father, George Webb Slaughter, and brother, C. C. (for Christopher Columbus) Slaughter, who became the largest individual landowner in all Texas. Pete also was a cousin of John Horton Slaughter, known as a fearless Texas Ranger and Confederate soldier who became a prominent cattleman and law officer in Cochise County, Arizona Territory.

Pete Slaughter drove cattle in Arizona Territory for years before establishing his PS Ranch headquarters at the head of the Black River. His ranch was fully operational by 1881, the year that Henry Antrim (aka Billy the Kid) died.

Whether or not Henry ever drew wages from Pete Slaughter during his time in Arizona Territory, the young man undoubtedly crossed paths with men who rode on both sides of the law. Merchants operating in the vast open country above Clifton made a living selling to Mormon settlers and outlaws alike. Stealing horses and cattle in southern Arizona Territory and then selling them to ranchers in the north could be profitable. Naturally the outlaws simply reversed the procedure and returned south with another herd of stolen stock to sell there.[21] Joseph A. Munk describes the scene in *Arizona Sketches*, published in 1905.

> Dishonest men are found in the cattle business the same as in other occupations and every year a large number of cattle are misappropriated and stolen from the range. Cattle have been stolen by the wholesale and large herds run off and illegally sold before the owner discovered his loss.
>
> The owner of cattle on the open range must be constantly on his guard against losses by theft. Usually the thief is a dishonest neighbor or one of his own cowboys who becomes thrifty at the owner's expense. Many a herd of cattle was begun without a single cow, but was started by branding surreptitiously other people's property. It is not an easy manner to detect such a thief or to convict on evidence when he is arrested and brought to trial. A cattle thief seldom works alone, but associates himself with others of his kind who will perjure themselves to swear each other clear.[22]

It did not take Henry long to resort to thievery himself. Leading the life of a saddle tramp, he moved from ranches and farms, gathering hay or herding cattle along the Gila River and San Simon Valley in southeastern Arizona Territory.[23] Because of his slight physique, Henry probably found the demands of range and farm life beneath the merciless desert sun particularly grueling. However, he soon discovered that all the gambling tips he had picked up from his brother, Joseph, and stepfather, William, in the gaming houses and saloons of Silver City were paying off.

It was easy to slip into a faro or monte game at the recently decommissioned army post of Camp Goodwin on the Gila River, not far from the San Carlos Apache Indian Reservation. Other opportunities awaited in the Mormon settlement of Safford and the nearby hamlet of Pueblo Viejo, where a skilled gambler could leave with more cash money than he would make in a hay field or out on the dusty range.

In early 1876 Henry heard talk of even riper pickings and a chance to make plenty of money at the expense of soldiers and cattle herders at gaming tables near Camp Grant, in the Sulphur Springs Valley, below the towering Pinaleno Mountains. All the young hustler had to do was get there. On March 19, 1876, Henry found his means of transportation. He stole a horse belonging to one Private Charles Smith, a soldier traveling on detached service, who had briefly paused at old Camp Goodwin on his way to Camp Apache.[24] Astride the stolen mount, Henry took off for Fort Grant, looking for whatever opportunities he could find.

The Hotel de Luna near Fort Grant, Arizona Territory, late 1870s

THE BOB BOZE BELL COLLECTION

TWELVE

KID ANTRIM

It was here in Arizona that Henry—or Billy—first became known as "Kid," an appellation which would naturally come to a boy working among mature men.[1]

—ROBERT N. MULLIN

AMERICA TURNED one hundred years old in 1876, and Henry Antrim turned seventeen. It was a pivotal year for both the nation and the young man.

In the United States the Republican candidate, Rutherford B. Hayes, was chosen president by a single electoral vote over Samuel J. Tilden in a highly disputed election marked by fraud and scandal. That year Americans flocked to the first National League baseball game, cheered Colorado's entry into the Union, and clucked their tongues when Mark Twain's newly published novel *The Adventures of Tom Sawyer* was banned at the Brooklyn and Denver public libraries.[2] To commemorate the nation's birthday, the Centennial Exposition was held in Philadelphia. The spectacle featured a wide variety of attractions and displays ranging from such revolutionary contraptions as Alexander Graham Bell's telephone and the Remington typewriter to George Washington's false teeth and such snack foods as hot popcorn and exotic bananas packaged in tinfoil that cost a whole dime.[3]

A popular display sponsored by the Smithsonian Institution and the Department of the Interior presented Indian "curiosities." This prompted William Dean Howells, then an observer for the *Atlantic Monthly*, to declare: "The red man, as he appears in effigy and in photograph in this collection, is a hideous demon, whose malign traits can hardly inspire any emotion softer than abhorrence."[4] Howells's commentary, coming from so public and respected an intellectual, reinforced every stereotype about Indians that was being promulgated across the nation, especially in the Southwest. In the territories of Arizona and New Mexico bands of Apaches continued their futile guerrilla warfare with white invaders who came with mining tools, great herds of cattle, and broken promises. For many years chroniclers of Arizona history perpetuated the myth of racial superiority by referring to white citizens as Americans while at the same time degrading the Indian and Hispanic populations.

This remained the standard until after the turn of the century. Joseph Munk, for instance, wrote in 1905:

> the bloodthirsty Apache, who seems to delight only in killing people. Cunning and revenge are pronounced traits of his character and the Government has found him difficult to conquer or control. The Mexican leads a shiftless, thriftless life and seems satisfied merely to exist. He has, unfortunately, inherited more of the baser than the better qualities of his ancestors and, to all appearance, is destined to further degenerate. The *American* is the last comer and has already pushed civilization and commerce into the remote corners and, as usual, dominates the land.[5]

Beyond the perpetuation of white supremacy beliefs, some of the most enduring myths of the American West were either reinforced or created in 1876.

On June 25, for example, near the Little Bighorn River, Montana Territory, a force of Lakota and Northern Cheyenne warriors annihilated the controversial Lieutenant Colonel George Armstrong Custer and 261 men of the Seventh Cavalry.[6] Hailed as Custer's Last Stand, this least understood yet most frequently depicted episode in American history inflamed the nation's passion and aroused further hatred of Indians. It became the subject of articles, dime novels, and illustrations that ingrained an inflated legend of a glorified and martyred Custer in the American imagination.

Six weeks later, on August 2, the picturesque character named James Butler

Hickok, better known by the colorful moniker Wild Bill Hickok, was shot and killed from behind at a poker table in Saloon No. 10 in Deadwood, Dakota Territory.[7] Already a legend thanks to dime novelists and his stage appearances back East, Hickok grew even larger in death.

Finally, on September 7, the James gang, led by brothers Jesse and Frank, were shot to pieces during a bank robbery in Northfield, Minnesota. Only Jesse and Frank escaped unscathed. Soon they were back on the scout, and before members of his own gang killed him in 1882, Jesse James had become a part of American folklore for all time.[8]

Given the spectacles of these three events, it is not surprising that young Henry Antrim's flight from the law drew minimal attention. Earlier that spring, on April 19, 1876, months before Custer, Wild Bill, and Jesse made bold headlines, Antrim showed up near Camp Grant, Arizona Territory, looking for work.[9] Anyone who saw him that spring day could never have guessed that the scruffy teenage horseman would become even more mythologized than Custer, Hickok, and James. As for Henry Antrim, at that moment he had no thoughts of myths or legends. After a long ride down a wagon road, all he wanted was a dry bed, cold water, and the chance to start all over once more.

"He may have started out as an Irish cowboy, but he became an American cowboy," writes Fintan O'Toole, examining the Irish roots of Henry's heritage in a superb article about Billy the Kid that appeared in the New Yorker. "For he embodied the greatest of American paradigms, that of an immigrant making a new life. He discovered that out here, where no one knows you, you are free to invent a new life and call it authentic, to spin a story and find that others will tell it for you, to escape from history and enter the vast playground of myth."[10]

For Henry, Camp Grant was in all likelihood as good a place as any to create a new life. Named for Ulysses S. Grant, the camp replaced an abandoned army post of the same name at the junction of the San Pedro River and Aravaipa Creek.[11] The old camp had been the site of the notorious Camp Grant Massacre, when in the predawn hours of April 30, 1871, a gang of nearly 150 vigilantes, mostly Hispanics and Papago Indians led by several prominent Anglos from Tucson, attacked a settlement of sleeping Pinal and Aravaipa Apaches. In less than a half hour the raiders raped, mutilated, and slaughtered more than 100 defenseless people, mostly women and children. At least 30 more Apache children were taken captive to be sold as slaves. Only 7 people survived the carnage.[12]

Citizens back East, stirred up by newspaper headlines, were horrified by reports of the grisly genocide, and President Grant angrily denounced the blood-bath. In Arizona Territory, however, few people were sympathetic. A trial for a hundred of those accused of murder was held less than a year later, but it was a sham. After just nineteen minutes of deliberation all the defendants, including a former Tucson mayor, were acquitted of all charges.[13]

In 1872 General George Crook, regarded by many white Americans as the greatest of all "Indian fighters," selected the site of the new Camp Grant (it became Fort Grant in 1879), at the base of towering Mount Graham in the Pinaleno Mountains some forty-five miles southeast of the original post. By January 1873 eleven companies of cavalry and infantry had been transferred to the new camp. They immediately started construction of a stone commissary building, officers' quarters, and a wagon road up the mountainside.[14]

Mounted troops from the camp patrolled southeastern Arizona and western New Mexico Territories, chasing small bands of Apaches and keeping the peace. Among the soldiers was the writer Edgar Rice Burroughs, who was stationed at Fort Grant in 1896 with Troop B, Seventh U.S. Cavalry (Custer's old regiment) long before he created the popular cultural icon known as Tarzan.[15]

The majority of troopers at Camp Grant and other army posts across the West bore no resemblance to Burroughs, who had been born into a prosperous Chicago family and attended private schools. Army recruits often were poor, illiterate, and foreign-born, mostly Irish and German immigrants. The pay was poor, as was the food. Desertion was common. Soldiers were mostly young bachelors, since during the 1870s the army discouraged enlisted men from marrying. Men who wed without permission could be charged with insubordination.[16]

Life was excruciatingly hard and often monotonous at frontier outposts. The men spent most of their time in manual labor. When they were in the garrison and not on patrol or on the parade field, boredom took its toll on off-duty soldiers. They yearned for more to do than seek out patches of shade beneath clumps of mesquites. Growing weary of waiting for letters and newspapers that often took weeks to arrive, they reread dime novels or took potshots at coyotes and skunks drawn to the garbage piles in nearby ravines. Troopers were more than willing to part with their pay for a game of chance, some strong drink, or a wildcat whore.

"The temptations to drink and gamble were indeed great, and those who yielded and fell by the way-side numbered many of the most promising youngsters in the army," wrote Captain John G. Bourke, a Congressional Medal of Honor recipient and aide-de-camp to General George Crook in Arizona Territory.[17] "Many a brilliant and noble fellow has succumbed to the *ennui* and gone down, wrecking a life full of promise for himself and the service. Of the two vices, drunkenness was by all odds the preferable one. For a drunkard, one can have some pity, because he is his own worst enemy, and at worst, there is hope for his regeneration, while there is absolutely none for the gambler, who lives upon the misfortunes and lack of shrewdness of his comrade."

A savvy gambler himself, Henry Antrim understood the behavior of soldiers, especially after they drew wages at the paymaster's table. Although he did pursue some ranch and range work, the chance to pocket money at the gaming tables was what really attracted him to the Camp Grant area.

Henry went directly to the settlement less than three miles southwest of Camp Grant known as McDowell's store. Close at hand and just outside the boundaries of the military reservation was a scattering of saloons, gambling dens, dance halls, and brothels. These establishments were of course frequented by soldiers and working stiffs from the area ranches.[18] "This place is a 'dead fall' [a low-class den of iniquity] hangout where soldiers from Fort Grant went for recreation and excitement—and generally found it," wrote Arizona author Will Croft Barnes, who as a young man was a telegrapher at Fort Apache.[19]

Barnes was not referring to Milton McDowell's store, George Atkins's lively cantina, or even the dance hall operated by Lou Elliott. The "dead fall" Barnes referred to was about one-quarter mile away, on the east side of Grant Creek. There George McKittrick managed a thriving red-light district that the soldiers called the hog ranch.[20]

A slang term popularized by frontier soldiers, hog ranches operated near the fringes of virtually every military fort and camp in the West. They pretended to be working hog farms, but they actually supplied whiskey, harlots, and other diversions to the troops and any cowhands or miners in the area. "Some of the men would stroll down to the settlement at the edge of the reservation for a shot or two, and a whirl at the dance hall with señoritas," recalled Anton Mazzanovich, who after his army discharge worked for the post sutler (civilian trader) and as a bartender. Mazzanovich introduced those taking their ease to mixed drinks and put pebbles in the shaker so that it at least sounded like ice, a luxury that was impossible to provide.[21]

Throughout his career as a cavalry officer John Bourke encountered scores of such hog ranches catering to enlisted personnel just beyond military jurisdiction. Each combined a saloon, a dance hall, and a bordello. Bourke described one "nest of ranches" as "tenanted by as hardened and depraved a set of wretches as could be found on the face of the globe. Each of these establishments was equipped with a rum-mill of the worst kind and each contained from three to a half a dozen Cyprians [sic], virgins whose lamps were always burning brightly in expectancy of the upcoming bridegroom and who lured to destruction the soldiers of the garrison. In all my experience, I have never seen a lower, more beastly set of people of both sexes."[22]

Bourke's lurid description could have easily applied to the hog ranches near Camp Grant. "Gambling and drinking saloons and dance houses were numerous," recalled John Bachelder, a construction worker who helped build many of them in 1873 after the army post moved to the site below Mount Graham.[23] "There were many noted bad men drifting in and out. Billy the Kid [still known as Henry Antrim] was there for a time. He was a young, light, green-looking fellow."

Besides patronizing the gambling dens and hard falls where he excelled at dealing monte and faro, Henry picked up more cowboy skills while living in Arizona Territory. He apparently did not stick with any one outfit too long. "Details of his movements at this time are understandably sparse," according to Billy the Kid scholar Frederick Nolan.[24]

Henry worked briefly at army beef contractor Henry C. Hooker's Sierra Bonita Ranch in the Sulphur Springs Valley, no more than an hour's ride from Camp Grant.[25] Hooker, of sturdy New England stock, was one of the first ranchers to recognize the great market potential in Arizona Territory. In 1866, after having established his family in California, Hooker had lost his entire mercantile business and home in a fire there. He had no insurance and was left with only a few hundred dollars and a mound of ashes.[26]

Instead of returning East, Hooker purchased five hundred turkeys at $1.50 each, and with the help of a hired man and some dogs drove the flock over the rugged Sierras to mining camps in Nevada, where he sold the birds at $5.00 a head. The profits from this transaction financed Hooker's fresh start in the cattle business in Arizona Territory.[27]

Hooker soon earned huge sums of money as a government contractor supplying beef to soldiers weary of dining on "sow bosom." The wise rancher also provided beef and other supplies to wandering Apache bands and became a close friend of Cochise, the principal chief of the Chiricahuas. Even after Cochise's death in 1874, when Geronimo became the new tribal leader, the Apaches never bothered the Sierra Bonita Ranch, which became a social retreat for officers and their wives from nearby Camp Grant.[28]

Working for Hooker could be demanding. He was proud of his luscious gamma grass ranges, high-grade saddle horses, and kennel of fine greyhounds used to chase down coyotes and wildcats. It was said of the rancher that he had "no use whatever for scrubs of either the human or brute kind."[29] Henry Antrim, in fact, quickly proved to be one of those scrubs when it came to wrangling on the Hooker spread. William Whalen, the ranch's first foreman and general manager and a future sheriff of Graham County, hired Henry but soon had to give him the boot when the young man showed himself to be a "lightweight," unable to handle the exacting work on the range.[30]

Henry almost certainly sought work at other ranches in the Sulphur Springs Valley and may have hired on for a short time at a few of them. Jerry Weddle writes:

Perhaps he found work at one of the roving cow camps belonging to John Chisum, the self-styled "Cattle King of the Pecos" from Lincoln County, New Mexico. Chisum had been driving cattle into the region in 1873 after the newly formed San Carlos and Chiricahua reservations created a market for beef in Arizona. His herds fattened on ranges near Camp Bowie, at Croton Springs near present-day Willcox, on the San Pedro River near Old St. David, and on the Empire ranch south of Tucson. He spent the summer of 1876 situating a large herd on the Eureka Springs Stock ranch, a new spread north of Hooker's. If Billy [Henry] did not meet Chisum, he probably sought work at Eureka Springs and made the acquaintance of George Teague, Chisum's foreman.[31]

By late summer of 1876, while working his way around the ranch circuit, Henry had picked up the nickname Kid, and often was called Kid Antrim.[32] The new handle was not surprising. Throughout the West, particularly in New Mexico and Arizona Territories, Kid had become the most common nickname for juveniles of the delinquent variety or at least teenagers who were handy with guns. In his book of recollections of Arizona, published in 1892, James Cabell Brown writes: "In New Mexico and Arizona, strange to say, the most deadly ruffians were seldom over twenty-five years of age; very many not over eighteen or twenty. One that was scarcely twelve years old had quite a reputation, and was responsible for the conduct of two extra heavy revolvers, and a bowie-knife large enough for a hay scythe." Brown went on to explain that the generic name for these youths of evil fame frequently was "Kid." According to Brown: "A newcomer, to whom the honors were shown, would, at a cost for refreshments of from twenty-five cents to one dollar and acquaintance, be introduced to New Mexican Kids, Wyoming Kids, Arizona Kids, Colorado Kids, Texas Kids, and such a variety of other kids, that he would be so bewildered between the effects of vile whisky and the Kid introductions, as to come to the conclusion that in Calabazas he had struck a human goat ranche [*sic*]."[34]

Long before Henry Antrim first became known as Kid in 1876 and well after his death, there was, as Brown pointed out, a plethora of Kids in the West. They came in all forms: Apache Kid, Texas Kid, Pecos Kid, Jimmy the Kid, Verdigris Kid, Ace-High Kid, Pockmarked Kid, Willie the Kid, Dutch Kid, and many more.[34] Most of them were so nicknamed because like Henry, they were actually kids. In some instances the name stayed with them into manhood.

In November 1876, Henry, sporting the new name of Kid Antrim, found himself back near Camp Grant, looking for a job so he could afford food and shelter and fund his gambling ways at the hog ranches. The Kid found just what he needed not far from McDowell's store at the Hotel de Luna. The modest adobe hostelry featured both sleeping bunks and a mess hall that served hot common food but no saloon and associated vices. The hotel and sutlers Norton & Stewart were the only two civilian businesses that were allowed to operate inside the military reservation.[35]

Miles L. Wood, the local notary public and justice of the peace, ran the hotel. A rugged Canadian native with a big drooping mustache, Wood had moved to Arizona in 1869 and worked for rancher Henry Hooker. Wood herded cattle for a time, then became a butcher and eventually resettled at the new Camp Grant.[36] Hired help was hard to come by in those parts, so when the teenager who introduced himself as Kid Antrim asked for a job, Wood immediately put him to work as a cook in the blazing hot hotel kitchen. Besides some salary, free room and board were provided.

His mother may have been a fine cook and baker, but Henry's only prior experience had been a stint as a hotel dishwasher in Silver City. Although the Hotel de Luna was not some fancy eatery in the East, even saddle tramps and soldiers seeking hot meals as hangover cures had some standards when it came to palatable food. As a result, Kid Antrim's culinary career was short-lived. The company he was keeping did not help matters either. "He worked for a few days," recalled Wood in 1911, "but he got to running with a gang of rustlers, this place was the headquarters of the gang."[37]

Just as in Silver City when he took up with George "Sombrero Jack" Schaefer, Henry's newest mentor was more experienced than was his criminal apprentice. John R. Mackie was a twenty-seven-year-old ex-soldier originally from Scotland who had been only a fourteen-year-old schoolboy when he enlisted in the Union army in 1862. For the next dozen or so years Mackie was in and out of the army, mostly serving as a musician, until he was discharged as a Sixth Cavalry private at Camp Grant on January 4, 1876, following a run-in with authorities.[38]

On September 19, 1875, Mackie had shot T. R. Knox in the throat in a card game dispute at Milton McDowell's. The badly wounded Knox survived, and Mackie was arrested and charged with attempted murder. He was locked up in the Camp Grant guardhouse, and McDowell was charged as an accessory to the crime. The following month, at an evidentiary hearing in Tucson, a bartender and cowboy who witnessed the shooting appeared on behalf of the defendants. Mackie and McDowell entered pleas of self-defense and were set free even though it was shown that the wounded Knox had been unarmed.[39]

Following his discharge from the army, Mackie joined a band of horse thieves operating between Tucson and the Salt River. Once he took notice of the youngster hanging around the Hotel de Luna, the wily Mackie acted quickly and recruited Henry for his gang. Mackie instructed him in the finer points of larceny and how to stay one step ahead of the law. Mackie taught him well, and Kid Antrim proved to be an able student.

Miles Wood, justice of the peace and owner of the Hotel de Luna

THE ROBERT G. MCCUBBIN COLLECTION

THIRTEEN

FIRST BLOOD

. . . he shot me in the belly.[1]

·

—DYING WORDS OF FRANCIS (FRANK) P. "WINDY" CAHILL,
AUGUST 18, 1877

IN ARIZONA TERRITORY, and throughout the West, no crime posed a greater risk than horse stealing. Those who depended on trusty mounts for their livelihood knew that the loss of a good horse could be devastating. Vigilante groups formed in some areas just to deal with the problem. A horse thief was an abomination, and anyone caught in the act or even suspected of such activity might end up "decorating a cottonwood," a popular expression for hanging. Sometimes it was easier to get away with cold-blooded murder than to make off with another man's horse.

Many people believed that citizen justice without due process of law was warranted because of inadequate courts, corrupt law officers and judges, lack of suitable jails, and the frontier's geographical remoteness. The summary punishment of culprits or suspects by hanging without a proper court trial gained currency throughout the American West. This practice became known as lynch law, a term dating back, in fact, to the American Revolution.[2]

It is worth observing that some late-nineteenth-century historians surreptitiously condoned or even whitewashed vigilantism through their criticisms of the formal justice system. "Courts of law are in bad repute these days," wrote the publisher and historian Hubert Howe Bancroft.[3] "Venality and corruption sit upon the bench in the form of dueling, drinking, fist fighting, and licentious judges. Where the people look for justice, they find too often jokes and jeers. It is not uncommon to see a judge appear upon the bench in a state of intoxication, and make no scruple to attack with fist, cane, or revolver any who offend him."

The threat of being the guest of honor at a lynching bee, as some called an illegal hanging, did not deter the individuals and gangs stealing livestock and horses. Several famous Old West figures, in fact, were said to have been horse thieves at one time or another. They included Belle Starr, John Wesley Hardin, and Harry Alonzo Longabaugh, who earned his nickname, Sundance Kid, when jailed for horse theft in Sundance, Wyoming. His partner at crime, Robert Leroy Parker, better known as Butch Cassidy, also served time in a Wyoming prison for stealing a horse. In 1871 even the vastly mythologized Wyatt Earp was indicted in Van Buren, Arkansas, for stealing two horses in nearby Indian Territory, just one of his dubious activities that were downplayed by countless admirers.[4]

While horse stealing was always a chancy business, Henry Antrim and his cohort John Mackie, like so many others, found it very profitable. The thought of easy money erased any memory Henry had of being a twelve-year-old in Kansas and hearing of a vigilante gang's shooting and hanging eight horse thieves not far from where his family lived. For Mackie and Kid Antrim the gain from stealing horses and saddles outweighed all the risks.

"Soldiers would come from Fort Grant and visit the saloons and dance halls here," explained Miles Wood, owner of the Hotel de Luna and Henry's former employer. "Billy [Henry] and his chum Mackie would steal the saddles and saddle blankets from the horses and occasionally they would take the horses and hide them out until they got a chance to dispose of them."[5]

By late 1876 the clientele at the hog ranch and surrounding establishments had grown weary of finding themselves horseless. Many years later Miles Wood remembered the day a lieutenant and a doctor from Camp Grant were outsmarted by the pair of brazen thieves. "They [the army officers] said they would fix it so no one would steal their horses," said Wood. "They had long picket ropes on the horses and when they went into the bar carried the end of the ropes with them. Macky [sic] followed the officers into the saloon and talked to them while Billy cut the ropes from the horses and run off, leaving the officers holding the pieces of rope."[6]

When he learned of the latest escapade, Major Charles E. Compton, commanding officer at Camp Grant, made the hog ranch off-limits to all troopers. Compton then ordered the post quartermaster, Captain Gilbert C. Smith, to swear out a formal compliant against Mackie and Henry before Justice of the Peace Wood at the Hotel de Luna. Three times Wood sent out an elderly constable to arrest the thieves, and each time he returned to the hotel claiming he could not locate the pair, causing Wood to remark, "I knew he did not want to find them."[7]

Despite their commander's order that all soldiers keep away from the hog ranch and environs, some men yielded to temptation. On November 17, First Sergeant Louis C. Hartman, Company G, Sixth Cavalry, tied up his horse near McDowell's store. When Hartman came out, he found his horse gone, along with the army-issue saddle, blanket, and bridle. Within days of reporting the loss to Major Compton, the embarrassed Hartman and four other enlisted men were ordered to scour the territory "in pursuit of horse thieves."[8] One of the other posse members was Private Charles Smith, the soldier who had had his mount stolen by Kid Antrim the previous March.

By talking to ranchers, herdsmen, and Indians along the way, Sergeant Hartman and the four privates followed the tracks of his stolen horse through the Aravaipa Valley and into the mountainous country surrounding the fast-developing mining boomtown of Globe City on Pinal Creek. On November 25, the soldiers caught up with Kid Antrim riding the stolen horse along the trail to McMillen's Camp, an illegal mining settlement that had sprung up just inside the San Carlos Apache Reservation. It is believed that at the time William Antrim was residing in one of the miners' tents at McMillen's Camp and that Henry was on his way there to see his estranged stepfather.[9]

Brandishing guns but lacking an arrest warrant, the soldiers simply ordered Henry to dismount, took the reins of the stolen horse, and rode off on their five-day return journey to Camp Grant. Undoubtedly grateful that he was not shot, lynched, or physically harmed, Henry nevertheless was afoot, a not insignificant situation when one was all alone in Apache country.

Eventually he made his way to Globe City. Founded in 1876, the town supposedly got its name (changed to just Globe in 1878) from the discovery of a large spherical-shaped nugget of almost pure silver that resembled the planet Earth.[10] Because of rich silver and copper strikes in the nearby Pinal Mountains, Globe

City was growing rapidly when Henry arrived. He made the rounds of at least a dozen saloons crowded with prospectors and miners itching to part with their money in games of chance.

In Globe City, Henry was reunited with Mackie and other fellow horse thieves. This meant that whenever Henry tired of dealing monte and playing poker and faro, he could always earn some illicit funds by filching horses. In fact, late on the night of February 10, 1877, Kid Antrim, as Henry now was generally called, and Mackie stole three horses from Cottonwood Spring, a rest stop known for its cool, sweet water. Again the horses they made off with belonged to soldiers. These were from Company F stationed at Camp Thomas, established in 1876 on the Gila River.[11]

This time the army definitely had had enough. On February 16, officers from both Camp Thomas and Camp Grant confronted Miles Wood at the Hotel de Luna, where he held civilian court, and lambasted him for not corralling the horse thieves. On the basis of Sergeant Hartman's complaint the previous November, an arrest warrant was sworn out charging "Henry Antrim alias Kid" with horse theft.[12]

Aware that Henry had been last known to be in the Globe area, Wood provided authorities there with a copy of the warrant and some hand-drawn wanted posters. "I sent the warrant to a constable in Globe but the Kid had slipped away from him," Wood recounted. "The next day the constable arrested him and brought him down as far as Cedar Springs, when he got away again."[13]

The same month William Antrim, perhaps embarrassed by his stepson's antics, beat a hasty retreat from McMillen's Camp and returned to Silver City. "Mr. Antrim has returned from Pinal," concisely reported the *Grant County Herald* of February 24, 1877.[14]

After his two narrow escapes from the law, Henry decided to lower his profile and perhaps make a peace offering by returning five stolen army horses to Camp Thomas. For some reason Henry and Mackie must have felt the heat was off them, for they soon appeared at their old stamping grounds around McDowell's store south of Camp Grant. They were totally unaware that hotelier/Justice of the Peace Miles Wood still held arrest warrants for them.

"The next morning, I saw two men coming in to breakfast so I told the waiter I would wait on them myself," recalled Wood about the morning of March 25, when he spied Henry and Mackie approaching the Hotel de Luna. "I had the breakfast for the two placed on a large platter and I carried it in to them. I shoved the platter on the table in front of them and pulled a sixgun [*sic*] from under it and told them to put their hands up and go straight out the door."[15]

Wood called for help from Caleb Martin, the hotel cook, and together they marched Henry and Mackie at gunpoint the two and three-quarter miles up the road to Camp Grant, where the sergeant of the guard locked up both culprits.[16] With Henry and Mackie safely confined to the guardhouse, Wood proceeded to the post hospital, where he was conducting an inquest into the killing of James W. Lockhart, one of cattleman John Chisum's cowhands, who had been shot out of his saddle during a drunken melee with some Sixth Cavalry soldiers.[17] His business completed, Wood returned to his hotel.

Meanwhile, Henry, emboldened by his former successful flight up a chimney, wasted no time in trying to escape. When he was being escorted to the privy, Henry somehow got hold of some salt, threw a handful into the guard's eyes, and made a break. He dashed toward Bonito Creek, but some soldiers, responding to cries for help, quickly ran him down and dragged him back to the guardhouse.[18]

This time, when he was summoned back to the post, Wood had blacksmith Francis Cahill rivet shackles on Kid Antrim's ankles and wrists. However, even iron restraints could not stop the lithe Henry from breaking free, as Wood learned just hours later, when he and his new bride attended a reception at the home of Major Compton.[19]

That evening, while officers and their wives danced to the regimental band in Compton's quarters, Mackie helped his young pal scale the guardhouse wall. Like John Nevil Maskelyne, the famous conjurer of the time, Henry squeezed his small frame through the ventilator and dropped to the ground. From there he skulked through the shadows away from the camp, past the Hotel de Luna, to Atkins's cantina, where bartender Tom Varley forced open the shackles. In the meantime, the sergeant of the guard learned of the escape and raced to the Compton reception with the news.[20]

Wood wasn't surprised by the news. As he later put it, "[Henry] was a small fellow not weighing over ninety pounds and it was almost an impossibility to keep him imprisoned or handcuffed."[21] On the scout once again, Kid Antrim procured a mount and headed toward the country near Camp Thomas. There he blended into the Arizona Territory cultural fabric and found work at a hay camp run by army contractor H. F. "Sorghum" Smith. "[Henry] said he was seventeen, though he didn't look to be fourteen," recalled Smith long after he hired the youngster. "I gave him a job helping around the camp."[22]

What Henry really wanted was another grubstake to finance his further adventures. According to Smith, "He hadn't worked very long until he wanted his money. I asked him if he was going to quit. He said, 'No, I want to buy some things.' I asked him how much he wanted and tried to get him to take $10 for I thought that was enough for him to spend, but he hesitated and asked for $40. I gave it to him. He went down to the post trader and bought himself a whole outfit: six-shooter, belt, scabbard, and cartridges."[23]

Given the hefty pay advance he received, Henry likely worked at Smith's hay camp through the first cutting and into the summer of 1877. Perhaps believing that for some unknown reason his transgressions would be forgotten and aware that he was fast becoming something of a local hero because of his daring escapes, Henry started showing up yet again with seeming impunity around Camp Grant.

His final appearance came on August 17, 1877, a Friday night, a so-called howling and prowling time at George Atkins's cantina. A description of what transpired came from Augustus M. Gildea. A tough Texan, who started working cows at the age of twelve, Gus Gildea also had ridden with the Ku Klux Klan and was a foreman for John Chisum's outfit.[24] By some accounts, Gildea, at that time drawing wages from cattle baron Henry Hooker, was one of the patrons taking it all in that night. Others said that Gildea showed up the following day.

Kid Antrim "came to town, dressed like a 'country jake' with 'store pants' on and shoes instead of boots," was how Gildea remembered it. "He wore a six-gun stuffed in his trousers."[25] At Atkins's cantina, Henry, whose appearance alone was a brazen act, joined a poker game in progress and settled in for the night. Before too long trouble started when Henry and Frank Cahill started exchanging words. The two men were hardly strangers. Cahill was the blacksmith who helped put Henry in shackles earlier that year at Camp Grant.

A survivor of the Irish famine, Francis P. Cahill had enlisted in the army at New York in 1868, when he was twenty-two. He served most of his three-year hitch in Arizona at Camp Crittenden, working as a horseshoer. After his discharge as a private in 1871, Cahill continued as a civilian blacksmith for the army at the old Camp Grant and later at the new camp when it was established below Mount Graham.[26]

Prone to telling tall tales, or "windies," Cahill answered to the sobriquet Windy since, as Gildea explained, "he was always blowin' about first one thing then another." Henry had had difficulties with Cahill long before the blacksmith bully secured him in shackles. "Shortly after the Kid came to Fort Grant, Windy started abusing him," said Gildea. "He would throw Billy to the floor, ruffle his hair, slap his face and humiliate him before the men in the saloon. Yes, the Kid was rather slender. . . . The blacksmith was a large man, with a gruff voice and blustering manner."[27]

If Cahill's army records are accurate, he was just five feet four and three-quarter inches tall.[28] Descriptions of him as a large man may have been references to his powerful torso and girth, hardly to his stature. No matter his size, Cahill was a hothead who did not fear altercations. Indeed, it was on that hot August night in the cantina that all of the physical and verbal abuse Cahill handed out finally pushed Henry to the brink. The argument became heated and then exploded into violence when Cahill called Kid Antrim a pimp and the Kid responded by calling the muscular smithy a son of a bitch. Cahill rushed at Henry and locked his arms around him. The pair wrestled their way out the cantina door and toward a cattle chute.

Miles Wood, one of the many onlookers who spilled outside to watch the fight, later said that "Cahill was larger and stouter than the Kid and threw him down three times which made the Kid mad."[29] In his account of the fight, Gus Gildea said that Cahill "pinned [Henry's] arms down with his knees and started slapping his face. 'You are hurting me. Let me up!' cried the Kid. 'I want to hurt you. That's why I got you down,' was the reply."[30]

At that moment Gildea and others in the crowd saw the Kid had freed his right arm. "He started working his hand around and finally managed to grasp his .45," said Gildea. "The blacksmith evidently felt the pistol against his side, for he straightened slightly. Then there was a deafening roar. Windy slumped to the side as the Kid squirmed free."[31] Before the smoke cleared, Henry jumped to his feet and ran. He dashed to a hitching post and mounted a fleet pony owned by a local man, John Murphey. Named Cashaw, for a desert shrub akin to the mesquite, it was said to be the fastest horse in the valley. In a flash Kid Antrim vanished into the moonlit night.[32]

Since there was no civilian doctor available, Cahill was taken by wagon to the post hospital just up the road at Camp Grant. Gravely wounded, he was made as comfortable as possible under the care of assistant surgeon Frederick Crayton Ainsworth. In the army since 1874, Ainsworth was a capable officer and physician who much later, in 1904, became a major general and adjutant general of the U.S. Army.[33] However, even a highly skilled doctor could do little to repair the damage Cahill had sustained that night. The slug from the Kid's gun had torn through vital organs, and it was difficult to stem the internal hemorrhaging. Being gut-shot at such close range not only was horrifically painful but usually guaranteed a slow and agonizing death.

By early morning the next day, August 18, Ainsworth knew that Cahill was going quickly. Justice of the Peace/Notary Public Miles Wood was summoned to the post hospital to scribble down a deathbed statement:

> I, Frank Cahill, being convinced that I am about to die, do make the following as my final statement. My name is Frank P. Cahill. I was born in the county and town of Galway, Ireland; yesterday, Aug. 17th, 1877, I had some trouble with Henry Antrem [*sic*], otherwise known as Kid, during which he shot me. I had called him a pimp and he called me a son of a bitch; we then took hold of each other; I did not hit him, I think; saw him go for his pistol and tried to get hold of it, but could not and he shot me in the belly; I have a sister named Margaret Flannigan living at East Cambridge, Mass., and another named Kate Conden, living in San Francisco.[34]

Soon after dictating this statement, the blacksmith Windy Cahill died. The following day he was laid to rest in the dusty camp cemetery.[35]

By then Wood had already convened a coroner's inquest at the Hotel de Luna. The six citizens on the panel were Milton McDowell, Bennett Norton, T. McCleary, James L. "Dobie" Hunt, Delos H. Smith, and George Teague. Their verdict did not take long to reach: "The shooting was criminal and unjustifiable, and Henry Antrim, alias Kid, is guilty thereof."[36]

Not everyone who knew Cahill and Henry agreed with the verdict. They thought the Kid was wise to flee the scene, given the large number of Cahill's friends, especially soldiers, who no doubt would have exacted revenge. Those who sided with Henry believed he had acted in self-defense and that the bully had had it coming. "He had no choice," said Gildea of Kid Antrim. "He had to use his 'equalizer.'"[37]

He had, and it would not be the last time.

The Kid returns to New Mexico Territory

ILLUSTRATION BY BOB BOZE BELL

— FOURTEEN —

AT LARGE

Cahill was not killed on the [military] reservation. His murderer, Antrim alias Kid, was allowed to escape and I believe is still at large.[1]

—MAJOR CHARLES COMPTON, AUGUST 23, 1877

IDING THE SPEEDY Cashaw, Kid Antrim made few stops that August night after leaving Windy Cahill gut-shot and dying. His new store-bought duds soaked with sweat, the fugitive rode long and hard through high desert country that had been refreshed from seasonal monsoons. He dared rein in the panting pony only when they were many miles from the scene of the crime. About a week after the fatal shooting of Cahill, a mounted traveler leading Cashaw, minus saddle and bridle, showed up at McDowell's store. The stranger explained that the Kid had asked him to return the horse to its owner, John Murphey.[2]

By then Henry Antrim was out of Arizona Territory. He had crossed the border back into New Mexico Territory by hedge hopping, the unorthodox practice of "borrowing" a horse, riding it a short ways, releasing it to return to its owner, then riding off on a freshly acquired steed. Gone on the scout once again, Henry made his way to familiar ground where he would feel safe. He showed up at the foot of the thorny Burro Mountains, southwest of Silver City just at the edge of the desert, where there was a ranch and a stage operated by his old friends Richard and Sara Connor Knight.[3] Henry's boyhood pal and Sara's little brother Anthony Connor, also was there at the time, delivering mail on horseback to small settlements and camps in the area. "He told folks what he had done," recalled Anthony. "He remained there about two weeks, but fearing that officers from Arizona might show up any time he left."[4] The Knights gave Henry plenty of food and some of Anthony's clothing to replace what he had worn since the night of the Cahill shooting. When Sara told Henry to pick any horse he wanted from the ranch corral, he supposedly choose the "scrubbiest" of the lot and rode off.[5]

In some ways Henry may have resembled the countless other rootless young men known as Kid who populated the western frontier at that time. Author J. Cabell Brown's depiction of the young ruffians given the generic name Kid comes close to describing at least a few of Kid Antrim's physical attributes:

> The genus "Kid" wore his hair long, and in curls upon his shoulder in cow-boy or scout fashion; had an incipient moustache, and sported a costume made of buckskin ornamented with fringe, tassels, and strings of the same material—the dirtier the better. His head was covered with a cow-boy's hat of phenomenal width of brim, having many metal stars, half moons, etc., around the crown. Upon his feet he wore either moccasins or very high heeled, stub toed boots, and an enormous pair of spurs, with little steel balls that jingled at each step. Buckled around his waist would be a cartridge belt holding two carefully sighted revolvers, and a bone handled bowie knife in his boot leg, completed his dress. He was the proud owner of a "cayuse" horse and Mexican saddle, a bridle with reins of plaited hair, and a "*riata*" [lariat] tied behind the saddle. The "cayuse" was never far from his master, for when that gentleman wanted a horse he wanted him badly; either to escape from a worst man than himself, or to escape the consequences of having killed one.[6]

In those waning days of August 1877 Henry Antrim had no time to ponder the consequences of fleeing Arizona as a wanted killer. Many people through the years have wondered what would have happened if he had stayed and not run away. Maybe he would have been able to clear himself with a self-defense plea, though an uneducated young man like Henry might not have been a credible witness. Then, again, he might have ended up hanged by either a court of law or vigilantes.

Like so many other questions in his life, this one remains unanswered. The reality was that Henry was no longer just a horse thief but had turned man-killer.

Henry did not know that a new code of behavior governing the ideology of violence and honor had become acceptable in parts of the nation, especially the American West. The code included the new doctrine of no duty to retreat, a clear departure from the tradition of medieval British common law that required a person under threat to retreat until his back was to the wall before using deadly force.[7]

In 1876 an Ohio court held that a "true man" if attacked was "not obligated to fly." The following year the Indiana Supreme Court, upholding the legality of no duty to retreat, stated: "The tendency of the American mind seems to be very strongly against the enforcement of any rule which requires a person to flee when assailed."[8]

Soon this code of behavior to settle disputes became known as the Code of the West across the cattle ranges of Texas, New Mexico, Arizona, and beyond. This was not the saccharine unwritten commandments governing behavior and ethics contrived by those who romanticized the West. That simplistic code, chronicled by Zane Grey, the popular pulp writer of melodramatic and improbable Old West tales, stressed self-reliance, accountability, and integrity while it celebrated the frontier values of the people. Instead, the Code of the West dictated that a man did not have to back away from a fight. It also meant a man could not only fight but also pursue an adversary until the threat was over, even if that resulted in death. "Stand your ground" was a popular battle cry for many years.

"Central to the Code of the West were the doctrine of no duty to retreat, the imperative of personal self-redress, and an ultrahigh value on courage, which often became, in the phrase of one historian, 'reckless bravado'—a bravado that, however, was praised for its courage and not derided for its recklessness," writes Richard Maxwell Brown, a historian who suggests America's high homicide rates could be traced back to this concept.[9]

In the Cahill shooting, the Kid had stood his ground, even if he ended up lying on his back with his opponent on top of him. However, not only did he choose to make an escape, but he broke another important rule when he shot an unarmed man even if he did not shoot him in the back. Still, given Cahill's brute strength superiority, perhaps Gus Gildea's argument in Henry's defense that Kid Antrim had no choice but "to use his 'equalizer' " might have worked.

Luckily for Henry, there were other distractions to keep law officers occupied besides pursuing a two-bit boy gun toter. On September 2, 1877, the tenacious

Apache warrior Victorio and large numbers of his Chiricahua and Warm Spring followers had slipped away from the San Carlos Reservation, sparking three years of mayhem and violence in the territories. Besides army patrols riding from camps and forts, law officers, such as Sheriff Harvey Whitehill from Silver City, formed civilian posses to search the mountains for Apaches.

Beyond the constant Apache threat, lawmen, themselves bound by masculine honor, faced other dangers. There were growing numbers of people from all levels of society ready and willing to use violence, including those who justified their acts as defending their properties and persons.

In the late nineteenth century, violence between a broad range of interest groups and factions was rampant across the nation. Cattlemen and farmers throughout the frontier fought over land and water. In some instances, local militias and even federal troops took sides in these wars, usually assisting the most powerful land and cattle barons. Much of the violence could be attributed to cultural feuds and outright racism. Self-appointed vigilantes attacked Indians for no reason other than that they were Indians. There also were frequent acts of terror against blacks and Hispanics.[10]

Debate has long raged about just how violent life on the American frontier really was in the decades immediately following the Civil War. Some historians have always maintained that much of the violence associated with the so-called Wild West was exaggerated, the stuff of legends. They contend this is especially true when it comes to the actual number of deaths attributable to guns, and they point to statistical data to back up their claims. Other historians challenge this argument with statistics of their own. They insist that the violent nature of the frontier was not only encouraged but also widespread. Sheriffs and outlaws often were made over into heroes as an essential part of American mythologizing.

"The world of the Wild West is an odd world, internally consistent in its own cockeyed way, and complete with a history, an ethic, a language, wars, a geography, a code, and a costume," writes Peter Lyon.[11] "The history is compounded of lies, the ethic was based on evil, the language was composed largely of argot and cant, the wars were fought by gangs of greedy gunmen, the geography was elastic, and the code and costume were both designed to accommodate violence. Yet this sinful world is, by any test, the most popular ever to be described to an American audience."

The Wild West that Lyon writes of was already a way of life when Henry was a lad in Kansas. In Wichita and the other cattle towns he and his family witnessed the ongoing struggle between those who wished to settle and civilize the West and those who wanted nothing to change. It was the phenomenon that came to be called the Western Civil War of Incorporation by some twentieth-century historians.[12] And at the forefront of this struggle were the gun sharks, man-killers, and shootists scattered throughout the West. They were the shock troops.

On one side of the battle were the corporate gunmen employed by big business, cattle barons, and mining syndicates and cheered on by merchants who wanted law and order. These hired guns, such as "Wild Bill" Hickok and Wyatt Earp and his brothers, were usually Republicans, ex-Union soldiers, or from northern states. On the other side were those who opposed corporate encroachment on their lands and vehemently fought against the incorporation of the West. They had the support of gamblers, saloon owners, and prostitutes concerned about earning a living. The populist gunslingers this faction hired were mostly Democrats, and many of them hailed from Texas. They included a large number of unreconstructed Confederates akin to the Missouri outlaws Jesse and Frank James.[13] This is not to say that the gunmen protecting corporate or establishment interests wished to do away with brothels and gambling dens. They simply wanted to control and regulate them.

Was Kid Antrim aware of these factions? He was educated to a degree, and he had been subjected to situations in which big business was ruling the land in Arizona Territory for example. He had seen the other side as well, the libertarians of the day who resented any organization or incorporation. At this point it is safe to say that he aligned himself with those that opposed organization.

"The cattle towns were run by a business elite, since the towns formed a nexus between large-capital investments in herds and in the government-supported railroads," writes Garry Wills. "They needed a controlled climate in which gambling and prostitution were regulated (secretly taxed but protected, to keep the cowboys coming up from Texas) while safety was guaranteed (to keep buyers and agents in town for the large cash or banking transactions involved in shipping such huge amounts of property)."[14]

Besides the cattle and mining boomtowns, other major theaters of war for these glorified gunfighters were the immense cattle ranges, especially those in Arizona and New Mexico Territories. This was precisely the dangerous and volatile land where Henry Antrim found himself in the autumn of 1877. It was also where he spent the rest of his days.

According to the best available evidence, having departed Knight's ranch and stage stop, Kid Antrim next showed up at Apache Tejo (often misspelled as Tejoe), a settlement and watering stop on the ruins of old Fort McLane, yet another abandoned army post south of Silver City.[15] The hot springs where Catherine Antrim had tried to regain her health shortly before her death were not too far from this site. Apache Tejo also had been infamous among the Apaches since the years when it was an army fort. It was there that U.S. soldiers had murdered the revered chief Mangus Colorado in 1863 when he was brought to what he was told would be a peace parley. After being shot down, he was scalped by a soldier wielding the camp cook's bowie knife. Later an army surgeon exhumed the corpse, severed the slain leader's head, and shipped it to Washington, D.C., for display in the Smithsonian Institution.[16]

At Apache Tejo Henry would have had no worries of being deceived like the old Indian warrior. The soldiers were long gone, and the closest law officer was Sheriff Whitehill in Silver City. Most folks who passed through only wanted grub and water and asked no questions, especially of an apparently rootless boy who did not appear to pose any real threat.

Still, the short time he was at Apache Tejo proved eventful for Henry. For while he was there, he likely took up with a bunch of hard-riding thieves and rustlers who were part of an outlaw network with tentacles throughout the territories of Arizona, New Mexico, and parts of northern Mexico. Made up of ex-soldiers, rogue cowboys, and pistoleros, the brazen band stole horses and cattle and whatever else it wanted and killed anyone who dared get in its way. They were best known as the Boys, and in a heartbeat Kid Antrim became one of them.[17]

John Kinney, outlaw boss

THE ROBERT G. McCUBBIN COLLECTION

FIFTEEN

BANDITTI

New Mexico was sparsely populated in the 1870's, but it is doubtful
whether there has ever been another place in the United States where so
many men were indicted for murder and so few convicted.[1]

•

—W. EUGENE HOLLON

ANY DIRECT TIE that Kid Antrim had with the outlaw band known
as the Boys may not have lasted very long, yet such a connection certainly had a
significant influence on the "career" that lay ahead of him. During the 1870s and
early 1880s the Boys were a key link in a chain of thieves that was the equivalent of
organized crime in the Southwest. During their rampage of terror these maraud-
ers accounted for an abundance of transgressions, including armed robbery, livestock rustling, and murder. Yet beyond a crash course in felony crime, the Kid's
passing association with the Boys also helped propel him further into the public
eye, whether he liked it or not.

The mastermind behind the gang was John Kinney, a Massachusetts native
and former cavalry sergeant who had joined the army in Chicago in 1867 and been
mustered out in Nebraska in 1873. He chose not to stay in Nebraska but instead
went south to New Mexico Territory and took up residence in Dona Ana County.

Kinney's ranch, just west of Mesilla on the Rio Grande, was known as the "head-quarters and rendezvous for all the evildoers in the country."[2] There Kinney planned the forays and called the shots for the Boys, who brought him all the cattle and horses they could steal. Kinney sold the horses to other cattlemen. Hoteliers, army suppliers, and anyone else who did not ask questions or require a bill of sale purchased the slaughtered cattle.

Within months of Kid Antrim and the gang meeting, the Kinney men became hired guns in a conflict that kept Lincoln County in turmoil for several years. In a twist of fate, the Kid ended up on the opposing side in that conflict. Even more ironic, in 1881 Kinney was one of the deputies, albeit a corrupt one, who escorted the Kid from La Mesilla to the jail in Lincoln following his murder conviction.

Although Kinney was the head of the gang, there was no question that the man who rode as undisputed leader of the pack was Jesse Evans, a Missouri-bred cowboy turned man-killer, thief, and scruffy barroom brawler. Evans had come to New Mexico Territory in 1872 and, before going outlaw, worked as a hand for various ranchers, including the powerful John Chisum, the Texan who created a cattle empire in the Pecos River Valley.[3] Chisum's vast herds became one of the Boys' favorite targets.

The Jesse Evans Gang, as some people called the Boys, fluctuated in size but at times numbered as many as thirty misfits and drifters. They were labeled Texas cowboys by one army officer who pursued them even though some were Hispanic or Indian.[4] Among the more notorious gang members were Charles Ray, alias Pony Diehl, or Pony Deal, who later tangled with the Earp brothers in Arizona, and Bob Martin, a bold thief and ruthless killer, reputed to be one of the most wanted bandits in northern Mexico. Frank Baker acted as Evans's right hand man and helped him boss such other hard cases as George "Buffalo Bill" Spawn, Jim McDaniels, Bill Allen, Nicholas Provencio, Dolly Graham, Tom Hill, Serafin Aragón, William "Buck" Morton, Manuel "Indian" Segovia, Dick Lloyd, Roscoe Burrell, Ponciano Domingues, and others known only by a surname or an alias.[5]

Now that he was on the scout once more, Kid Antrim found hooking up with this wild tribe appealing since they offered employment of a sort and appeared to be impervious to the law. For his part, the young man would have made a promising recruit for the gang. When he fled New Mexico Territory as a petty thief, he was a fifteen-year-old boy, but during the time he spent in Arizona the Kid had come of age. Reputation on the outlaw level traveled fast, and the fact that the Kid had killed a man in Arizona Territory was a mark in his favor. In only two years before returning to New Mexico Territory, the Kid had picked up enough survival skills and frontier savvy to make him a competent stock thief. His association with hardbitten cowboys and rustlers in Arizona Territory initiated him in a lawless culture that stressed that every man must ride and shoot well and above all abide by the Code of the West.[6]

Kid Antrim could hold his own. Windy Cahill, moldering in an Arizona grave, was not the last man to learn that young Antrim was more than willing to stand his ground, especially when his temper was aroused. Despite some reports that he was a scrawny runt, firsthand accounts from the Kid's associates generally agreed that he had a lean but muscular physique. Many described him as wiry. Others recalled him as being as lithe as a cat, especially on the dance floor.[7] Full grown, he stood at least five feet seven inches tall and weighed about 135 pounds, meaning he was about the same height as many of his compañeros, such as Jesse Evans, who was just five feet five and three-fourths inches tall.[8] The Kid had wavy brown hair, a light beard, clear blue eyes, and two slightly protruding front teeth. He kept himself as neat as possible and took to wearing an unadorned Mexican sombrero, in the style of his boyhood criminal mentor Sombrero Jack Schaefer.[9]

According to several of the Kid's acquaintances, he was gregarious and affable with most folks he met, relished a good joke, and had plenty of charisma. His mind was agile, and unlike some of the crowd he ran with, he could read and write a decent hand. Although he shunned tobacco and seldom, if ever, drank spirits, he enjoyed the company of pals at a gambling table or saloon. The Kid also took pleasure in the festive music at lively bailes, where on the dance floor a flash of his fetching smile invariably charmed the women, especially the señoritas.[10] Of course, it helped that he spoke Spanish as fluently as a native, a proficiency that served him well with Hispanics for the rest of his life.

This, then, was the Kid Antrim who took up with what was one of the most notorious gangs in New Mexico Territory and beyond. In September 1877, when the Boys, led by the bullet-scarred Evans, rode into Apache Tejo with a herd of horses and mules stolen from Lincoln County ranchers and Mescalero Apaches, it would have been an impressive sight to a promising teenage brigand watching from the shadows.

"He [Kid Antrim] got in with a band of rustlers at Apache Tejo in the part of the country where he was made a hardened character," his boyhood friend Louis Abraham said in 1937.[11] Abraham, by then an elderly man remembering bygone days, further stated there was no justification for his friend's further descent into lawlessness. "Billie [sic] had no reason, only fear, for he hung around Apache Tejo quite a while, and Sheriff Whitehill could have gotten him if he wanted him punished for there was law and order in Silver City and even if sometimes the gun did speak too soon, the killer was tried."

On October 1, 1877, Kid Antrim purportedly was one of nine foot soldiers riding with Evans when the Boys swooped down on the L. F. Pass coal camp in the Burro Mountains, only sixteen miles southwest of Silver City.[12] The Kid knew this country well since it was near the Richard Knight ranch he often visited.

At the coal camp the gang promptly stole three horses and hastily departed. Two of the horse owners, Colonel A. G. Ledbetter, a customs inspector, and John Swisshelm, a rancher and one of the earliest prospectors in the area, decided to track the thieves but soon lost their trail on the road to Apache Tejo.[13]

The following day, however, C. A. Carpenter, of Silver City, encountered the outlaws with the stolen horses on the road, which snaked its way through Cooke's Canyon, to Mesilla. Named for nearby Cooke's Peak to the north, this rugged canyon had been the site of several Apache ambushes and was known as the Journey of Death by soldiers. As Carpenter passed near the gang, he was able to get a good look at some of the riders. He recognized the Kid as one of them, as area newspapers soon reported. One news item describing the horse theft at the coal camp read in part: "Sometime on Tuesday, the party of thieves, among whom was Henry Antrim, were met in Cook's [sic] canon [sic] by Mr. Carpenter."[14]

After passing Carpenter, the Boys continued on the road to Mesilla, acquiring more horses along the way. Seven miles east of old Fort Cummings, an abandoned army post and water hole near the mouth of Cooke's Canyon, they halted a westbound stage and demanded money from the driver. The frightened man assured them that he carried no bullion and had nothing of great value other than his life. They reluctantly let him continue his journey, but not before Evans made him take a pull from a bottle with the gang.[15]

Stagecoaches were the preferred transportation of the land, carrying passengers, mail, and many times large deposits of money. In retrospect the stagecoach era is often depicted as romantic and exciting, but that was not the case. Road conditions were poor, and the coaches uncomfortable. As the going got rougher, passengers and mail were often hauled in Celerity wagons, also known as mud wagons. Boxlike with open sides, these wagons were lighter than the Concord stagecoaches and were designed for the worst road conditions and mountain routes. A real danger for stagecoach drivers and travelers was the threat of robbery by mounted bandits. This was especially true since stages regularly carried cash payrolls and bank transfers were regularly made by scheduled stage lines that operated far away from any telegraph service.

The stage driver near Cooke's Canyon later told a newspaper reporter that when he was stopped, there were only nine men in the gang, including Evans, and that each one was armed with two revolvers and a Winchester rifle and carried two gun belts with cartridges. The news story went on to report that shortly after the stage incident the nine gang members took some potshots at rancher George Williams, "but as George promptly returned their fire, they left without unnecessary delay."[16]

Within days, however, the gang's numbers increased to at least twenty-six as other heavily armed members showed up with more stolen horses. This gave the Boys enough firepower to drive off easily an approaching six-man posse carrying only pistols. The steady barrage of gunshots forced the posse to seek refuge in a canyon and wait for reinforcements. Intent on delivering their herd of horses to one of the ranches that was a clearinghouse for stolen stock, the gang rode off and yelled a "shout of derision."[17]

The Boys' escapades throughout the autumn of 1877 did not go unnoticed. Nor did the series of their criminal acts go unreported, thanks to Albert Jennings Fountain, the editor of the *Mesilla Valley Independent*. Unafraid of retribution from the outlaw network, the plucky Fountain relentlessly pressured local authorities to arrest the outlaws. He also published story after story about the widespread crime spree and called for swift justice, even if that meant vigilante action. "This gang is constantly on the road, and it is time that the citizens turned out and strung them up," wrote Fountain in one of his blistering editorials.[18]

As much as Fountain despised the lawless elements running rampant at the time, one day he would become an advocate for Kid Antrim and even represented him during a trial in which the Kid's life was on the line. In the autumn of 1877, however, he and his future client had not met, and it is doubtful if the newspaper publisher knew who Henry Antrim was since the young outlaw's name appeared only once in the Mesilla newspaper. Fountain was more concerned about exposing the leaders of the network of outlaw gangs. And expose them he did, much to the consternation of Jesse Evans and John Kinney.

Fountain's courage came from the fact that he was a genuine maverick. Born in 1838 on Staten Island, New York, to a sea captain father and French Huguenot mother, Fountain traveled the world as a young soldier of fortune and had an exotic background, even for the Old West. He had been a prisoner in Canton,

China, panned for gold in California, and in 1860 narrowly escaped execution in Nicaragua while reporting on the slave trade for a Sacramento newspaper. He managed to escape a firing squad only by disguising himself as a woman and slipping aboard a ship bound for San Francisco.[19]

Back in California, Fountain studied the law, and he had just been admitted to the bar when the Civil War broke out. He was commissioned a lieutenant in what became known as the California Column, under the command of General James H. Carleton. After marching into New Mexico Territory to regain control of the Rio Grande Valley from the Confederacy, Fountain and his troops fought in skirmishes against Cochise and his Apache warriors. Wounded in what was described as a "desperate encounter" with Apaches, Fountain decided to stay in the area after his mustering out.[20]

He married a young woman from a prominent Hispanic family and started a law practice in El Paso. Later he served a term in the Texas Senate as a crusading Republican. He held several other public offices and soon became a political force to be reckoned with. Fountain firmly believed that although the Civil War was over, any of the root causes of rebellion lingering among unreconstructed Confederates and southern sympathizers had to be eradicated. That became evident early in his career, when as a customhouse officer in El Paso Fountain examined the land titles of former Confederates and often confiscated their properties and sold them at auction.[21]

In 1873, when Texas Democrats regained control of both houses of the state legislature after having shaken off the rigors of Reconstruction and punishment for having been part of the Confederacy, Fountain, under constant attack and accused of being a carpetbagger, knew it was time for him to leave the Lone Star State. He served the rest of his term in the senate battling trumped-up charges leveled at him by Democrats and conservative Republicans. When his term ended, Fountain moved his family back to Mesilla, New Mexico Territory, where the Republican Party was in control.[22]

Fountain quickly earned a reputation as a skilled bilingual orator in the courtroom and often addressed the mostly Hispanic juries in Spanish. From 1876 to 1878 he served as probate judge and county court clerk and became the editor of the *Mesilla Valley Independent*, his short-lived bilingual newspaper.[23] "Fountain knew nothing about the practical side of newspaper work, but he was fearless and at times wrote editorials with a pen dripping blue vitriol instead of ink,"[24] writes William A. Keleher.

The crusading editor doggedly chronicled the escapades of Jesse Evans's gang members, whom he branded the banditti, a name for rogues of any kind, especially outlaws who lived by plunder. "Banditti" appeared as a heading in one of Fountain's October 1877 editorials that described the gang's nefarious activities during the brief time that Kid Antrim rode with them.[25]

Fountain wrote of how the Boys crossed into Lincoln County, where they were able to obtain fresh horses and the "choicest viands" from the larders of ranchers friendly to their cause. He described their terrorizing Tularosa, where they drank all the liquor they could find and rode off after firing "a hundred or more shots promiscuously about the town as a parting salute."[26] From there the gang proceeded to the home of a man who had once testified against one of them. The frightened man pleaded for them to spare his wife's and sick children's lives, and the outlaws did, but only after shooting the man's dog and riddling the house with bullets.

During their ride the Boys stopped at various roadhouses and trading posts for food and drink. Whenever the bills were presented, the gang smugly told the proprietors to "chalk it up" on credit. At one such stop, they spied a copy of the *Independent* containing one of Fountain's denunciations of the banditti. Angered by what he read, Evans told the others that he would reward Fountain with "a free pass to hell."[27]

On the afternoon of October 9, 1877, the Boys stopped for provisions at the trading post run by John Ryan near the Mescalero Apache Indian Agency. Ryan worked for J. J. Dolan & Co., a mercantile establishment in the town of Lincoln, the seat of Lincoln County.[28] Formerly named L. G. Murphy & Co., the name had changed in April when Murphy severed his ties with the business. The two remaining partners, James J. Dolan and John H. Riley, took over the operation, which included the branch store at the Mescalero agency managed by Ryan.[29]

By that evening the gang had made its way to near the summit of the Sacramento Mountains and stopped to make camp beneath the pines. Fires were built for cooking and warmth, and Evans posted sentinels to guard against surprise visitors. Around eight o'clock a buggy appeared on the rocky trail, and one of the lookouts hooted like an owl to warn the others drinking back at camp.[30] When the buggy drew closer, the sentry recognized the two men inside as John Riley, partner in the mercantile firm, and James Longwell, one of his employees. Both men were well known to the Boys, who put on a humorous show on horseback to welcome their guests' arrival. Perhaps such antics even allowed Kid Antrim to recall his boyhood experiences onstage in Silver City.

"Riley and Longwell passed within a few feet of the guard, an American, who responded to their greeting in Spanish, and on passing, the entire party, number-ing seventeen well armed and mounted men, paraded on the roadside,"[31] wrote Fountain. The cordial greeting that Evans and his men gave the pair of Lincoln County merchants was to be expected. After all, one of the gang's best customers when it came to purchasing stolen livestock was J. J. Dolan & Co. The cattle were then sold to fulfill the Murphy firm's beef contracts with the army and reservation Apaches.[32]

Dolan & Co. owned and ran a cattle-clearing business in the Pecos country near Seven Rivers and was known to have dabbled in rustling. "It was understood that Jesse Evans and his associates, the most formidable and consistent band of cattle thieves then operating in Lincoln County, were on a secret payroll of the Murphy firm and were to earn their income by steadily stealing from the [John] Chisum herds,"[33] writes Maurice G. Fulton.

The next morning the Boys, including Kid Antrim, bade Riley and Longwell so long, and the two parties continued their separate paths. The revelry of the night before at the mountain campsite, however, was published for all to see. This brazen contribution written by an anonymous source named Fence Rail, appeared in the same issue of the *Independent* as Fountain's column describing how the Evans gang and their guests had carried on.[34] The unsolicited story from "Fence Rail" was entitled "Grand Reunion Of 'The Boys.'"

I am requested to furnish you with a copy of the proceedings of a reunion held "at rendezvous in the Sacramento Mountains" on this day, which are as follows: "At a reunion of 'prominent citizens' of Southern New Mexico held at one of their numerous rendezvous on this 9th day of October A.D. 1877, Captain Jesse Evans took the stump (which served as a chair) and after having congratulated the gentlemen of the road present on the bril-liant record they had recently made in the line of their profession, announced that the object of the present reunion was to compare notes, perfect their organization, and prepare a plan for the upcoming cam-paign. Nor was this all; they had received valuable assistance in their labors from citizens who were not so prominent as they, and it was but *justice* (here a murmur was heard, Captain Evans begged pardon for hav-ing made use of that unpalatable word, and proceeded) it was but right that they should award honor where honor was due. The first thing to be done was to perfect their organization.

No doubt that "Fence Rail" was mimicking this gathering of outlaws in the most civilized way. The justice he alludes to is probably the law of the land and the man—and in this case the men—with the most guns. The article continues:

This business was concluded with the following result. Captain Jesse Evans was promoted to the colonel. Nick Provencio and Frank Baker, on account of their proficiency in horse stealing, etc., were elected captains, and all the balance of the band were made captain by brevet. The following resolutions were then adopted:

"Resolved: That those who have so generously and continually warned us of every effort being made by the despotic, tyrannical and arbitrary authorities of Southern New Mexico to deprive us of our liberties and incarcerate us in their vile dungeons, we return thanks, and add that in the opinion of this band, an occasional beef steer is inadequate compensation for the invaluable information furnished us by there faithful friends."

Fountain's sword was sharp and he had no fear in outright accusing these men of being renegades and cow thieves.

"Resolved: That that portion of the press of New Mexico which notwithstanding our many open and notorious robbers and murderers has persistently denied that organized lawlessness exists in South New Mexico and which has held us to the public as paragons of virtue and honesty, is entitled to favorable mention. Having no further use for the services of such champions, however, (we having reached the conclusion that even murder and horse stealing can be made respectable by our friendly newspaper correspondents and editors) we hereby reconsider our intention to present each one of our said champion editors and correspondents with one of the next bunch of horses that we shall appropriate."

In conclusion, "Fence Rail" took some swipes at the pesky Fountain and his newspaper.

"Resolved: That we shall take the first opportunity of getting even with the 'Independent clan' and regret that an unwillingness to experience the

⁂

disagreeable sensation of 'pulling hemp' [hanging] has operated as an obstruction to carrying into execution heretofore our intentions in this regard. In the meantime we applaud those newspapers who abuse the *Independent* in our interest.

"Resolved: That the public is our oyster, and that having the power, we claim the right to appropriate any property we may take a fancy to, and that we exercise that right regardless of consequences."

These resolutions having been adopted Captain Nicholas Provencio produced a copy of the *Independent,* a huge fire was built, and the obnoxious paper was thrown into the flames. The gang, headed by Colonel Evans, now marched around the pyre to the inspiring strains of the "Rogues' March" performed by Captain Baker on a fine tooth comb.

Although the satirical account of the so-called reunion of the banditti was published with just the pen name Fence Rail, there was little doubt that the actual author was John Riley.[35] Fountain, who must have known who penned the story, but who had guts enough to run it, must also have been aware that Riley's arrogant and sarcastic ramblings were only a hint of the chaos to come. The stage for pure mobocracy and bedlam was now set in Lincoln County. It was now only a matter of who the actors were going to be.

James Joseph Dolan (left) and
Lawrence Gustave Murphy, 1871
THE ROBERT G. MCCUBBIN COLLECTION

Sixteen

SEVEN RIVERS

There was no one part of the remoter west which could claim the monopoly in the product of hard citizens, but there can be small challenge to the assertion that southeastern New Mexico, for twenty years after the Civil War was without doubt, as dangerous a country as ever lay out of doors.[1]

•

—EMERSON HOUGH

THROUGHOUT THE SHORT time that Kid Antrim rode with the Jesse Evans Gang in the autumn of 1877, violence and bloodshed were widespread across southern New Mexico Territory.[2] The same was true in western Texas.

Records reveal that outlaws killed more than ninety law officers in Texas from 1868 through 1878. Disputes and feuds during the commission of crimes led to massive numbers of civilians being massacred. Most of the violence went unrecorded and unpunished. The worst shootists and killers of the day were either born or raised in Texas. Some of them were embittered ex-Confederates, who had poured into the state after the war and directed much of their racist hostility against Indians, blacks, and Mexicans, although northern soldiers were hardly unprejudiced. Vicious crimes saturated the Mexican border, creating a precarious future for Hispanic citizens already discriminated against by most Anglos, who not only failed to comprehend that the Mexican War had ended thirty years before, in 1848, but also perpetuated discrimination against Mexicans and Mexican-Americans that continues to this day.[3]

No small amount of the violence that seared the Texas countryside came from gang members known as the banditti. Throughout September and October 1877, as the banditti committed a slew of felonies, an ongoing dispute known as the Salt War erupted in bloodshed at the sleepy little town of San Elizario, an old settlement near El Paso. Several participants in future clashes involving Kid Antrim earned their stripes in this conflict. The violence was the culmination of a long disagreement caused by Anglos' persistent attempts to take over and control salt-mining rights at the foot of Guadalupe Peak, east of El Paso. The extensive and ultradry salt flats were considered communal property, available as a salt source to all comers particularly the many Hispanics who had enjoyed free harvest of the life-sustaining staple since the mid-1700s. Some of the pilgrims pushing hand-carts traveled up to a hundred miles across arroyos and sandhills just to collect the salt. Several villages near El Paso depended on the salt trade for sustenance. They were outraged when the self-styled Salt Ring, a collection of contemptible Anglo politicians and lawyers, tried to acquire title to the salt deposits for their own profit.[4]

That autumn of 1877, when mobs of angry Hispanic residents rebelled and responded with firepower, retaliation from the Anglos was swift. The feud eventually resulted in the looting of San Elizario and death and destruction on both sides. One outspoken Confederate veteran, Thomas Coke Bass, went so far as to request formally that Texas Governor Richard B. Hubbard grant him the authority to organize a regiment of soldiers to take on the insurgents.[5] "From latest indications it seems that our country has to give the Mexicans another thrashing and of course we old Texans will take particular pride in doing that work," Bass wrote to Governor Hubbard on October 9, 1877.[6] Hubbard chose not to grant the bellicose request, and the cantankerous Bass died less than a year later during a yellow fever epidemic in Memphis, Tennessee.

Others, however, did take up arms and join the fight. A small force of freshly recruited Texas Rangers led by Lieutenant J. B. Tays headed to San Elizario, and later an all-black troop of the Ninth Cavalry arrived on the scene. These troopers from Fort Bayard were popularly called buffalo soldiers, the appellation given them by Indians who perceived a similarity between the hair of the black soldiers and the buffalo.[7]

Citizen posses, little more than vigilantes, also entered the melee in the days before Christmas 1877 and besieged the Texas Rangers, forcing them to surrender. El Paso Sheriff Charles Kerber put out the call to New Mexico Territory for help, and criminal mastermind John Kinney responded, although some historians question the extent of his participation in the conflict.[8] At the time Kinney, a recurring figure in Kid Antrim's life, was on the dodge after being indicted for murder in Dona Ana County in the shooting death of one Ysabel Barela in Mesilla on November 2, 1877. The timing was right for Kinney and some of his followers to form a force of hired killers and head to Texas.[9]

"Capt. John Kinney now has an independent command of about 70 men and has issued a call for 30 more well armed and mounted to join him at or near El Paso," reported the *Grant County Herald* in early 1878. "Pay $40 per month and forage, by state of Texas. With 100 well armed and mounted men Capt. Kinney is liable soon to have a world wide reputation and lay Lieut. Bullis in the shade."[10]

The newspaper's comparison of Kinney with Lieutenant John Lapham Bullis appeared entirely unwarranted, given that Bullis was a hero highly decorated for his "gallant service" while commanding the Black Seminole Scouts in several campaigns against renegade Indians.[11] Needless to say, Kinney and his gang did not live up to the accolades. At San Elizario in late December 1877 and early January 1878, the deputized Kinney men murdered and terrorized "greasers" and "gringos" alike. The Kinney riders were so cruel that even the Texas Rangers, hardly an outfit known for compassion when it came to enforcing the law, stayed clear of the mercenaries.

"We didn't stay with them or camp with them, but tried to keep separate from them, and I ordered my men not to mix with them, or have anything to do with them, because I knew that a great many of them were bad men, that they were acting badly, and didn't appear to have any restraint," Lieutenant Tays testified during a subsequent congressional investigation of the matter.[12] However, the Rangers did not manage to escape criticism from some historians for their role in the war. "When the fighting was over, Ranger reinforcements arrived after the nick of time," according to David J. Weber, editor of *Foreigners in Their Native Land*, a collection of essays examining Hispanic roots in America. "They killed some 'escaping' Mexicans, raped a woman, and committed other atrocities in revenge. Curiously, no Mexicans were ever brought to trial for their role in the Salt War, but in the long run they lost the war. All, eventually, had to pay for salt."[13]

The experience at San Elizario proved useful to Kinney and the hired gunmen and helped prepare them for their role as mercenary fighters in the upcoming Lin-

coln County War. That dark chapter in New Mexico history and its aftermath catapulted Kid Antrim into the public eye, but in October 1877 he was still merely a
minor player struggling to survive.

Conjecture abounds about the Kid's exact whereabouts at this juncture in his
life. As usual, any precise dates and details regarding his movements in late 1877
vary greatly even among credible eyewitnesses who encountered him at the time.

One of those sources was Eugene Van Patten, an ex-Confederate and Mesilla
Valley rancher who in the late 1870s built a resort called the Dripping Springs
Hotel near Ice Canyon in the Organ Mountains, east of Las Cruces. In his later
years Van Patten told Gustave Dore Griggs, a member of a prominent Mesilla family, of meeting Kid Antrim sometime in the fall of 1877, when the young man
sought work at his ranch. Van Patten explained to Griggs that he was greatly surprised that the boy named Antrim turned out to be a notorious outlaw.[14]

At this time, when Kid visited Van Patten's ranch, it remains unclear if he was
traveling on his own or still riding with the Boys. What is known is that sometime
in October 1877, Kid Antrim entered Lincoln County, New Mexico Territory, his
turf for the rest of his life.

About the middle of that month Jesse Evans and some of the Boys made their
way to the Lincoln County settlement of Seven Rivers, named after the seven
springs that fed into the Pecos River. Dick Reed founded the community in 1867,
when he realized it was a good stopover place for the many cattle drivers passing
through the Pecos River valley. Reed built a trading post, which he named Dog-
town because of the abundance of prairie dogs, but by 1878 the name had been
officially changed to Seven Rivers.[15]

A favorite gathering spot for ranchers and drovers, Seven Rivers also had a
reputation as a hangout for cattle rustlers, rowdies, and gamblers. According to
local legend, there were so many shootings in the town that all the saloon doors
had removable hinges so they could be easily removed and used as stretchers for
the wounded.

Seven Rivers proved to be an especially good haven for anyone who preyed on
the herds of Texan John Chisum. Unquestionably the principal cattle owner in the
region, Chisum, along with his brother, Pitzer, and their cowboys, muscled their
way into New Mexico Territory in the late 1860s and began selling beef to the
army. Like other cattle kings, John Chisum was known to steal livestock from the
smaller ranchers as he claimed squatter and homestead rights along the Pecos. "In
the time-honored New Mexico tradition, Chisum dominated lush grasslands that

were not his own; these public domain lands were free for the claiming, but Chisum's men treated anyone who tried as an interloper,"[16] writes environmental historian Hal K. Rothman.

The enormous Chisum ranch was known as the Jinglebob (later the Jinglebob Land and Cattle Company), after the distinctive earmark on Chisum cattle, made by cutting two-thirds of each ear so the lower part dropped down in a dewlap.[17] In the late 1870s Chisum was running a herd of one hundred thousand longhorns on open range that spanned more than two hundred miles, from Fort Sumner in the north all the way to the Mexican border.

This area, the Trans-Pecos, was wide-open, unfenced territory. Scattered among the high plains were mountains that had springs and canyons, perfect places for outlaws to hide out, and very little law enforcement. Some said it was a rustler's dream, with few, if any, roads (mostly trails along arroyos and dried-up riverbeds) and 365 days of sunshine every year. Cattle roamed free, and to the thieves and rustlers, they were there for the taking. No questions asked.

The Jinglebob herds were a tempting target for thieves. Around Seven Rivers people said that "no man could live there who did not steal from Chisum."[18] With that in mind, Evans and his gang headed straight to Hugh Mercer Beckwith's ranch, only a few miles north of Seven Rivers.

A Virginian by birth, Beckwith had come to New Mexico Territory over the Santa Fe Trail in 1849. Later that year he wed Refugia Rascón y Piño, a sixteen-year-old beauty from a well-connected New Mexico family.[19] Beckwith began acquiring farm and ranchland throughout the territory and started a cattle operation. In the early 1870s the Beckwith family, by now including three sons and two daughters, established the cattle ranch near Seven Rivers. Beckwith, with help from his older boys, Robert and John, built a fortresslike adobe house and put out herds of cattle to graze on free-range blue gamma grass.[20] Before very long Beckwith had become the acknowledged patriarch of Seven Rivers and Chisum's most outspoken competitor.

After arriving in the Seven Rivers region, Evans and those gang members still with him went directly to the security of Beckwith's ranch for some rest and recuperation. It remains debatable, but most historians believe that by then Kid Antrim was no longer with the Boys. According to solid testimonial evidence, it is almost certain that when he first came to the lower Pecos country, the Kid stayed with the Heiskell Jones family.[21]

In 1877, after a stint running a freight business in Texas and Arizona Territory,

Jones returned to New Mexico Territory and took over the trading post and ranch owned by Dick Reed, the Seven Rivers pioneer who the previous year succumbed to dropsy, also known as edema.[22]

The Kid, who was on the run again, turned up in the Pecos Valley. Apaches had stolen his horse, forcing him to walk many miles to the nearest settlement, the Heiskell Jones house. Barbara Culp Jones, called Ma'am Jones by all who knew her, nursed the Kid, who was near death, back to health. The Jones family, which included nine sons and one daughter, developed a strong attachment to Billy and gave him one of their horses.

To her dying day in 1905, Ma'am Jones firmly maintained that she was the first person to encounter Kid Antrim in Lincoln County. Oral historian Eve Ball compiled and eventually published her vivid recollections of that meeting and Jones's memories of other events in late-nineteenth-century Lincoln County.[23] According to the Ball account, when in the predawn darkness the fearless Ma'am Jones, whose husband, Heiskell, was away on business, heard rustling in the mesquite outside the cabin, she reached for her Winchester and peered through a slit in the wall. She saw movement and ordered whoever was there to come forward. Kid Antrim obliged.[24] Bell writes:

> A slender boy arose and stumbled unsteadily toward the house. Ma'am dropped her rifle, unbolted the door, and ran to meet the boy. She half-carried him to the kitchen and eased him into her big chair before the fire. When she had a good blaze she put the kettle over it and turned to find the boy tugging at his boot. She knelt, took it in her hands—a very small boot—and pulled it off. Then she removed the other. He wore no socks and his feet were raw and swollen. How foolish to wear boots too small! Those blisters! He'd never got them riding a horse. He'd walked, and he'd walked a long distance.[25]

Recognized throughout the Pecos Valley for her generosity and nursing ability, Ma'am Jones tended to the young man's bleeding feet and, despite some protests, made him drink a cup of warm goat's milk, before tucking him into a feather bed with her own boys. The next morning the Kid told Ma'am Jones that he had reached her place after walking many miles from the Guadalupe Mountains. He said that he had been traveling with a companion named Tom O'Keefe when a band of Mescalero Apaches attacked them.

"They warned us at Mesilla to come through the reservation, but we wanted to see the country," the Kid allegedly told Ma'am Jones. "When we got to the top of the ridge and saw the stream below, I left O'Keefe with the horses and went down to fill the canteens. Just as I started back, the Indians struck. I waved O'Keefe to ride out of it, and I hid. I stayed under cover till dark and then worked my way downstream till it began to get light. For three days I lay out in the daytime and walked at night."[26]

According to the Ma'am Jones narrative, while Kid Antrim spent several days recuperating at the Jones home, he helped with the chores and engaged in some friendly target practice with John Jones, one of the nine Jones boys. Later it was learned that O'Keefe had safely made his way back to Mesilla.

Although there is surely some truth in the Ma'am Jones story as told in the Ball book, other historians, including those who used some of the material in their own books about the Kid, have expressed skepticism. Robert Utley was one of those who wrote about this dilemma. He said: "On one hand, Eve Ball obtained the story from the Jones boys (mostly Sam) in the 1940s and 1950s, and their recollections must be taken seriously. On the other hand, the story is presented in grossly romanticized fashion replete with contrived conversation. Separating the Jones boys and Eve Ball is impossible."[27]

Utley and other historians appear to have put more stock in *My Girlhood among Outlaws*, another of Eve Ball's contributions to the body of work chronicling the New Mexico frontier during the brief years when the Kid made his mark. This book by Lily Casey Klasner was published only after Ball discovered the manuscript, lost after Klasner's death in 1946, inside a trunk in an old adobe hut and then undertook the editing and annotation of the work.

Lily was the daughter of Robert Casey, who in 1867 brought his family from Texas to a ranch near the village of Picacho on the Rio Hondo, where he ran cattle and operated a gristmill. Casey was a close friend of John Chisum's, putting Casey at odds with the cattle king's enemies, Lawrence Gustave (L.G.) Murphy and James J. (J. J., Jimmy) Dolan, owners of the largest mercantile store in Lincoln County.[28] William Wilson shot and mortally wounded Casey on the streets of Lincoln in 1875 just hours after a convention staged by Murphy-Dolan opponents came up with a slate of candidates that seemed likely to remove the grip of the powerful political machine that controlled the county.[29]

Wilson was apprehended, quickly convicted of first-degree murder, and sentenced to hang. "Almost no one took seriously Wilson's claim that he killed

Casey because the latter owed him eight or nine dollars in wages," wrote Maurice Fulton. "Casey had consistently opposed the Murphy machine, and Casey's friends imputed his killing to the antagonism he had aroused by his verbal attack on the Murphy organization at the convention earlier that day."[30]

Ironically, given the amount of pure anarchy that had reigned there for so many years, Wilson had the dubious honor of being the first person legally hanged in Lincoln County. A huge crowd of gawkers and invited guests turned out for the occasion on December 10, 1875. The proceeding, however, turned into a macabre event when it turned out that the condemned man actually had to be hanged twice.[31] "After hanging nine and a half minutes, the body was cut down and placed in the coffin, when it was discovered that life was not yet extinct," reported "A Rolling Stone," the pen name used by a special correspondent for the *Santa Fe New Mexican*. "A rope was fastened around the neck, and the crowd drew the inanimate body from the coffin and suspended it from the gallows where it hanged twenty minutes longer. It was then cut down and placed in the coffin and buried."[32]

Justice had been served, but Casey's murder left his widow, Ellen, to fend for her five children. She began to dispose of property, and early in 1877 most of her cattle was sold at a sheriff's auction to satisfy mounting debts. Soon the widow decided it would be best for her family if they returned to Texas.

Later that year she packed her children and their few belongings in a wagon, rounded up what remained of the cattle, as well as some that had already been sold, and headed in October down the Pecos. Toward the end of that month the Caseys paused at Seven Rivers and stayed with Heiskell and Ma'am Jones for about three weeks. While at the Jones place Lily Casey and her family first met Kid Antrim.[33] The fourteen-year-old girl clearly was impressed with the Kid's antics: "The Kid was active and graceful as a cat. At Seven Rivers he practiced continually with pistol or rifle, riding at a run and dodging behind the side of his mount to fire, as the Apaches did. He was very proud of his ability to pick up a handkerchief or other object from the ground while riding at a run."[34] Lily's older brother, Robert, who usually went by the nickname Add, was not as impressed with the Kid as his kid sister was. "When I knowed him at Seven Rivers, you might call him a bum," Add recalled many years later. "He was nothing but a kid and a bum when I knowed him back then."[35]

The Kid tried to swap his horse for one of Ellen Casey's mares, but the widow turned down the trade when she learned that his horse had been stolen from John Chisum. Then the Kid and Ellen's sons Add and William tried in vain to convince

Ellen to let him accompany the family to Texas. "Both of my brothers urged Mother to take him to Texas with us but she refused," recalled Lily. "Then he left for the Murphy-Blake Spring [the Murphy-Dolan cow camp] where Billy [Buck] Morton was in charge. Upon returning he told Will that Morton had given him a terrible 'bawling out' for some trivial offense and that he intended to get even with him. Again he broached the subject of accompanying us, and again Mother courteously refused."[36]

In other memories she left behind, Lily provided more details concerning the Kid's run-in with Buck Morton, foreman for Jimmy Dolan and the "cow boss of all the Murphy-Nolan [sic] Co. cow camps." The "trivial offense" she had alluded to turned out to have been a disagreement over a female.[37]

"Morton had a girl," Lily explained. "She was a beauty in every way; she was called the 'Bell' [sic] of the Pecos Valley. And the Kid he got to meddling in, and Morton, although a fine man in many ways, yet he was very jealous hearted, he just could not take good naturedly the Kid's trying to cut in on him, the Kid then was only considered a little outlaw tramp just hanging around any where he could get to stay."[38]

The fact that Ellen Casey had not wanted the Kid to go with her family to Texas and this squabble over the Belle of the Pecos Valley kept him from joining back up with the Jesse Evans Boys again.

On October 17, 1877, a posse out of Lincoln County working on a tip it had gotten from an undisclosed source, surrounded a *choza* (adobe hut) near Hugh Beckwith's Seven Rivers ranch house. Following a brief exchange of gunfire, the men took into custody Jesse Evans, Frank Baker, Tom Hill, and George Davis. Dick Brewer, the deputized foreman of the Lincoln County grand jury and a foreman for John Tunstall, the Englishman whose horse and cattle herds had been raided by the Evans Gang, led the posse. The prisoners were hauled back to Lincoln and placed in a new cellar jail with six round-the-clock guards posted.[39]

The posse immediately hit the road again and caught up with the Casey family just before they reached the Texas border. It demanded the return of the 209 head of stolen Tunstall cattle. Ellen Casey quickly and wisely complied. She then turned her caravan around and returned to Seven Rivers and soon after to the Casey ranch on the Hondo. Later the posse came to the family's place and took Will and Add Casey to the Lincoln jail, where they lingered for a short time until John Chisum saw to it that they were released.[40]

During all this, Kid Antrim was on his own and avoided capture. He remained in what historian Robert Utley calls "a shadow world along the fringes of the law."[41] Although Lily Casey Klasner conspicuously avoids any mention of the posse in her book, she does repeat something Kid Antrim told her. "Once I heard him say, 'He who fights and runs away will live to fight another day.' "[42]

Did he really utter these words of eighteenth-century Irish poet and dramatist Oliver Goldsmith to Lily Klasner or was this something she imposed on him to heighten the romance and mystery of the Kid? He might have heard the words from his mother, who was, for all practical purpose, a learned woman. Or it may have been from his schooling days back in Silver City or something he picked up along the trail.

The completion of the stanza of Goldsmith poetry, by the way, is: "But he who is in battle slain can never rise and fight again."

William H. Bonney, circa 1880

Seventeen

BILLY BONNEY

Making his own way had brought out a self-reliance and a willingness
to dare anything. Eager for adventure, the newly christened William H.
Bonney rode with the Banditti into Lincoln County.[1]

•

—Jerry Weddle

AT THE END of 1877 Kid Antrim became acquainted with Lincoln County, which was on the cusp of a battle between owners of the county's largest general store and its competitors. The Kid was anticipating another clean start and had already concocted a new alias. He still answered to the Kid, but by then and for the balance of his life he introduced himself as William H. Bonney.

In large part because of the many books riddled with myths, inaccuracies, and barefaced lies that were written about the Kid after his death, this became the moniker that for many years most people accepted as his true given name. Few ever realized that he was not branded with his more famous sobriquet until 1881, the final year of his life.

Just prior to the Kid's appearance in southeastern New Mexico Territory, he had been known sometimes to use the given name of his stepfather, William Henry Antrim, and refer to himself as Billy Antrim. The middle initial H., which he inserted between William and Bonney in his newly invented name obviously stood for Henry, both his given name and Antrim's middle name. Why he picked the last name Bonney has never really been explained.

Many writers and researchers, as well as Bonney family genealogists hoping to make a case for a "celebrity" kinship link, have offered all sorts of hypotheses about the name. People surnamed Bonney from across the nation and beyond maintain they have a direct relationship to the Kid from both his paternal and maternal lines. Many of them argue that they are distant cousins to the Kid or that he was born with a different surname and later acquired the Bonney name through adoption into one of the branches of the Bonney family.[2] The majority of these claims cannot be corroborated and are not considered reliable.

Some imaginative genealogists have suggested that the Kid's birth father was a descendant of the Thomas Bonney who immigrated to Plymouth, Massachusetts, in 1635 and supposedly lived next door to Miles Standish.[3] A more romanticized version of the Kid's place in Bonney family history, once again without any proved link, suggests that Billy Bonney was somehow related to Anne Bonny (née Cormac and with no *e* in her last name), possibly the most infamous of all female pirates.[4]

Born in 1700 in County Cork, Ireland, Anne was the illegitimate daughter of a prominent lawyer and his wife's maid. The ensuing scandal forced him to flee Ireland with his lover and their child and take refuge in the Carolinas. At age sixteen, Anne wed a sailor named James Bonny, who took her to a pirate lair in the Bahamas. When she caught the eye of Calico Jack Rackham, a notorious buccaneer rogue, she left Bonny and joined Rackham's pirate crew, which included another fiery female named Mary Read. Together they made pirate history on the high seas until Mary succumbed to a fever and Anne Bonny mysteriously vanished.[5]

More than likely Billy Bonney never even heard of this alleged ancestor, Anne the pirate, although the notion of being related to a female sword-wielding swashbuckler might have been exciting for the young man to ponder. On the other hand, the Kid may have been aware of yet another illustrious Bonney, the popular dime novelist Edward Bonney.

A native New Yorker, known to be devious, if not outright fraudulent, in his business practices, Edward Bonney settled not coincidentally in Indiana, where he started a gristmill and a sawmill on the Elkhart River. His dream was to develop a city to be named Bonneyville, but that scheme never materialized after Bonney ran afoul of the law. He was arrested by Elkhart officials for counterfeiting in the mid-1830s, escaped on the way to his arraignment, and fled to the Illinois frontier.[6]

To prove his innocence, Bonney became a bounty hunter and tracked down an assortment of crooks, thieves, and killers. The exploits brought him much notoriety, and in the decade leading up to the Civil War, he became a writer of dime novels and for newspapers, churning out countless stories loosely based on his adventures. His best-known work, *The Banditti of the Prairies, or, The Murderer's Doom*, published in 1850, was very popular and came out in at least six editions over a span of eight years.[7] Some historians conjecture that the Kid may have read one of Edward Bonney's adventure books and borrowed the author's surname.

"I concluded a long time ago that the reason there is no trace of the origins of the Kid and his family in any of the 'traditional' locations is, ipso facto, because they were never there, but how to go about proving it is a horse of a different color," Frederick Nolan, the British author and acknowledged expert on Billy the Kid, wrote this author. "The key to the mystery has always been (in my mind, any-way) the name 'Bonney.' Although of course it might have been nothing more than a name he saw on the cover of a dime novel (Edward Bonney was very popular then) my gut instinct is that it was the Kid's (or perhaps his blood father's/mother's) original family name. But whether there is a link, and whether there is any way of establishing that link . . . the question would be, as in the song, where do I begin?"[8]

Of all proponents of the premise that Henry McCarty was born a Bonney, the most credible was Herman B. Weisner. A respected New Mexico historian and longtime genealogical researcher on William H. Bonney, Weisner devoted much of his career to investigating the life and legend of Billy the Kid. Prior to Weisner's death in 1993, some of his revelations about the illusive outlaw's genealogy were closely examined by several leading Billy the Kid scholars, including Nolan, Robert Utley, Jerry Weddle, and Leon Metz.[9] None of them refuted Weisner's preliminary findings, and Weddle was quoted as saying he was "impressed by Herman's research."[10]

Much of Weisner's research into the Bonney name was unveiled publicly for the first time during a Billy the Kid symposium cosponsored by the Lincoln County Heritage Trust and Recursos de Santa Fe. More than fifty noted Billy the Kid scholars and devotees attended the conference, which was held in Ruidoso and

Lincoln, New Mexico, September 11–15, 1991.[11] Weisner's revelations about the Kid's lineage during the five-day conference were described as "bombshells" in one of the subsequent newspaper reports.[12]

On the basis of preliminary research, mostly into census data and family oral histories, Weisner told the symposium participants that in his judgment, the Kid had been born a Bonney in Missouri at least two or three years earlier than previously believed. He also theorized that the Kid and his mother, Catherine, were linked by blood to a Hispanic family living in Lincoln County.[13]

"When Billy the Kid fled Arizona for New Mexico after killing his first man, he was not fleeing the law—he was going home to family, a research expert says," wrote John R. Moore in a front-page story for the *El Paso Times* following the conference. "He's [Weisner's] answered, for me, why Billy fled Arizona and went almost in a bee-line to Lincoln County," El Paso historian and author Leon Metz told Moore.[14]

According to Weisner's preliminary findings, Catherine was born in Missouri, not Ireland. Weisner further declared that her father was James Bonney, either an Englishman or an Irishman, who immigrated to the United States and settled near the start of the Santa Fe Trail in Missouri. There he fathered children with an unidentified woman. According to Weisner, one of those offspring was the Kid's mother. For several years Bonney reportedly ran a successful freighting operation on the Santa Fe Trail and made countless trips to the ancient city of Santa Fe and then back to los Estados Unidos.[15]

Eventually Bonney abandoned his family in Missouri and settled in northern New Mexico Territory. He married Juana María Mascarenas, the daughter of Miguel Mascarenas, one of the grantees of the extensive Mora Land Grant. Bonney and his wife had three children, Cleofas, Santiago (James Bonney, Jr.), and Rafaelita.[16] He built a trading post on land given to him by his father-in-law near La Junta, the future site of the town of Watrous. Bonney's blue eyes and red hair and beard quickly made him a well-known figure in the mostly Hispanic region.

Bonney was busy running his trading post in 1846, when Brigadier General Stephen Watts Kearny and his Army of the West claimed the territory New Mexico for the United States from Mexico. His battalions marched through La Junta and quenched their thirsts from the acequia, or irrigation ditch, called the Bonney Ditch, a name it has carried even into the twenty-first century. The night of August 13, 1846, Kearny and some of his troops were Bonney's supper guests and were fed his choicest beef.[17]

"The first settlement we had seen in 775 miles," Lieutenant William H. Emory, the noted surveyor and cartographer under Kearny's command, wrote of Bonney-ville, as it was then called. "Mr. Boney [*sic*] . . . has been some time in this country, and is the owner of a large number of horses and cattle which he manages to keep in defiance of wolves, Indians and Mexicans. He is a perfect specimen of a generous, openhearted adventurer, and in appearance what, I have pictured to myself, Daniel Boone of Kentucky must have been in his day. He drove a herd of cattle into camp and picked out the largest and fattest, which he presented to the Army."[18]

By the time of the American soldiers' arrival Bonney had taken up with a new woman, Maria Bibiana Martin, the attractive young daughter of another prominent local family.[19] In 1846 she gave birth to a son they named Ramon.

The boy never knew his adventuresome father. In early October 1846 Bonney rode off to recover some horses that had been stolen by Indians. He took along an Indian servant to translate and a bag stuffed with freshly baked tortillas to use for barter. He never returned. His body, studded with arrows, was found beside a creek, and the servant was never heard from again. In time Bonney's young widow, Bibiana, left with Ramon to raise, married a Swiss-German named Daniel Eberle and had more children.[20]

Several generations later Bibiana and Daniel's great-great-granddaughter Jan Girand, a journalist from Roswell, New Mexico, began investigating a possible connection between Ramon Bonney, her mother's half great-uncle, and the Kid. It was her belief that Uncle Ramon might have been a half brother to Catherine, one of James Bonney's offspring from his Missouri family.[21] Jan shared the Bonney family information with Herman Weisner.

"I first became acquainted with Weisner in the early 1990s when he came to Roswell to visit my mother and me," wrote Girand in her online Web magazine. "He had a theory and came seeking information because he heard my mother knew something about an Englishman named James Bonney. For several reasons, Herman Weisner believed that James Bonney was possibly Billy's grandfather, and the source of his adopted name. However, because of his failing health, Herman was unable to fully prove his theory."

Weisner, however, contended that the Bonney family line connected the Kid to a family named Salazar living in Lincoln County. When this theory was first presented at the 1991 Billy the Kid symposium in Ruidoso, rancher Joe Salazar verified that the story of Billy the Kid being a relative "has been known for a long time by my family."[22]

According to Weisner's research, one of Catherine's sisters married a Salazar and ended up living in Lincoln County. Those findings about Catherine's sibling were consistent with some local beliefs based on oral tradition that when the Kid first entered Lincoln County in 1877, he carried a letter of introduction from a Bonney aunt that he was to present to the Salazars. Although some family members chose not to acknowledge any kinship to the Kid, "the Salazar family in Lincoln accepted him," Joe Salazar told reporters.[23]

Despite all of Weisner's hard work, doubts about the Bonney-Salazar link to the Kid will always linger. "I knew Herman Weisner quite well," Frederick Nolan relates in correspondence. "We talked and talked and argued and argued but I could never get him to put down what he knew on paper. He was a painfully dogged and honest man who had at one time or another talked to most of the families (Anglo and Hispanic, and it was the latter that I thought valuable) in and around Lincoln County and, I am sure, gathered up a terrific amount of oral history. The trouble was, he kept it all inside his head and unless you sat down with him and wheedled it out, it stayed there."[24]

Still, as Nolan writes in *The West of Billy the Kid*, the quest for finding out more about Billy the Kid will always continue. "It might be pertinent to ask why any of this matters," says Nolan. "It might be relevant to propose that even if we knew now exactly where Billy the Kid was born and raised, or indeed, his complete genealogy, it would not add a scintilla to our understanding of him. Yet doubtless the search will go on, and perhaps one day someone will find the answers."[25]

Whether or not those questions are answered, the complicated theory of the Kid's having some Hispanic blood, which may never be proved, clarifies even more the Kid's simpatico relationship with the Hispanic people of New Mexico. For many Hispanics, the Kid was and always will be one of their own.

Christopher "Kit" Carson

EIGHTEEN

EYE OF THE STORM

Lincoln County held within its boundaries all the props, trappings, and paraphernalia needed for staging an out-of-doors theatrical production of huge proportions.[1]

•

—WILLIAM A. KELEHER

THE KID FABRICATED a new identity as William H. Bonney in New Mexico Territory's Lincoln County, long a stronghold of violence and treachery. Without the rapid succession of events that unfolded in Lincoln County over a whirlwind three years starting in 1878, there never would have been a Billy the Kid.

Against a backdrop of ethnic hostility, greed, and corruption dating back years before the Kid's arrival, Lincoln County epitomized the desires of the lawless. Crooked politicians, ruthless cattle lords, and hired gunmen cohabited there in a milieu of unspeakable cruelty and vindictiveness. Exploitation became the norm, and the distortion of truth was commonplace. Any means, however unscrupulous, could be justified to realize ambitions or retain power. The county became the harbor of the reckless and brazen and, in so doing, an especially fertile ground for spawning myth.

The place was made to order for anyone choosing mayhem as a way of life.

Bloodshed was even associated with its chosen name. Created by an act of the territorial legislature on January 16, 1869, the county was named in memory of the martyred President Abraham Lincoln, killed by John Wilkes Booth just four years earlier.[2]

By 1878 Lincoln County had grown in size until it was the largest county in the United States. Its 20 million acres sprawled over a vast expanse 160 miles wide and 180 miles deep, making it about one-fourth of the entire territory of New Mexico and two-thirds the size of England.[3]

Part of Lincoln County encompassed a great plateau that extended south of the Canadian River for four hundred miles. This landform, bounded on the west by New Mexico's Pecos River Valley, and known as the Llano Estacado, or Staked Plain, stretched beyond the boundaries of Lincoln County across the Texas border toward Indian Territory (Oklahoma). The meaning of its name remains open to debate. Some historians believe that the Spanish *Estacado* describes the rugged caprock that surrounds the plateau like a rock stockade. Others contend the name came from the wooden stakes that were driven into the sand and soil to mark a route for early traders or was the result of the profusion of yuccas, commonly called Spanish bayonets, that thrust their sharp-pointed stalks into the air.[4]

Lincoln County was composed of both unsurveyed public domain and Spanish land grants that dated back to long before the appearance of any Anglos. The eastern plains, adjoining Texas, were arid and largely unfit for raising livestock, but in the western plains and mountain valleys the grazing was excellent. Through time, all manner of humankind traversed the region: roving Comanches and Mescalero Apaches; wily comancheros, who bartered trade goods, including slaves; native shepherds and farmers; soldiers; cattlemen; Anglo traders and merchants; and scoundrels and opportunists of every stripe.[5]

A village on the Bonito River in a narrow valley just south of the Capitan Mountains was chosen as the county seat. Largely settled by Hispanics in the mid-1800s, it was originally named La Placita del Rio Bonito, "the village by the pretty river," after the nearby stream that flowed east from the Sacramento Mountains to join the Rio Ruidoso and form the Rio Hondo, which empties into the Pecos.[6] The settlers usually referred to their town as La Placita, Bonita Plaza, or simply Bonita. Most of the citizens had migrated from Manzano, a community in the foothills well to the north that, according to legend, took its name from two ancient apple orchards established by Franciscan friars in the seventeenth century. In fact, the orchards were probably planted no earlier than 1800.[7]

By the 1870s the town of Bonita was supporting a few stores and there was a scattering of adobe and rock houses as well as some jacals, huts with walls made of rows of vertical poles filled in between with mud, lining the plaza and town's only road. Central to the settlement was a stout rock torreón, or defense tower, constructed by the Spanish villagers as a place of refuge and protection from Mescalero Apache raids.[8] During such assaults the village women and children crowded into the first floor of the watchtower while the men took up positions on the second floor, where they fired at their attackers through slits in the thick walls.

Shortly after the creation of the county and the arrival of more Anglo settlers, the village assumed the name of Lincoln in honor of the slain president. Local residents also pointed out that a nearby rock formation strongly resembled a craggy profile of Honest Abe.[9]

Because of its proximity to Fort Stanton, the village was chosen as the county seat over rival towns, such as Tularosa to the west and San Patricio in the Ruidoso Valley. Just the act of picking the site for the fort in 1855 had been cause for celebration. On that auspicious day Private James A. Bennett dutifully scribbled in his diary: "The officers all got drunk."[10] The young soldier made no mention of any beverages' being dispensed to the enlisted ranks.

Situated in the rolling piñon-covered hills just nine miles up the Rio Bonito from the town of Lincoln, Fort Stanton was named for Dragoon Captain Henry W. Stanton, killed in 1855 in an ambush by Apaches in the Sacramento Mountains.[11] From its beginnings, Fort Stanton's location encouraged settlement in the area despite the constant fear of Apache raids and the numerous bands of Hispanic and Anglo outlaws, including some who masqueraded as Indians.

When the Civil War extended to New Mexico Territory in 1861, invading Confederate forces from Texas threatened to overtake the fort. Retreating Union troops set the post on fire to prevent its falling into enemy hands, but a rainstorm put out most of the blaze. Apaches and local citizens looted the remaining buildings, including the commissary, before the arrival of the Confederates, who remained only a short time before they too abandoned the post.[12]

Most of the Confederate troops had been driven back to Texas by the spring of 1862. With no Johnny Rebs to fight, Brigadier General James Carleton, the newly appointed commander of the Department of New Mexico, turned his attention to what was commonly referred to as the Indian problem.[13] A native of Maine and son of a sturdy ship captain, Carleton in his younger years had harbored literary aspirations and corresponded for a time with Henry Wadsworth Longfellow and Charles Dickens. Ultimately, Carleton took up the sword and began a thirty-year career of soldiering, mostly in the American West.

In 1861 Carleton led two thousand volunteers known as the California Column into Arizona and New Mexico Territories to reassert U.S. control of the Southwest. He had turned into a hardbitten officer, and soon after his arrival his steadfast contempt for and distrust of Indians became evident. "An Indian is a more watchful and wary animal than a deer," Carleton once told a comrade. "He must be hunted with skill."[14]

Beyond his pathological hatred of Indians, the shrewd Carleton had an ulterior motive for declaring open season on Indians: greed. Like many others, Carleton took note of the gold and silver strikes that had been made in the Southwest and was very much aware of the mineral riches waiting to be harvested from beneath the Indian lands.[15] Stricken with a hard case of mine fever, he wanted his share and then some.

Early on in New Mexico Territory, Carleton told his soldiers to prospect for precious minerals as much as possible and to report any significant finds. He also actively lobbied for mining interests, advising politicians in Washington, D.C., of "the national importance of settling Indians on Reservations, so that the country now inhabited by many bands of them may be left open to the enterprize [sic] and skill of the miner."[16]

Besides those questionable activities, Carleton encouraged eastern investors to explore obtaining capital to develop mines in New Mexico Territory. If that were not enough, Carleton even sent a gold nugget to Treasury Secretary Salmon Chase. In an accompanying letter, he asked Chase to present the nugget to President Lincoln along with a request for roads to be built in order to conquer the Indians and expand mine development.[17]

Carleton first set his sights on the Apaches. To vanquish them, he tapped the well-known trader and scout Colonel Christopher "Kit" Carson. Much like Billy the Kid, Carson was transformed into a legend in nineteenth-century America by dime novelists and others who frequently exaggerated his exploits.

The dutiful Carson and his five companies of New Mexico Volunteers marched off to the Mescaleros' traditional hunting grounds in the Sacramento Mountains and took over the vacant Fort Stanton. Carleton's orders to Carson were explicit: His troops were to kill all Mescalero men whenever and wherever they were encountered. All surviving Apache women and children were to be rounded up and held at Fort Stanton until further orders.[18]

"Carleton's idea, and a very sensible one, was to chastise the savages thoroughly, and show them that there was to be no more trifling," wrote historian Hubert Howe Bancroft in 1888. "No treaties were to be made, and no terms except unconditional surrender as prisoners of war."[19]

Carson waged a vigorous punitive campaign, and in less than three months his troops had crushed the Mescaleros. In January 1863 the more than 450 Mescaleros who had surrendered at Fort Stanton were herded like cattle more than 130 miles to Bosque Redondo (round wood), a dense grove of cottonwood trees near an old trading post on the Pecos River.[20]

Soldiers at the newly constructed Fort Sumner guarded the perimeters of the reservation. Named for General Edwin Vose Sumner, who died while the fort was being built, the site was 140 miles southeast of Santa Fe on an empty plain. Less than twenty years later Fort Sumner figured prominently in the life and death of the Kid and became his final resting place.[21]

At Fort Sumner, Carleton, like many others of his generation, expected the exiled Indians to learn the white man's ways and become peaceful, self-sustaining Christian farmers. In the summer of 1863, with the Mescaleros ensconced on farms scattered up and down the Pecos near Fort Sumner, Carson and his troops headed west to conduct what he called a scorched earth campaign against the Navajos.[22]

Carson gave no quarter. His men laid waste to everything the Navajos needed for survival, including log hogan dwellings, food stores, horses, and sheep. The soldiers destroyed wheat and corn crops and cut down hundreds of peach trees. In a short time many Indians perished, and the great Navajo Nation was starved into submission.

By the end of 1864 some ten thousand Navajo prisoners of war began a desperate 450-mile forced march from their sacred homeland to join the Apaches, their hereditary foes, at Bosque Redondo. This horrific journey came to be known as the Long Walk.[23] Large numbers of Navajos died during the trek. Harsh weather and lack of adequate clothing and food took a heavy toll. Many of the old and injured and other stragglers, including pregnant women, were shot pointblank or left behind.

By the time the Navajos reached the reservation at Fort Sumner, no more than eighty-six hundred of them had survived.[24] During the next four years of confinement hundreds more died from outbreaks of malaria and measles, dysentery, malnutrition, and sheer loneliness. Officers often took pretty Navajo girls as mistresses, and many women were routinely raped and brutalized. Soldiers infected the Navajos with syphilis and gonorrhea, which spread throughout the camp and the tribe. It was estimated that as many as one-fourth of the Navajos died during their internment at Bosque Redondo.[25]

Despite good efforts, the Navajos and Apaches had little success at farming. Continued animosity between the two tribes did not help the situation, and neither did nature. Drought, hailstorms, and cutworms took a heavy toll on crops. Firewood was scarce, and Comanches raided the livestock. Food and such basic creature comforts as medicine and blankets were always in short supply. Out of desperation, the Indians were forced to eat skunk, gopher, and rat meat. They picked kernels of undigested corn from the army horses' manure and cooked crude soups made from river water and flour.[26]

Even the soldiers finally recognized that keeping the Navajos captive was wrong. Eventually word of the deplorable conditions reached the War Department in Washington, D.C., and in 1868, under terms of peace, the Navajos were released and returned to their beloved homeland.[27]

By then the Mescaleros had already broken free of the confines of Bosque Redondo. In 1865 they fled the prison camp and returned to their spiritual home in the Sacramento and White mountains.[28] They were never recaptured, and in the 1870s they received reservation lands in their traditional stronghold. The task of supervising the Mescaleros once more fell to the troopers stationed at Fort Stanton. After the Civil War the post had fallen into increased disrepair until only the rock walls remained. With the return of the Apaches to the area, however, Fort Stanton was rebuilt, and by 1876 it housed more than two hundred soldiers in stone barracks.[29]

The mere presence of soldiers, many of them drifters, men on the run, or immigrants who spoke little or no English, presented problems for the army. Even before the Civil War, hog ranches had already sprung up near Fort Stanton just as they did around the remote posts in Arizona and throughout the West.[30] For many years peddlers along the Bonito, Peñasco, lower Rio Grande, and other streams supplied illicit whiskey, fresh horses, and firearms to Indians. So did army deserters, who frequently sold their government-issue mounts, guns, and ammunition to Apaches to make a little "traveling money." Cheap whiskey, known as the soldier's curse, provided the troopers with a balm for boredom and low pay. Diarrhea, dysentery, and venereal diseases were common among the soldiers. Alcoholism, suicide, and illness proved as deadly as hostile Indians.[31]

Another problem was the great expense of maintaining the garrison. In the 1870s just the cost of keeping the soldiers fed and clothed was exorbitant. Fort Stanton was nearly two hundred miles from its primary supply depot in Albuquerque, making the transportation of contract goods a high-priced proposition. Even after the crude roads and trade routes were improved, the shipping fees remained steep, and the army constantly sought ways to reduce expenses.[32]

Just prior to the Kid's arrival in Lincoln County, area farmers and ranchers also were looking for a way to cut shipping charges for their produce and beef to such distant markets as Albuquerque, El Paso, and Mesilla. They discovered Fort Stanton could be a profitable market and began providing the garrison with locally grown staples for men and beasts, including corn, beans, oats, wheat, and hay. The army annually purchased tons of hay and grain to feed its work and cavalry horses. By the early 1870s oak, piñon, juniper, ponderosa pine, and mesquite roots supplied by private contractors replaced coal as the heating fuel at Fort Stanton and other military posts.[33]

Irish potatoes, a favorite of the many soldiers originally from the old sod and a food valued by the army to counteract scurvy, were grown for the first time in New Mexico Territory as early as 1859 by farmers around the Rio Bonito.[34] The post quartermaster snapped up bushels of the spuds along with plenty of fresh beef to supplement the fort's cattle herd. For civilians living in the vicinity, especially cattlemen and farmers in the river valley, Fort Stanton provided a ready market for livestock and crops and became a magnet for people who sought to provide the army with the commodities needed to feed, clothe, and shelter soldiers and to fulfill its obligations to reservation Indians.

Many Fort Stanton soldiers, either honorably or dishonorably discharged from the army, decided to stay in the area and make a go of it. Some of them came from the ranks of Carleton's California Column volunteers who were mustered out as their terms of enlistment expired after the Civil War. Frequently both the officers and enlisted men married local women and became influential in the business and civic life of Lincoln County.[35] They realized there were fortunes to be made in cattle, land speculation, mining, and, very important, mercantile companies. By the late 1870s the rivalries for the lucrative army contracts had become fierce and often brutal.

Fort Stanton officers and friends
(far right, L. G. Murphy);
inset: Emil Fritz, 1871
THE BOB BOZE BELL COLLECTION

NINETEEN

DREAM KILLERS

Everything *in New Mexico that pays* at all . . . *is worked by a "ring."*[1]

•

—JOHN TUNSTALL

TARTING OUT AS a bit player in the Lincoln County War, one of the most notorious and memorable dramas in nineteenth-century Southwest history, the seventeen-year-old William H. Bonney was first a supporting actor, before unwittingly attaining star billing as Billy the Kid. Yet this sanguinary conflict, which helped create his myth, was just one of several open battles between warring factions in Lincoln County. Violence had been rampant in the region for many years and seemed only to increase once the county was organized.

To understand how the Kid was ensnared in the Lincoln County War and quickly became a household name in his short lifetime, it is important to recognize some of the personalities and circumstances responsible for perpetuating not only the violence but also the myths. Lincoln County's geographical remoteness and corrupt legal system worked against law and order and inevitably played a big part in the creation of Billy the Kid.

By the 1870s, sparsely populated New Mexico Territory accounted for at least

15 percent of all murders in the nation and by 1880, the last full year of the Kid's life, the homicide rate in New Mexico Territory was forty-seven times higher than the national average, with gunshot wounds as the leading cause of death.[2] Much of that violence occurred in Lincoln County. The appearance in 1873 of the Colt .45 revolver, or the Peacemaker, a weapon that used metallic cartridges, caused the violence to increase ever more rapidly.[3]

"In frontier New Mexico," according to New Mexico historian Warren Beck, "life was cheap and killing was not considered a particularly heinous crime. Men hardened by shedding blood during the Civil War found it difficult to break the habit of fighting. Killing became an accepted means of settling disputes. The improvement of firearms greatly augmented the resort to a gun in time of need. No longer was there any fear about the reliability of a gun. Seldom did the six-shooter misfire."[4]

The regular consumption of hard liquor also contributed to the epidemic of violence in Lincoln County. Liquor was a frontier staple that was always in great demand. Although the Kid seldom, if ever, had a drink of alcohol, many of those who took part in the Lincoln County War were hearty imbibers.

"A mixture of alcohol and kids with guns always causes problems, and that was sure the case in the Lincoln County of the 1870s," explained Jack Rigney, former manager of the Lincoln State Monument. "There were plenty of hard drinkers out of control. Alcohol was the drug of choice back then, and it was everywhere."[5] All sorts of strong drinks were available throughout New Mexico Territory, ranging from Taos Lightning to cactus wine made from a mix of tequila and peyote tea.[6] Beer, served warm since there was no ice to chill it, was also popular, particularly with soldiers, but straight whiskey was the beverage most in demand. Nearly all the rotgut was "full of fight," in the parlance of the time. Barkeeps had to cut the stuff with ammonia, turpentine, cayenne, or even gunpowder, which was no surprise since typically liquor could be purchased in the same establishments that sold guns and ammunition.[7]

Around Lincoln County in the 1870s and 1880s, whiskey drinkers were reported to knock back so many shots of S. N. Pike's Magnolia, Old Joe Gideon, and Double Anchor that they developed calluses on their elbows from leaning on wooden bars.[8] Almost anyone who swilled what appropriately became known as a bravemaker was well armed, or "heeled," with at least one gun and plenty of attitude.[9]

"In Lincoln County it was necessary for every man to protect himself and assert his rights," Lily Casey Klasner wrote in her memoirs. "The cheap whiskey that was commonly drunk contributed to the confusion. Men who drank it became quarrelsome, and were settling their difficulties with some sort of fight, using fists, knives, or shooting irons."[10]

A glut of firearms and generous doses of liquid courage potent enough to get any man all "roostered up" certainly incited much of the over-the-top behavior in Lincoln County. Still, racial strife coupled with pure meanness also played a significant role.[11] One of the worst episodes of violence took place in 1873, just four years before Billy Bonney showed up in Lincoln County. Known as the Horrell War, this clash of cultures began soon after five felonious brothers named Horrell (sometimes spelled Harroll) and a pack of their renegade followers fled a series of cold-blooded murders in Texas for the refuge of Lincoln County.[12] Almost immediately the inherent animosity and tension between the Texans and the Hispanic community turned to bloodshed. "The result was a race war, in which the Horrells seemed bent on ruthlessly exterminating the Mexicans [the universal name most Anglos used for all Spanish-speaking New Mexicans], and the Mexicans determined to retaliate as much as was in their power," remembered Klasner.[13]

On December 20, 1873, the Horrell gang rode into Lincoln with guns blazing and broke into an Hispanic wedding celebration in an old dance hall.[14] Four citizens were shot and killed, and two others wounded. Among the victims was Isidro Patrón, the father of Lincoln County Clerk Juan Patrón, who fled to Santa Fe to seek help from Territorial Governor Marsh Giddings.[15]

The slaughter of the wedding guests led to more acts of revenge and terror. For a time the frightened residents of Lincoln cowered every night inside the old torreón. Originally built for protection from the Apaches, the stone tower became a refuge from rampaging Texans, who shot and killed an Anglo deputy sheriff in front of his home simply because he had a Mexican wife.[16] Several reporters began using the term "guerrilla warfare" to describe the ambushes and raids, and some of the nervous locals formed a vigilante committee. Finally a plea for help reached President U.S. Grant and members of his cabinet requesting their assistance in what the *Santa Fe New Mexican* called "the unfortunate war . . . between the Texans and Mexicans."[17]

Federal intervention did not come, but as the conflict intensified, many of the Anglos in Lincoln County soured on the Horrells. By the end of March 1874, the troublesome clan and their followers had returned to Texas.[18] In their wake, they left a pattern of armed violence and discord that persisted in the county for years.

The unbridled violence in Lincoln County sparked tension among the citizens and acted as a prelude to the Lincoln County War and the emergence of Billy the Kid.

"Lincoln County had more than its share of people of very questionable integrity," explained Jack Rigney. "There were lots of southerners coming here, especially Texans, and many of them were bitter and mean. They didn't like blacks, didn't like Mexicans, didn't like Indians, and really didn't like anybody except their own kind."[19]

Besides the frequent and often deadly disputes between various factions of newcomers and natives, it seemed even nature itself had turned against the people of Lincoln County. Throughout the 1870s a succession of relentless insect plagues and an epidemic of black smallpox ravaged the land and the people.[20]

The grasshoppers came first. Hordes of locusts laid waste to the Great Plains and prairies including southeastern New Mexico Territory. Vast clouds of flying hoppers actually darkened the sky.[21] They stripped barks and leaves from trees, devoured gardens, chewed crops down to stubble, even ate clothes hanging on washlines. They gnawed harnesses and the wooden handles of spades and plows soaked with palm grease. Tree branches snapped under their weight. Swarms of the insects flew into the faces of cattle and horses, driving them wild.

After the plague of grasshoppers subsided, Lincoln County was assailed by fleas so persistent that residents dreaded the painful bites of the blood-sucking parasites more than the bites of rattlesnakes and rabid skunks. "Where the millions came from nobody knew, but they were there, and they made life a burden," was how Lily Klasner recalled the flea infestation. "Nobody could sleep at night nor find peace by day. They chewed viciously on both people and animals, and seemed to move constantly."[22] Scrubbing with lye soap had little effect. Nearly everyone resorted to an old frontier remedy of placing tins of water under the bed legs to prevent nocturnal flea attacks. It took a few hard freezes to kill off the tiny pests.

Following the grasshopper and flea invasions, an epidemic of infectious black smallpox spread throughout Lincoln County and took many lives.[23] The few crops that had managed to survive the scourge of insects shriveled up from neglect since most folks not stricken with the pox had to nurse the sick and bury the dead. "One who has not seen a case of black smallpox cannot believe its loathsomeness," recollected Klasner. "Flesh rots to a mass of putrid corruption which affects eyes, nose, or any other part of the body, and becomes a mass of pus. If the disease breaks out in the mouth or throat the patient suffers intense pain."[24]

Billy's stepfather, William Antrim
(1842–1922)

THE ROBERT G. McCUBBIN COLLECTION

Billy's brother, Joseph McCarty Antrim (only
existing photo), Denver Post, *April 1, 1928*

THE ROBERT G. McCUBBIN COLLECTION

*Earliest-known photo of the Lincoln County Courthouse, formerly the
L. G. Murphy & Co. store known as the "The House," circa 1887*

THE ROBERT G. McCUBBIN COLLECTION

Dolan store, formerly the Tunstall store, Lincoln, New Mexico Territory, 1886

THE ROBERT G. McCUBBIN COLLECTION

*Charlie and Manuela Bowdre,
Las Vegas, New Mexico Territory,
1880; photo carried by Bowdre
when he was killed in 1880
at Stinking Springs (note
blood stains)*

The Robert G. McCubbin
Collection

*Tom O'Folliard, the Kid's pal, born in
Uvalde, Texas, in 1858, and killed at Fort
Sumner, New Mexico Territory,
December 19, 1880*

The Robert G. McCubbin Collection

Regulator Fred Waite (1853–1895)

The Robert G. McCubbin Collection

BELOW *Dick Brewer (circa 1870), the first Regulator captain, born in Vermont, 1850; killed at Blazer's Mill, April 4, 1878*

The Robert G. McCubbin Collection

Regulator Josiah "Doc" Scurlock (1849–1929), circa 1920

The Robert G. McCubbin Collection

Regulator Henry Brown (1857–1884)

The Robert G. McCubbin Collection

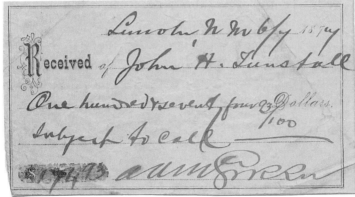

Alexander McSween and receipt to John Tunstall, signed by McSween

John S. Chisum, 1880s
THE ROBERT G. MCCUBBIN
COLLECTION

*Susan McSween, photograph by
Fromhart & Benson, Kansas
City, Missouri, circa 1895*

THE ROBERT G. MCCUBBIN
COLLECTION

John H. Tunstall and receipt to Alexander McSween, signed by Tunstall

THE ROBERT G. McCUBBIN COLLECTION

*John Riley (1850–1916), partner of
James Dolan, 1885*

THE ROBERT G. McCUBBIN COLLECTION

*Colonel Emil Fritz, shortly before forming
partnership with L. G. Murphy at Fort
Stanton, New Mexico Territory, circa 1866*

THE ROBERT G. McCUBBIN COLLECTION

*Sheriff William Brady, shortly before he was
shot and killed in Lincoln, New Mexico
Territory, April 1, 1878*

THE ROBERT G. McCUBBIN COLLECTION

*William Rynerson, district attorney for Doña
Ana, Grant, and Lincoln Counties and
member of the Santa Fe Ring*

THE ROBERT G. McCUBBIN COLLECTION

Augusta "Gus" Gildea, cowboy who witnessed the Kid kill Frank "Windy" Cahill in Arizona, 1877, and who later took part in the Lincoln County War

James Dolan (seated) and Bob Olinger, circa 1879

Godfrey Gauss, former cook on Tunstall ranch who witnessed the Kid's daring escape from the Lincoln County Courthouse, April 28, 1881

Juan Batista Patrón, circa 1874, prominent citizen of Lincoln and opponent of the Santa Fe Ring

San Patricio
Lincoln County
Thursday 20th 1879

General. Lew. Wallace;

Sir, I will keep
the appointment I made.
but be sure and have men come
that You can depend on I am not
afraid to die like a man fighting
but I would not like to be killed
like a dog unarmed, tell Kimbal
to let his men be placed around
the house. and for him to Come in
alone; and he can arrest us. all I am
afraid of is that in the Fort we
might be poisined, or killed through
a Window at night, but You can
arrange that all right. Tell the
Comanding Officer to Watch) Let Goodwin
he would not hesitate to do anything
there Will be danger on the road of
Somebody Waylaying us to kill us on the
road to the Fort.

Letter written March 20, 1879, from the Kid to Governor Lew Wallace

INDIANA HISTORICAL SOCIETY, LEW WALLACE IN NEW MEXICO (M0292)...1ST PAGE

You Will never Catch those fellows on the road Watch Fritzes. Captain Bacas. ranch and the Brewrys they Will either go to Seven Rivers or to Picarillo Montians they Will stay around close untill the Scouting parties come in give a Spy a pair of glasses and let him get on the Montain back of Fritzes and Watch and if they are there ther will be provisons carried to them, it is not My place to advise you, but I am anxious to have them Caught, and perhaps know how men hide from Soldiers, better on you please Excuse me for having so much to say and I still remain Yours Truly

P. S.   W. H. Bonney

I have Changed my mind Send Kimbal to Gutierese just below San Patricio one mile. because Sanger and Ballard are or were great friends of Camels Ballard told me yesterday to leave for you were doing every thing to Catch me. it was a blind to get me to leave

Letter written March 20, 1879, from the Kid to Governor Lew Wallace

Maxwell family residence, Fort Sumner, New Mexico Territory, 1882, where the Kid met his death at the hand of Pat Garrett, July 14, 1881

THE ROBERT G. McCUBBIN COLLECTION

Paulita Maxwell Jaramillo (1864–1929), the Kid's favorite "querida," who was laid to rest in the old Fort Stanton military cemetery beside her brother Pete's grave and close to the Kid's

THE ROBERT G. McCUBBIN COLLECTION

Deluvina Maxwell, a Navajo who was a longtime Maxwell family servant and who cherished the Kid and for many years left flowers on his grave during the summer, died in Albuquerque, New Mexico, November 27, 1927

THE ROBERT G. McCUBBIN COLLECTION

Fort Sumner, N. Mex
March 20th 1926

I Deluvina Maxwell do hereby
state that the Butcher knife now
in possession of Adelina J. Melton
is the original that Billy the
Kid held in his hand at the
time of his death

Deluvina X Maxwell
(her mark)

The above Deluvina Maxwell
was an indian slave of my
grandfather Lucien B. Maxwell

Adelina J. Melton

*Butcher knife the Kid carried when he was killed by Pat Garrett in Pete Maxwell's
bedroom, July 14, 1881; with Deluvina Maxwell's statement of authenticity
dated March 20, 1926*

THE ROBERT G. McCUBBIN COLLECTION

Pat Garrett, circa 1881

The Robert G. McCubbin Collection

IS NOW READY
AND ON SALE.

Advertisement for Pat Garrett's book
about the Kid, from the Santa Fe Daily
New Mexican, *July 18, 1882*

THE ROBERT G. MCCUBBIN COLLECTION

*Marshall Ashmun "Ash" Upson,
Pat Garrett's ghostwriter*

THE ROBERT G. MCCUBBIN
COLLECTION

No one was safe. Coffin makers, clergy, *curanderos* (healers), and the few available doctors stayed busy with the sick, dead, and dying at Santa Fe, Tularosa, Las Vegas, Anton Chico, Tecolote, Arroyo Hondo, Socorro, and all across the territory. At Santo Domingo Pueblo, on the east bank of the Rio Grande, more than 120 men and boys died from smallpox in 1877 alone.[25]

Black pox also struck the already demoralized Mescaleros, as well as soldiers, prominent citizens, and everyday ranch hands. Powerful cattleman John Chisum was stricken at his Bosque Grande Ranch but eventually recovered. So did English gentleman turned cattleman John Tunstall, his ranch foreman, Dick Brewer, and several others who soon were entangled in the Lincoln County War and whose names are forever linked to Billy the Kid. Although Tunstall and Brewer survived the pox, both succumbed to "lead poisoning" during that vicious tussle.[26]

Most Catholic Hispanic residents, and those Anglos of a God-fearing nature, believed the scourge of insects and disease, as well as the many acts of violence, were sent from the Almighty. Years later Lily Klasner recalled that many folks looked at the maladies and bloodshed as retribution for the wicked and also believed that "a puny creature like man" could do nothing to stop divine punishment.[27] "This argument was accepted by many, including officers at the Fort [Stanton]; and people quoted Scripture to prove their contention," wrote Klasner. "Had not God visited plagues upon the Egyptians because of their treatment of the Israelites?"[28]

Sadly for those whose beliefs were rooted in the Old Testament, there was no latter-day Moses to rescue them from the series of events, man-made and natural, that culminated in the Lincoln County War. Nothing was honorable, noble, or even vaguely romantic about the conflict. It was as horrendous as the Horrell War, the Salt War, the Pecos War, and all the other gun battles and bloodbaths in the Seven Rivers country.

As in all the earlier clashes, those who fought in the Lincoln County War were motivated by personal gain. It was not a fence-cutting war or a range war, as some have said. It was a war of greed and corruption waged by profiteers, charlatans, and hired guns. As a rule the actual combatants were drunk or close to it, armed to the teeth, and without any conscience. Historian Maurice Fulton's assessment was right: "Scratch beneath the surface and you will find one thing as the prime mover in most of Lincoln County troubles—money."[29]

Like some of the other young bucks, Billy Bonney ended up riding for both main factions in the war. In the fall of 1877 he had come to the Seven Rivers country with the banditti, the wild bunch of thugs and thieves controlled by John Kinney and headed by Jessie Evans. It was not very long before the Kid had a change of mind and heart and joined the other side. In the end it really did not matter which side he fought for. The line separating the two was not sharply defined. Nothing about the war was black or white.

The two main alliances and the various splinter groups were made up of Anglos and Hispanics and included politicians, ranchers, and merchants. Both sides employed gangs of mercenaries who fought solely for wages. L. G. Murphy, at one time a county probate judge and owner of the largest mercantile store in the town of Lincoln, led the establishment faction and had the clear advantage over any rivals. It was the so-called Murphy men who became the bitter enemies of the Kid and those he eventually rode for during the Lincoln County War.

Murphy and his cohorts controlled local politics, law enforcement, and economic life in Lincoln County. Murphy was widely suspected of being a force behind the Horrell War and had organized the vigilantes that drove the Texans out so he could take over their property and possessions.[30]

Juan Patrón, whose father had been killed by the Horrells, dared challenge Murphy and questioned his nefarious activities in Lincoln County. Patrón branded him a divisive and tyrannical despot who brazenly dictated which candidates could run for office. According to Patrón, during an especially stormy political convention in Lincoln, Murphy, a short-tempered heavy drinker, went into one of his tirades and shouted: "You might as well try to stop the waves of the ocean with a fork as to try and oppose me."[31]

Born in County Wexford, Ireland, in 1834, Murphy, like Catherine McCarty Antrim and tens of thousands of other refugees, came to the United States as a young man because of the potato famine.[32] Following the lead of many Irish lads, he quickly enlisted in the army and eventually found himself a commissioned officer serving as quartermaster and regimental adjutant in New Mexico Territory during the Civil War. In the course of the campaign to relocate the Navajos to Fort Sumner, a report filed by Colonel Kit Carson described Lieutenant Murphy as "a most efficient and energetic officer" noted for both his "zeal and intelligence."[33] General Carleton took notice of Carson's flattering words and promoted Murphy to the rank of brevet major of volunteers for his meritorious service in the wars against the Navajos and Mescalero Apaches.[34]

Murphy served as the commander of Fort Stanton for only seven months before he was mustered out of the volunteer service on September 16, 1866. As soon as he packed away his uniform, he formed a partnership with Emil Fritz, another army officer who was discharged that same day.[35] Fritz was a native of Stuttgart, Germany, and had had some military experience in his homeland before moving to the United States as a young man. While mining in the goldfields of California, he joined Carleton's Volunteers, bound for glory and gain in New Mexico Territory. He served under Kit Carson. In recognition for bravery in battle against the Comanches and Kiowas, Fritz was promoted to brevet lieutenant colonel and immediately preceded his friend Major Murphy as commanding officer of Fort Stanton.[36]

Mustered out of the army, both Murphy and Fritz decided to stay in Lincoln County, and by 1867 the entrepreneurial civilians had become the post sutlers, or traders, at Fort Stanton. Operating as L. G. Murphy & Co., they sold goods to soldiers and also had a contract for supplying beef and flour to the Mescalero Apache agency.[37]

Following a modest start, their business turned a profit, but the two army comrades were anxious to earn even more and beat out any competitors who might emerge. Their desire for wealth and power resulted in questionable business methods that often were outright fraudulent. This was the case when it came to the fulfillment of government contracts for beef and every other staple imaginable for man and beast, including corn, coffee, flour, charcoal, sugar, lumber, and hay.[38]

Murphy and Fritz shrewdly cultivated their close ties to the commissioned officers at Fort Stanton. Through their business as post traders, they lent money to financially strapped officers, offered sage advice based on their own army experience, and supplied guides for scouting forays into Apache territory. As a result, their post store became what has been described as "a resort for officers and [enlisted] men alike."[39] Such strategies also bought plenty of goodwill, and before long Murphy & Co. became the dominant economic force in the region.

Fritz, beset with chronic poor health, began spending time relaxing at his ranch outside Lincoln. Meanwhile, Murphy continued his often unscrupulous business practices. He frequently overcharged clientele for supplies and repeatedly inflated the number of Mescaleros drawing rations at the agency. When questioned about such practices, Murphy, who usually operated under the influence of spirits, threatened to stir up an Indian uprising.[40]

By 1873 even Murphy's cronies at Fort Stanton had finally had enough of his deceptions. In the fall of 1873 the army unceremoniously evicted L. G. Murphy & Co. from the post, although the firm retained many of its government contracts.[41] By then the ailing Fritz had left New Mexico to visit relatives in Germany. He had hoped to return to the United States, but on June 26, 1874, he died of dropsy at his father's house in Stuttgart, not far from the Black Forest.[42]

Murphy was not fazed by the loss of Fritz. He already had a handpicked protégé in place. On April Fool's Day, 1874, more than two months before Fritz died, Murphy had made James Joseph Dolan a partner.[43] J. J. Dolan was nobody's fool. Cut from the same cloth as Murphy, the cocky Dolan possessed a fiery temper and a penchant for liquor.

Born in County Galway, Ireland, in 1848, Jimmy Dolan, about ten years older than the Kid, was six years old when his family moved to New York. During the Civil War, the young man left his job in a dry goods store to enlist as a drummer boy with the New York Zouaves.[44] In 1866 he reenlisted in the regular army, and after serving at various posts in the West, Dolan was mustered out at Fort Stanton in 1869.

He immediately joined L. G. Murphy & Co. as a clerk. Murphy soon became so fond of Dolan it was rumored that he had secretly adopted the younger man.[45] Some local folks even gossiped that the two men had a physical relationship.[46] As junior partner the diminutive and feisty Dolan wasted no time in expanding the firm's economic stranglehold on Lincoln County.[47] In so doing, he proved to be every bit as deceitful and cunning as his mentor.

"From the beginning Jimmie Dolan had been suspected of using practices that were dark and devious," recalled Lily Klasner. "He seemed gifted in concocting and carrying through crooked and underhanded deals, usually getting someone else to do the dirty work and take the consequences. If compelled to do it himself he cleverly concealed his actions. He was suspected of complicity in many discreditable occurrences in Lincoln but proving his participation was difficult."[48]

Murphy's questionable business practices aside, it was Dolan whose actions had resulted in the final expulsion of L. G. Murphy & Co. from Fort Stanton. In a fit of anger Dolan had drawn his gun and fired a shot at Captain James F. Randlett after the officer had intervened in a beef contract dispute between Dolan and a competitor.[49] In a letter to the War Department following the incident, Randlett branded the Murphy store as "nothing more or less than a den of infamy" that overcharged for goods sold to enlisted men.[50] He further accused the traders of swindling the government and recommended their immediate removal from the reservation.

After their ouster from Fort Stanton, Murphy and Dolan followed a contingency plan they had earlier devised. They gave their full attention to the three-room branch store they had established in nearby La Placita, soon to be renamed Lincoln. They also operated Samuel Wortley's Mess, a combination eatery and boardinghouse that offered lager beer from another Murphy & Co. subsidiary, the Rio Bonito Brewery.[51]

Then, in the autumn of 1873, with the eight thousand dollars they made from selling the sutler's buildings at Fort Stanton, Murphy and Dolan built a new two-story adobe just across the road from the "mess." The new building, said to be one of "the most pretentious structures in the county," housed the mercantile store as well as offices, and a combination saloon and gambling hall on the first floor.[52] The second floor provided living quarters for bachelor members of the firm, and the entire west wing was designated as the Lodge Room, a meeting place for members of the Masonic order.

Some people called the imposing structure with a pitched roof and long balcony over a wide front porch the big store or the Murphy store. The name that stuck was "The House," both words implicitly capitalized.[53] This building eventually housed the jail where the Kid in shackles gunned down two law officers and made one of his most daring escapes in 1880. It would also be his last escape.

The House of Murphy, while doing a profitable business, was always a source of controversy. It supplied all Lincoln County "with the necessities of life, but it held the population in what was approximately peonage," according to Lily Klasner.[54] Operating much like a company store, Murphy and Dolan were able to keep so many of their customers in debt that it was said the new building was constructed by the forced labor of citizens owing money to the business.[55]

"It [The House] sold merchandise at extremely high prices which the owners attributed to the expense of having merchandise hauled by teams from Santa Fe and Las Vegas, although much of it was owing to exorbitant charges," recalled Klasner. "The people had to have necessities and could get them nowhere else; consequently the company had accounts with almost every person who came into the county, and the outcome was usually an indebtedness surprising to the customer who brought his product for sale."[56]

As The House grew richer by monopolizing government contracts and charging outrageous prices, Murphy slid deeper into alcoholism.[57] Lily Klasner recalled that by the time the Lincoln County War actually erupted, Murphy "was so besotted with liquor he was almost a negative quantity in the trouble."[58]

As Murphy's health steadily declined, Dolan's value to the business greatly increased. In 1877, when Murphy learned he had terminal cancer of the bowels, he stepped up his consumption of whiskey, attempting to ward off his pain. Consequently he spent most of his time in an "alcoholic stupor."[59] One of his associates mused that "old man Murphy was dissipated and got so he couldn't do business, just drink whiskey."[60]

On March 14, 1877, a despondent, dying Murphy officially retired from The House.[61] Dolan immediately took over the store with junior partner John Henry Riley. They renamed the firm J. J. Dolan & Co., also known as Dolan, Riley & Co.[62] Many people continued to call the mercantile business the Murphy store and referred to Dolan's followers as Murphy men, despite Murphy's spending most of his time in isolation at his Carrizo Springs ranch until he moved to Santa Fe, where he died nearly destitute on October 20, 1878.[63]

Like Murphy and Dolan, Riley was pure Irish. Born in 1841 on Valentia Island in Dingle Bay in County Kerry, he immigrated to America when he was twelve. In 1861 Riley enlisted in the army in California and came to New Mexico Territory with Carleton's California Column.[64] After his discharge at Fort Stanton, Riley was one of the many soldiers who stayed in Lincoln County. He quickly found gainful employment as a clerk at The House. Riley, every bit as hotheaded as Jimmy Dolan, was considered to be "a smart devil and regular confidence man," recalled Frank Coe, a longtime Lincoln County resident in a 1931 interview.[65]

One of Riley's most malicious outbursts came in 1875, when he used a rifle to shoot Juan Patrón in the back following a confrontation in Lincoln. Patrón, a staunch foe of The House, pitched from his horse with what was thought to be a fatal wound. According to newspaper accounts, "the ball entered near the spine and passed into the abdomen, from which place it was removed by the physician, who says Patrón cannot live."[66]

Patrón miraculously survived, but he was badly crippled. He walked with a limp until that day in 1884 when he was shot and killed under suspicious circumstances at the village of Puerto de Luna.[67] The 1875 shooting of Patrón was quickly handled at a preliminary hearing before a friendly magistrate, where Riley pleaded self-defense and was cleared of any charges.[68]

Riley first encountered young William Bonney in October 1877, although it is doubtful the young man would have made much of an impression at the time. That was when the Kid was reported to have ridden for a brief time with Jesse Evans and the Boys, and Riley and Jim Longwell, one of his employees, stopped at Evans's outlaw camp in the Sacramento Mountains.[69] Shortly after that rendezvous, Riley, under the pen name "Fence Rail," wrote his satirical story extolling the virtues of the banditti.[70]

Anyone in Lincoln County with a bit of sense knew that Captain Evans and his gang were on The House's payroll. They rustled livestock, mostly from John Chisum's Jinglebob herd, and regularly furnished the stolen cattle at bargain prices to Dolan and Riley so they could fulfill their beef contracts. Besides stealing cattle and horses, Evans and his men provided armed protection and carried out clandestine acts for The House.[71]

Above and beyond their hired gunmen, Dolan and Riley really had no worries about the strong arm of the law's coming down on them. That was because they *were* the law in Lincoln County, or at least they controlled it. The high sheriff himself, William Brady, had long been a Murphy supporter and transferred that same allegiance to Dolan, Riley, and other associates of The House.

Still another of Lincoln County's Irish immigrants who came to America and found employment as a soldier, Brady served in the enlisted ranks of the U.S. Army for ten years. In 1861 he left the regular army and joined the New Mexico Volunteers as a commissioned officer.[72] In 1864, like his friends Fritz and Murphy, he became the commanding officer at Fort Stanton and then stayed in the area after he was mustered out in 1866. Major Brady married a Hispanic widow, Maria Bonifacia Chaves Montoya, and together they raised a brood of children and farmed a homestead east of Lincoln.[73]

Brady soon became a respected community leader, and in 1869 he was chosen as the first sheriff of newly organized Lincoln County, although he initially had to become a naturalized citizen in order to run for office. He held other political posts, including U.S. commissioner and legislator, and in 1876 was reelected for yet another term as sheriff.[74]

"As county sheriff, Brady dispensed a brand of law enforcement typical of first-generation frontier communities all over the West," writes historian Robert Utley. "Personal, pragmatic, capricious, physical, and final, it expressed the finer points of the law rather than the instincts of the man behind the badge. Because of the vast distances and nonexistent transportation, it prevailed mainly in the county seat and the immediate vicinity, and only there when Brady came to town from his farm three miles down the valley."[75]

In spite of frequently proving himself a capable officer of the law, Brady maintained a close relationship with Murphy and other fellow Irish army veterans. Brady also was bound in allegiance to Murphy and his partners because he was heavily in debt to The House for years.[76]

For many people just trying to make a living there must have been little hope of getting free from the tentacles of The House. Yet after years of unbridled domination of Lincoln County, the Murphy-Dolan-Riley crowd, firmly entrenched as the ruling patrons, at long last were challenged. In early 1877 an opposing faction not only competed head-on with The House but also threatened to break its iron grip on every aspect of life in the county.

The new alliance was an unlikely trio: Alexander Anderson McSween, of Scottish descent and from Canada who was a Presbyterian divinity student before becoming a lawyer; John Henry Tunstall, a polished English dandy with a wad of cash in his frock coat; and John Simpson Chisum, the rough-and-ready Texas rancher whose Jinglebob spread had become prime pickings for every Pecos Valley cattle thief.[77] Regardless of their completely different backgrounds and their obvious dissimilarities, the three men stood united in a common ambition: to create a financial empire in Lincoln County.

McSween, born in Canada in 1843, studied for the ministry but turned to law and completed half of a two-year course at Washington University in St. Louis. He moved to Kansas and briefly taught school before opening a law office in 1873. About that same time, he wed a lively redhead with protruding eyes and plenty of moxie named Susanna Ellen Hummer but better known as Susan.[78] The McSweens resided in Eureka, Kansas, until what has been described as a reversal of fortunes caused them to skulk off under cover of darkness for New Mexico Territory.[79]

Arriving in Lincoln in March 1875 and ready for a fresh start, McSween was the first attorney to establish a residence in the county seat.[80] Despite being shrewd and often overbearing, the ambitious McSween quickly amassed an impressive collection of clients and, for a brief time, acted as legal counsel and debt collector for none other than the reigning political and economic boss, Lawrence Murphy.

That working relationship was short-lived. Murphy accused McSween of mishandling the settlement of the estate of Emil Fritz, Murphy's late partner. At the same time, McSween disputed many of the claims on the estate made by The House and vehemently disapproved of its methods of doing business. All ties with McSween were severed. In late 1877 the Fritz heirs and Jimmy Dolan went so far as to have McSween and his traveling companion John Chisum falsely arrested and briefly jailed in Las Vegas, New Mexico. They claimed McSween had absconded with ten thousand dollars of the Fritz insurance money.[81] Relations between McSween and Chisum and members of The House became so acrimonious that both sides began forming battle plans.

By that time a violent confrontation had been inevitable ever since November

1876, when John Tunstall, a twenty-three-year-old Englishman, came to Lincoln looking for investment opportunities in grazing lands. McSween, almost ten years older than Tunstall, took an instant liking to the patrician Londoner who, after leaving Great Britain in 1872 to add to his fortune in Victoria, British Columbia, and later California, found himself landlocked in the secluded highlands of New Mexico Territory.[82]

Tunstall immediately allied himself with McSween and Chisum in their concerted effort to create a ranching-mercantile empire all their own. In spite of many warnings, Tunstall and McSween, with Chisum's support and financial backing, proceeded to establish their own store and banking operation just down the road from The House.

In an April 1877 letter to his father in England, Tunstall explained the rationale behind his business plan:

> *Everything* in New Mexico, that pays *at all* . . . is worked by a "ring," there is the "Indian ring," the "army ring," the "political ring," the "legal ring," the "Roman Catholic ring," the "cattle ring," the "horsethieves ring," the "land ring" and half a dozen other rings; now to make things stick "to do any good," it is necessary to either get into a ring or to make one out for yourself. I am at work at present making a ring & have succeeded admirably thus far. . . . My ring is forming itself as fast & faster than I had ever hoped & in such a way that I will get the finest plum of the lot. . . . I proposed to confine my operations to Lincoln County, but I intend to handle it in such a way as to get half of every dollar that is made in the county *by anyone*.[83]

What the stubborn and naive Tunstall did not realize was that his determination to challenge Dolan and Riley put him and McSween in a precarious position. Tunstall predicted that his ring would be in full control of Lincoln County in only three years. It was not to be. The fates of Tunstall and his partner were sealed. Within less than a year from the time that Tunstall's letter was written both he and McSween were dead and buried. William Bonney, who by then was firmly aligned with the Tunstall-McSween faction, would continue the ride that ultimately led to his own demise.

Thomas B. Catron, boss of the Santa Fe Ring,
photographer Brands Studios, Chicago, date unknown
THE ROBERT G. MCCUBBIN COLLECTION

TWENTY

THE UNFORTUNATE WAR SPAWNS THE MYTH

The Lincoln County War did more for the Kid than he for it. For the Kid of legend, the war provided a setting for feats of prowess and adventure and acts of excessive character that would be endlessly chronicled with creative hyperbole. For the Kid of history, the war provided the influences that shaped his personality from adolescence to manhood.[1]

—ROBERT M. UTLEY

THROUGHOUT THE AUTUMN of 1877 the Kid, high atop a borrowed horse, scoured the countryside of Lincoln County, looking for work. No record has been found, but he may have stayed for a short while at John Chisum's ranch. From there he probably made his way up the Rio Hondo and through the Ruidoso country, pausing at ranches and farms along the way to earn a grubstake.[2]

We do know that during this time the Kid struck up a friendship with George

Coe, his cousin Frank Coe, and Frank's brother-in-law James Albert "Ab" Saunders, three men who remained close friends with the youngster throughout the Lincoln County War. This first meeting with the Coes and Saunders took place after the Kid purportedly was jailed at Lincoln for the theft of a team of "dapple grey" buggy horses from John Tunstall's newly established ranch on the Rio Feliz, about thirty miles south of Lincoln.[3] If this incident did occur, as some credible historians believe, then more than likely Dick Brewer, the Tunstall foreman, apprehended the Kid. He is reported to have taken Bonney to the Lincoln jail, at that time a deep earthen pit often described as a dungeon. The Kid was soon released for lack of evidence and eventually showed up on the payroll of none other than John Tunstall.[4]

"When he got out [of jail] in the fall of 1877 [the Kid] came over to my farm on the Ruidoso, which was fifteen miles above Glencoe," Frank Coe said in a 1923 interview with the *El Paso Times*.[5] "Charlie Bowdre had a farm at the site of Tully's Store. The Kid came to Bowdre, who had a good corn crop laid by, and Bowdre brought him up to my place. I expect he wanted to get rid of him. Bowdre had a Mexican woman and the Kid could talk Mexican better than he could."

Coe's observations about Bowdre are noteworthy since the Kid and Bowdre became close pals and ended up riding together first in the Lincoln County War and afterward on the outlaw trail. The Kid was with Bowdre at Stinking Springs, not far from Fort Sumner, just a few years later when Bowdre was shot dead by a posse led by Pat Garrett. Of even more importance, Coe's comments reveal more about the Kid's linguistic ability. It was his ability to converse in Spanish with the Hispanic population that served him well and made him a champion in the eyes of many native citizens long after his death.

Coe offered additional insight into the Kid's personality and manners. His memories shed light on the human side of a young man who, owing to events often out of his control, was catapulted into the public eye as either a superhero or Satan incarnate. "We became staunch friends," Coe recalled much later in 1923. "I never enjoyed better company. He was humorous and told me many amusing stories. He always found a touch of humor in everything, being naturally full of fun and jollity. Though he was serious in emergencies, his humor was often apparent even in such situations."

A few years after his newspaper interview Frank Coe had yet more to say about his old compadre Billy Bonney. These comments came during a visit with Miguel Antonio Otero, the two-term governor of New Mexico Territory from

1897 to 1907 and the sole Hispanic to hold the office prior to statehood.[6] Coe told Otero:

> I found Billy different from most boys of his age. He had been thrown on his own resources from early boyhood. From his own statement to me, he hadn't known what it meant to be a boy; at the age of twelve he was associated with men of twenty-five and older. Billy was eager to learn everything and had a most active and fertile mind. He was small and of frail physique; his hands and feet were more like a woman's than a man's. He was not the type who could perform heavy labor. . . . Billy explained to me how he became proficient in the use of firearms. He said that his age and his physique were handicaps in his personal encounters, so he decided to become a good shot with both rifle and six-shooter as a means of protection against bodily harm.[7]

Numerous historians have written off as unreliable comments from those who reportedly knew the Kid, such as the Coes. Skeptics have been especially critical of the Federal Writers' Project interviews of New Mexicans in the 1930s. There is good reason for such an attitude.

Much of the criticism about the flaws and pitfalls of oral histories compiled about the Kid is merited. The dutifully recorded memories of elderly people about him contain embellishments, factual errors, and untruths. Some of the gathered information was entirely hearsay, secondhand speculation passed down like family myth to the next generation. Many of the inaccuracies have been perpetuated again and again by Billy buffs and detractors alike.

Not all recollections of the Kid should be dismissed. While there may have been much bravado, mythmaking, and conjecture added to the major historical episodes—tales of gunfights, jailbreaks, and daring bandit deeds—the simplest memories of the Kid often make sense. Stories of one-on-one encounters, the Kid at a community dance, sharing a meal or campfire, or other everyday events, frequently ring true. For example, Frank Coe's straightforward memories of the Kid told to the former governor do not excuse the Kid's behavior and actions altogether, but they provide some needed nuance. Through the years many historians and writers have lost sight of the fact that the Kid was just that: a *kid*. He was indeed a kid who had been left rudderless after his mother's death. He was on his own at a vulnerable age. He was a kid who fended for himself and lived by his wits.

He was a kid too often used and abused by older men and authority figures. He was a kid who was frequently impetuous and made errors in judgment.

Coe's memories as well as those of several others who knew the Kid were included in the Otero book *The Real Billy the Kid: With New Light on the Lincoln County War*, originally published in a limited edition in 1936. Otero explained that he met the Kid, who was in shackles, one cold December day in 1880. Billy was awaiting train transport from Las Vegas to Santa Fe shortly after Pat Garrett took him prisoner at Stinking Springs, where Charlie Bowdre died.[8]

"I liked The Kid very much," Otero recalled of that encounter. "Nothing would have pleased me more than to have witnessed his escape. He had his share of good qualities and was very pleasant. He had a reputation for being considerate of the old, the young and the poor; he was loyal to his friends and above all, loved his mother devotedly."[9]

For a large number of Hispanic people in New Mexico Territory, especially the poor and disenfranchised but also some of those from prominent and well-connected families such as Governor Otero's, the Kid was the ultimate underdog and a tragic hero.[10] This young man spoke their native tongue, played alongside their children, treated them as equals, and savored their culture. Inevitably, he became both their favorite outlaw and venerated champion.

Frederick Nolan, as noted earlier, perhaps the most dogged Billy the Kid researcher, agrees that the Hispanic viewpoint deserves further examination. "The idea of emphasizing his [the Kid's] folk-hero status in Hispanic culture is attractive," Nolan wrote to the author. "I have always said we will never understand this story until someone tells it from that side of the cultural divide."[11]

Yet most writers have ignored the Hispanic perspective on Billy the Kid. They have generally disregarded the non-Anglo interpretations of the time when the Kid roamed the land of the Hispanics and of the Indians who dwelled there long before the Spanish. Governor Otero's writings about the Kid and his period of history remain an important source of a viewpoint that warrants closer scrutiny. Otero and the voices of other Hispanic contemporaries help define the image of Billy the Kid more clearly.

According to scholar-essayist John-Michael Rivera:

> Otero's recreation of the life and history of Billy the Kid not only reexamines and exposes the colonial past of New Mexico. It also deflates and undermines the dominant Anglo-American Western narratives about

Billy the Kid that helped shape the popular imagination of America as being only Anglo-American in culture and history.[12]

Despite Otero attesting to the factual representations of his sources and his personally transcribed interview with Billy the Kid, Pat Garrett and the other individuals who knew Billy the Kid, historians who have studied this period of the frontier have ignored Otero's documentation and primarily concentrated on the Anglo historical version of the life of the infamous outlaw.[13]

Otero, who came from an elite Hispanic family, traced his roots in the political and economic life of New Mexico generations back. When he challenged the popular Anglo image of Billy the Kid, Otero defied the accepted history as portrayed by historians representing the traditional Euro-American power structure. He extracted a bit of revenge by further exposing the invincible and corrupt Anglo regime that stole his people's land, honor, and dignity. This uncompromising cartel of politicians, business leaders, and land speculators was known as the Santa Fe Ring. For most of the last half of the nineteenth century they dominated every aspect of life in New Mexico Territory. Even some of Otero's most vocal detractors agreed that this mostly Anglo coalition fanned the sparks that ignited the Lincoln County War and begot the undying myth of Billy the Kid that rose from those ashes. Otero wrote:

> . . . the all-powerful Santa Fe Ring, political powerhouse of New Mexico and the most lawless machine in that territory's history, became actively involved in the Lincoln County slaughter, lining up solidly behind the Murphy-Dolan-Riley faction. Headed by Attorney Thomas B. Catron, ruthless overlord of all the southwest racket interests, the Santa Fe Ring numbered among its more notorious members, Samuel B. Axtell, Territorial Governor; and J. B. (Billy) Mathews, Clerk of the District Court. The allegiance of the Santa Fe Ring gave to the Murphy clan a semblance of legality and lawfulness that only the cold facts belied. The McSween-Chisum party were, as a logical outcome, declared the desperadoes and law-breakers.[14]

Thomas Benton Catron, his law and banking partner, Stephen Benton Elkins, and their Santa Fe Ring cohorts were true sons of the Gilded Age. They were every bit as ruthless and greedy as the robber barons back east who had amassed great fortunes through ruthless business deals. William Keleher writes: "No man ever crossed swords with Tom Catron in New Mexico, in a lawsuit, a political row, or in a business transaction, who was not willing to admit that Catron was an expert swordsman, and aggressive and powerful adversary."[15]

Instead of making a fortune in steel and oil, Catron's Santa Fe Ring became spectacularly rich by acquiring valuable New Mexico land grants from their owners through fraud, encroachment, trickery, and violence. Catron and his legal, political, and banking allies further enriched themselves by pressuring small ranchers and pushing them off the open range. They used law enforcement to punish competitors and all others who dared oppose their interests. For Otero and others who opposed the ring, renegade Apaches, outlaw gangs, and the likes of some young colorful saddle tramp who called himself the Kid were nowhere as dangerous as the men of the Santa Fe Ring.

Catron, who built a huge fortune through land ownership, developed his sense of the soil on the family farm near Lexington, Missouri, where he was born in 1840. He later enrolled at the Masonic College in Lexington, where he met Steve Elkins.[16] Regardless of some political and philosophical differences, Elkins became Catron's lifelong associate, and the young men later roomed together while attending the University of Missouri in Columbia.[17]

Following graduation the two friends returned to their respective homes, and both briefly taught school and prepared for the law until the Civil War.[18] Catron enlisted as an officer in the Confederate army while Elkins became an officer in the Union army, even though his father and some of his brothers took up arms for the Confederacy.[19]

After the war Catron and Elkins reestablished their friendship despite their having fought for opposing sides. Elkins had relocated to New Mexico Territory and established a law practice in Mesilla. A short time later he moved his practice north to Santa Fe, and once settled, he encouraged Catron to join him there as a partner. Catron agreed, and while traveling west on the Santa Fe Trail in a prairie schooner loaded with flour, he diligently studied a Spanish grammar book. Like Elkins, who also tutored him after his arrival, Catron became proficient in Spanish, a skill that helped both men in their business dealings.[20]

Although he had been brought up in a staunch Democratic household in Missouri, the ever-opportunistic Catron promptly changed his political affiliation when he learned the Republican Party was gaining power in New Mexico Territory. Following his partner Elkins's lead, Catron quickly emerged as a dominant force in New Mexico politics and was pegged as an emerging Republican leader. He quickly rose through the party ranks and served in many public offices over the next half century before his death in 1921. He was attorney general of New Mexico Territory, a U.S. attorney, the mayor of Santa Fe, and, upon the admission of New Mexico into the Union in 1912, a U.S. Senator.[21]

Elkins also enjoyed a noteworthy political life in New Mexico Territory, first as district attorney, then as territorial attorney general and U.S. district attorney. He then served two terms as territorial delegate to the U.S. Congress. Urbane and bright, Elkins was known as Smooth Steve by friend and foe alike. After his last term in Congress, Elkins practiced law and served as president of the Santa Fe National Bank for a while before moving to Elkins, West Virginia, a town he had founded earlier, where he pursued his coal and railroad interests. He later was appointed secretary of war by President Benjamin Harrison and went on to serve several terms representing West Virginia in the U.S. Senate until his death in 1911.[22]

Santa Fe Ring sycophants, such as the historian and lawyer Ralph Emerson Twitchell, considered Catron and Elkins pillars of society, although Twitchell did write that "Mr. Catron is possessed of great strength of character and has as many enemies as he has friends."[23] Twitchell, who was believed to belong to the ring, failed to note that the majority of those enemies were citizens who had lost their land grants through loan foreclosures and swindles orchestrated by Elkins and Catron. From most accounts, for every person who considered Catron a great leader and financial wizard, ten more regarded him as a greedy land grabber and a ruthless politician.

Fearful of retaliation, most newspapers carefully avoided coverage of anything that concerned the ring. The *Santa Fe New Mexican* for many years was actually a mouthpiece for Catron and his associates.[24] There were a few exceptions. The most vocal critic was Simeon Newman, a crusading newspaper editor who moved to New Mexico Territory in 1871 and apprenticed at the *Las Vegas Weekly Mail*. Six weeks into his apprenticeship, Newman bought the newspaper from Ashton Upson, the future ghostwriter of Pat Garrett's book about the Kid.[25]

Newman feared no one, including Tom Catron and Smooth Steve Elkins. The strong-willed Democrat reformer took on the ring with a vengeance, exposing the land frauds, range wars, and corruption. Miraculously he survived. Although the ring used its political clout to have him jailed for a time, the scrappy Newman edited the paper from his jail cell for sixty-three days. In 1881 Newman left New Mexico Territory on his own terms when some Texas businessmen paid him a thousand dollars to relocate to El Paso and help turn around their corrupt city.[26]

When it came to Santa Fe Ring vindictiveness, Newman was an exception. Other journalists, such as those who dared take on the ring and their associates during the twenty-year battle over the sale of the Maxwell Land Grant in Colfax County, were not nearly so fortunate.[27] When sold by Lucien Bonaparte Maxwell in 1870, this land grant, more than two times larger than Rhode Island, was the single largest tract of property in private ownership.[28] The syndicate that purchased it served eviction notification to settlers, miners, and small ranchers with the full backing and blessing of the Santa Fe Ring. When that had little effect, pastures were burned, cattle were stolen, public officials were threatened, and ranches were raided and pillaged under the cover of darkness.[29]

Acts of retaliation broke out on both sides. Local residents formed the Colfax County Ring and recruited Clay Allison, a psychotic shootist, to lead the vigilantes in battle against gunslingers riding for the Santa Fe Ring allies.[30] No one was safe. In September 1875, after an outspoken Methodist preacher wrote a letter to the *New York Sun* exposing the Santa Fe Ring and naming Catron, Elkins, and others as members, he was found dead in a remote canyon with two bullets in his back.[31]

"In the Colfax County War, the dissidents rallied around one of the West's most fearsome resister gunfighters, Clay Allison," writes historian Richard Brown. "Anchored by the powerful political support of Republican nabobs in Santa Fe and Washington D.C., the Maxwell Land Grant Company outlasted the violent resistance of Allison and others. As a result, they erected a land, cattle, and mining empire of nearly two million acres that dominated the county until the 1960s."[32]

By the 1880s Tom Catron had become the largest landowner in the entire United States. At one time or another in his lifetime he controlled, gained an interest in, or held clear title to thirty-four land grants, totaling more than six million acres.[33] Helping him accumulate that wealth, while taking hearty shares for themselves, was a loose-knit cabal of lawyers, land speculators, merchants, investors, high-ranking government officials, and officers of the court. From the late 1860s to 1885 nearly every territorial governor was believed to belong to the ring.[34] The majority of "ringers" were Republican and Anglo, but prominent Jewish businessmen and both Democrats and Hispanics from the upper classes also played roles in the ring.

Regardless of ethnic heritage or political stripe, nearly every member of the

Santa Fe Ring had something in common: Each belonged to a Masonic lodge. As Freemasons, a group that was especially dominant in late nineteenth-century and early twentieth-century America, these men bonded as brothers in the oldest and largest secret fraternity in the world. Freemasonry first came to New Mexico Territory during the Mexican War in the mid-1840s, when military lodges were attached to U.S. army regiments stationed there. Most of the lodges in the territory were known as traveling Masonic lodges, made up of transient soldiers given a dispensation so they could hold lodge meetings wherever at least seven Masons could gather.[35]

The Grand Lodge of Missouri chartered the Montezuma Lodge in Santa Fe in 1851. The new lodge, the only one in the territory for nine years, counted among its members Kit Carson, who bequeathed his rifle to his Masonic brothers as an expression of his affection.[36] The first Masons in New Mexico Territory were Anglos. Most Hispanics were Catholic and were restricted by long-standing papal law from becoming Freemasons under penalty of excommunication.[37]

Instead of the saloons, cantinas, and gambling halls, the Masonic lodge offered men of like minds a comfortable and safe place for socializing, exchanging business information, and fostering political alliances. The more observant brothers frowned on such business-related activities. They believed that using the lodge as a place to conduct business violated the core principles of Freemasonry.

"The ties of brotherhood are so close in Masonry that every opportunity and inducement is [sic] offered to the man of mercenary spirit who would prostitute it to personal uses," a Masonic official told a Grand Lodge gathering in 1914. "The result is that nearly every Lodge has those who are continually calling upon their brethren to turn their grindstones. There are those who would capitalize their membership for business purposes; there are those who capitalize their Masonic affiliations for political ends. Such persons are the panhandlers of Masonry."[38] Although his oration came years later, the speaker could have been describing many of the Masons in Santa Fe and throughout New Mexico Territory in the late 1800s.

Tom Catron was a longtime member of Montezuma Lodge No. 1. So were the territorial governor Samuel Axtell, the future governor L. Bradford Prince, District Attorney William Rynerson, and wealthy Santa Fe merchants Abraham Stabb and the Spiegelburg brothers. The Masonic-Santa Fe Ring network extended throughout the territory to Lincoln County, where Catron reigned supreme and pulled all the strings controlling The House.[39]

It was no coincidence that Emil Fritz, L. G. Murphy, James Dolan, William Brady, John H. Riley, and others tied to The House also were Freemasons and faithfully met in the Masonic Room on the second floor of the Murphy-Dolan store.[40] It could be safely inferred that this band of rascals discussed far more than Masonic matters.

"Unquestionably the Masons played a big part in the Lincoln County drama," says Gwendolyn Rogers, exhibit coordinator at the Lincoln State Monument. "The Masons provided huge political and business connections. Just being a Mason gave Murphy, Dolan, and the others a lot of credibility and invaluable contacts. The Masonic ties made all of them more cohesive."[41] For that reason, both Dolan and Riley, who raised their children Catholic, just as they had been brought up, turned their backs on the church when they realized the ring hierarchy was almost exclusively Masons. Years later Dolan's death came so suddenly that there was no time to summon a priest to administer last rites. To make sure he did not suffer the same fate as his old partner, Riley left the Masonic order and returned to Catholicism, believing that sometimes it is actually wise to swap horses when crossing a stream.[42]

Perhaps Billy Bonney and the bunch he rode with would have fared better if they too had changed horses, changed their stripes, and signed on with Jimmy Dolan and the big shots in Santa Fe instead of with John Tunstall, a naive Englishman who never stood a chance. That never happened. Instead all the power and might of Tom Catron, The House, the Santa Fe Ring, the brotherhood of greed and pain, the lying judges and lawyers, and the crooked politicians crashed down on Tunstall, McSween, Chisum, and their followers.

As this happened, a myth was created. But for that myth to grow and have consequence, the Kid had to die. The boy, Billy Bonney, who sang and danced and rode like a comet, would have to be eradicated. When that came to pass, the greedy power brokers and their scheming puppets figured they would escape the limelight. The story of the Kid's outlaw ways, rather than the realities of the struggle against corruption that fueled the vicious war, would become the legend of Lincoln County.

*Lincoln, New Mexico Territory, circa 1885; the Lincoln
Courthouse, formerly the Murphy-Dolan store,
known as The House (center)*
THE ROBERT G. MCCUBBIN COLLECTION

TWENTY-ONE

ENDLESS WAR

The war is raging now as fiercely as ever. The country is overrun by horse & cattle thieves & there is no law in force. . . .[1]

•

—GODFREY GAUSS

IN KEEPING WITH an annual tradition Abraham Lincoln had started fourteen years earlier to soothe a country at war with itself, President Rutherford B. Hayes declared November 29, 1877, Thanksgiving Day.[2] His decree included the entire nation, even all those souls, both lost and found, dwelling in rowdy New Mexico Territory.

Billy Bonney, who turned eighteen six days before the holiday, had plenty to be thankful for. First and foremost, he was not dead, crippled, or in jail. He had found steady work at John Tunstall's ranch on the Rio Feliz. Although his English boss did not observe the American feast day, meaning he had no wild turkey stuffed with oysters shipped from afar or spicy mince pie, the Kid at least briefly was at ease. For the first time in a long while he had three square meals each day, a job of sorts, a warm bunk inside a crowded but cozy adobe, and a decent horse to ride. The wages he drew allowed him to procure a dime novel or two, a tin of pomade for slicking back his hair before a dance, and maybe even a slim grubstake for a game of three-card monte.

During this time the Kid often visited with George and Frank Coe, Ab Saunders, and the others he had met since coming back to New Mexico Territory. George Coe recalled:

> Billy lost no time getting to know the other people in the valley. He was the center of attention everywhere he went, and though heavily armed, he seemed as gentlemanly as a college-bred youth. He quickly became acquainted with everybody, and because of his humorous and pleasing personality grew to be a community favorite.
>
> In fact, Billy was so popular there wasn't enough of him to go around. He had a beautiful voice and sang like a bird. One of our special amusements was to get together every few nights and have a singing. The thrill of those happy nights still lingers—a pleasant memory—and tonight I would give a lot to live through one again. Frank Coe and I played fiddles, and all of us danced, and here Billy, too, was in demand.[3]

The Kid spent a lot of his spare time with Coe's nearest neighbors, Charlie Bowdre and his wife, Manuela, at their place on the upper Ruidoso. Through the Bowdres, the Kid met Josiah Gordon Scurlock, an Alabama native who supposedly had studied medicine in New Orleans, thus earning him the nickname Doc. Known to be quick-tempered and "a scrapping fool," he took pleasure in scribbling poetry and reading the classics.[4] Scurlock had drifted to Mexico at age twenty but relocated to New Mexico Territory the following year after he killed a man who had shot out Scurlock's front teeth during a card game squabble. Scurlock was hired by John Chisum for a while, and in 1876 he married Manuela Bowdre's sixteen-year-old half sister, Antonia Miguela Herrera, making him Charlie's brother-in-law. Scurlock turned to farming in the Ruidoso Valley and raised a family that eventually numbered ten children.[5]

The Kid liked keeping company with his new friends, and the pleasure was mutual. For a bit of sport and some extra money, they hunted bear, turkey, and deer and sold or traded the meat at Fort Stanton. According to Coe, the Kid "became quite expert as a deer slayer" as well as a popular dancer at the local bailes and often said that he wished his mother were still alive to enjoy those high times with him.[6]

"He was a mighty nice dancer and what you call a ladies' man," said Coe. "He talked the Mexican language and was also liked by the women." The Kid danced waltzes, polkas, and squares and almost always requested that the musicians play "Turkey in the Straw," one of his favorite tunes. "He'd come over and say, 'Don't forget the *gallina* [hen],'" remembered Coe.[7]

One of the Kid's preferred haunts was San Patricio, a small Lincoln County village on the Rio Ruidoso just above its junction with the Rio Bonito. Originally called Ruidoso, the name was changed in 1875 when a church named San Patricio, for the patron of Ireland, was built under the supervision of an Irish priest.[8] The mostly Hispanic population embraced Billy Bonney, especially the young señoritas who looked forward to his appearances at the bailes.

During the ten short weeks he worked for Tunstall, the Kid treated his employer respectfully, but the two men were not particularly close. None of the many letters that Tunstall wrote to family in England mentioned Billy Bonney by name. Tunstall frequently was away from the ranch on business trips or tending his store in Lincoln and had more on his mind than a teenage cattle hand.[9]

For someone often described as innocent and idealistic, Tunstall could be just as Machiavellian and greedy as his enemies at The House and others in the brotherhood of the Santa Fe Ring. When the Tunstall outfit hired Bonney, it was clear that Tunstall's employees, besides possessing competent ranching abilities, had to handle firearms skillfully. The Kid prized his Winchester '73 rifle, and he carried several kinds of pistols, but the compact .41-caliber Colt double-action Thunderer, was his favorite. It was a gun that did not have to be manually cocked and could be fired rapidly.[10] That was just fine with Tunstall, who wanted nothing but capable gunmen riding for him, even if keeping them was expensive. "It cost a lot of money," Tunstall complained in a letter to his family in England, "for men expect to be well-paid for going on the war path."[11]

Francisco Gomez, a resident of Lincoln County for seventy-five years and a former McSween employee, spoke many years later of the Kid's know-how with a gun and his competence as a horseman. "He used to practice target shooting a lot," said Gomez. "He would throw up a can and would twirl his six-gun on his finger and he could hit the can six times before it hit the ground. He rode a big roan horse about ten or twelve hands high all that winter and when that horse was out in the pasture Billy would go to the gate and whistle and the horse would come up to the gate to him. That horse would follow Billy and mind him like a dog. He was a very fast horse and could out run most of the other horses around here."[12]

Although he was well known by many people throughout the county, Bonney was most drawn to the fellows working for Tunstall, who became his best pals.

They included a few that the Kid had little in common with, such as Rob Widenmann. A hanger-on with some family connections back East, Widenmann drifted to New Mexico Territory, struck up a friendship with Tunstall, and in the process wrangled a commission as a U.S. deputy marshal. Mostly remembered as a speculator with an appalling reputation, he was described by one writer as "acting the role of friend, valet, and general handy man" for Tunstall and by the *Santa Fe New Mexican*, an instrument of the Santa Fe Ring, as "a first class liar and fraud."[13]

In the evening after supper the Kid listened to the tales of fighting Indians and cattle stampedes told by Godfrey Gauss, an old German employed as camp cook and ranch helper.[14] Billy also grew especially close to other hired hands nearer his own age. There was Fred Waite, a part Choctaw cowboy from Indian Territory, called Dash by his saddle mates. Waite and Bonney became constant companions and were even talking about operating a spread on the Peñasco someday. Henry Brown, a former buffalo hunter who had worked for both The House and Chisum, also was a close friend of the Kid's. After the Lincoln County War, Brown left the territory and became a lawman in Tascosa, Texas.[15] John Middleton, described by Tunstall as "about the most desperate looking man I've ever seen," was yet another of the Kid's pals. When the shooting started with The House, Middleton was indicted in the killings of Sheriff Brady and Andrew "Buckshot" Roberts. That was when he "cleared out" of Lincoln County and became a grocer in Kansas.[16]

Dick Brewer, the ranch foreman for Tunstall, had hired Billy despite the Kid's former but brief affiliation with the Boys. A powerfully built man from St. Albans, Vermont, Brewer had settled in the Peñasco Valley in 1870 and eventually bought the old Horrell Ranch on the Ruidoso.[17] He was a close friend and supporter of Tunstall, with whom he shared an interest in breeding horses and a hatred of The House. He also became a kind of big brother figure to the Kid, but only for a short time. "After he [the Kid] got in with Tunstall, he paid his way, and was a different man altogether," Add Casey told an interviewer in 1937. "He had more sweethearts on the creek than a little."[18]

It would seem the Kid's luck had turned for the better. Early in 1878 the fierce competition, aggravated by legal squabbles between Tunstall and McSween and the gang at The House, reached fever pitch. Besides the business rivalry, there was an ongoing dispute over the settlement of a life insurance policy that pushed Dolan and Riley to the edge. In late January, money got so tight Tunstall was forced to mortgage his store and everything in it, including the land it stood on, and he and McSween had to turn over all their livestock to Tom Catron, the boss they answered to in Santa Fe. Catron's brother-in-law, Edgar Walz, who had just arrived from Minnesota to oversee Catron's interests at the Dolan store, witnessed the transaction.[19]

Much of the conflict stemmed from court maneuverings in Mesilla that favored The House when they filed a civil suit for ten thousand dollars against their chief rivals, McSween and Tunstall. For security purposes, Judge Warren Bristol issued writs for the seizure of property and livestock belonging to McSween and Tunstall. In Lincoln, Sheriff William Brady happily confiscated McSween's property, Tunstall's store, and put together a posse to serve an attachment writ on Tunstall's livestock at the ranch.[20] "Tunstall and McSween didn't stand a chance against The House," explained Jack Rigney, former manager of the Lincoln State Monument. "They were in way over their heads. New Mexico was the last haven for lawlessness, and both camps hired renegade men who killed at the drop of a hat and without any real reason."[21]

In February 1878, the Kid and Tunstall's other hands were involved with riders for The House in several confrontations stemming from the recent legal actions. After the Dolan faction raised a gang of almost fifty men from the Seven Rivers area along with some of Jesse Evans's gunmen, the Tunstall forces were on constant alert for raids on their cattle and horse herds as well as attacks on themselves.[22]

After breakfast on February 18, Tunstall, accompanied by Bonney, Brewer, Waite, Brown, Middleton, and Widenmann, left the ranch bound for Lincoln.[23] The group drove a herd of nine horses whose ownership was in dispute, including six that supposedly had been exempted from seizure by Brady and a mare that by some accounts the Kid had stolen. As Tunstall and his men headed to Lincoln, a posse deputized by Sheriff William Brady and led by Jimmy Dolan and Billy Mathews, a silent partner in The House, rode to Tunstall's ranch, clutching writs of attachment to seize livestock as ordered by the court.[24] Finding only Gauss and another old-timer at the Feliz ranch, Dolan and Mathews decided that the nine horses being trailed to Lincoln had to be included in the attachment even though the horses had been specifically exempted. A band of riders from the posse was dispatched to track the Tunstall party. Buck Morton led the force, which included Jesse Evans, Tom Hill, and Frank Baker. Late that afternoon they caught up with Tunstall's men, who had scattered in pursuit of a flock of wild turkeys, leaving Tunstall alone with the herd.[25]

Some of Tunstall's hands yelled for him to run for cover, but instead he approached the posse as if to parley. It was a fatal mistake. When Tunstall drew near, Buck Morton leveled his rifle and shot the Englishman through the upper chest. Tunstall tumbled from his horse to the ground. As the gravely wounded man thrashed about, Tom Hill dismounted, picked up Tunstall's pistol, and shot him pointblank in the back of the head. Hill then shot and killed Tunstall's prized bay horse.[26]

"Hill had Tunstall's revolver, with two chambers empty, in his hand, and it was passed around the members of the posse and then replaced in the dead man's scabbard," Nolan writes in his biography of Tunstall. "His body was neatly covered with a blanket, and the bloody head was pillowed on his folded overcoat. As a wry and macabre joke on Tunstall's great affection for horses, the dead bay's head was then pillowed on his hat."[27]

Deciding against an attack on the hilltop defenses of Tunstall's men, the posse rode off with the herd of horses and returned to the Feliz ranch. Stunned by the sudden assault, the Kid and the men concealed themselves among the rocks and trees. They never forgot John Middleton's words: "Boys, they have killed Tunstall."[28] Most historians maintain that the cold-blooded execution of Tunstall in a patch of scrub oak marked the official start of the Lincoln County War. Technically, they are right. Yet in some ways, the war started long before that solitary act of violence. The endless battles and acts of cruelty waged for so many years before and the series of catastrophes and crimes of vengeance all merged into one war, without glory or purpose.

It was a war fought in Lincoln County in the late nineteenth century, but it had been spawned long before in Ireland and England, in boardrooms and court chambers, in saloons and places of worship. It was a war of race and religion and class, Protestant and Catholic, Anglo and Hispanic, rich and poor. It was a war fought for years and years by Texans, soldiers, ranchers, merchants, Indians, Mexicans, politicians, judges, lawyers, and a legion of the unnamed who died hard and with the passage of time were forgotten. It was a war described as a "sagebrush passion play" featuring private armies of paid killers.[29] As always, the end product of the war was widows, orphans, the homeless, and mothers burying their sons.

"Truly, the Lincoln County War was a war without heroes," writes Robert Utley, the former chief historian and assistant director of the National Park Service. Utley is right. It was a war without heroes, and that included Billy the Kid.[30] "Yet it was a significant war," according to Utley. "It captured the thought and behavior of a range of frontier personalities. It dramatized economic forces that underlay most frontier conflicts. It demonstrated the immensity and varieties of frontier crime and violence. And it gave the world Billy the Kid, a figure of towering significance, not for the part he played in the war, but for the standing he achieved in American folklore."

If Bonney had died along with Tunstall, there still would have been a Lincoln County War but there would not have been a Billy the Kid. He emerged from the ashes and the blood, riding a wave of illusion and deception created by the true perpetrators of both sides of the war. The truth was neatly covered up through sleight of hand with historical facts by a host of dime novelists, journalists, and hacks. What was left was the lone figure, all at once romantic and daring but also dark and lethal. He was no longer Henry McCarty, Henry Antrim, Billy Bonney, or even just the Kid. He had become Billy the Kid—both outlaw myth and mythical hero. He was then and forever after a mirage.

With Tunstall's death and the events that quickly followed, the die was suddenly cast for the Kid. While news of the murder spread throughout Lincoln County and farther, the young Englishman's body was recovered and laid on a table in the parlor of his former partner McSween. The Kid, sombrero in hand, came to pay his respects. Frank Coe was there and remembered that the "Kid walked up, looked at him [Tunstall] and said, 'I'll get some of them before I die,' and turned away."[31]

McSween became the leader of those opposed to Dolan and his gang. Instead of turning loose the "40 men armed in full fighting trim" who were angrily plotting revenge in his home, the lawyer, a man with little patience for or interest in violence, devised a scheme using the law.[32] He bypassed the district judge, district attorney, and county sheriff—all on the enemy side—and obtained warrants for the arrest of Tunstall's killers from John B. Wilson, the local justice of the peace. Besides murder warrants for five outlaws and a dozen members of the Mathews posse, Wilson issued warrants for Sheriff Brady and others for larceny at the Tunstall store.[33]

As the newly deputized Bonney and Fred Waite, accompanied by a reluctant Constable Atanacio Martinez, trooped to the Dolan store to serve the warrants, they were greeted by Brady and several others, their guns at the ready. Instead of placing Brady and his associates in custody, the Kid and his companions were marched down the street to the jail.[34] There is little doubt that this action contributed to Brady's own death several weeks later since the Kid and Waite were jailed just long enough to miss Tunstall's funeral on February 21. Tunstall was buried behind his store in Lincoln. The Reverend Taylor Ealy, a Presbyterian min-ister who had arrived in town just two days earlier, preached the sermon, which Squire Wilson translated for the many Hispanic townspeople in attendance. Hymns were sung, and although Susan McSween was out of town, her organ was carried to the gravesite for the preacher's wife to play during the solemn ceremony.[35]

In response to the Tunstall killing and the belligerence that followed, McSween and Widenmann carried out a letter-writing campaign in hopes of convincing credible authorities to investigate the dire situation in Lincoln County. When Widenmann claimed that the Dolan faction had tried to poison him and the threat of more violence increased, McSween wrote out his will and fled with his wife to a refuge in the mountains.[36]

Dick Brewer, Tunstall's capable and aggressive foreman, stepped forward and on March 1 was appointed "special constable" by Squire Wilson with the power to make arrests.[37] Brewer immediately formed the Regulators, a term some say may have come from the Kid's reading of dime novels.[38] Captain Brewer's deputized posse included Billy Bonney, Charlie Bowdre, Fred Waite, Doc Scurlock, the Coe cousins, Henry Brown, John Middleton, Jim French, Frank McNab, Sam Smith, and John Scroggins. The number of these active Regulators varied from as few as ten to as many as sixty, including Hispanics sympathetic to the cause. The core group was about twelve Anglos, each bound by an oath they called the "iron clad." The essence of the oath was that members were never to divulge any information about their activities or bear witness against the other Regulators.[39]

For the next five months, operating only with the promise of four dollars a day in pay, the Regulators considered themselves a lawful posse, not vigilantes, as they set out to avenge the Tunstall slaying.[40] The Kid was singled out as one of the most loyal Regulators faithfully taking part in every armed engagement.

In early March 1878, while searching the countryside for Dolan men, the Reg-ulators came upon some horsemen at a crossing on the Peñasco. A chase ensued, and eventually the posse captured Buck Morton, leader of the riders who had killed Tunstall, along with Frank Baker, one of Jesse Evans's boys. While heading up the Pecos for John Chisum's South Spring Ranch with their two prisoners, the Regulators encountered William McCloskey, a former Tunstall hand. Brewer and the others distrusted McCloskey, known to be one of Morton's friends, but he was allowed to ride with them back to Lincoln.[41]

McCloskey, Morton, and Baker did not survive the ride back. The three were shot and killed in what the Regulators claimed was an aborted escape attempt by Morton and Baker, who were gunned down after they had supposedly killed McCloskey. The trio was more than likely executed by the Regulators, who feared if they were returned to Lincoln alive, Sheriff Brady would release them or permit them to "escape."[42]

On the same day the Regulators disposed of McCloskey, Morton, and Baker, a concerned governor Samuel Axtell arrived in Lincoln to investigate the stories of lawlessness that pervaded New Mexico Territory. His visit resulted from Sheriff Brady's asking for help in Lincoln County. "Anarchy is the only word which would truthfully describe the situation here for the past month," Brady had written in a letter to U.S. Attorney Tom Catron that was then passed on to Axtell.[43] A summary was sent to Washington, and President Hayes was asked to authorize the use of army troops to assist the local law enforcement officers. Hayes agreed, and the commanding officer at Fort Stanton was put on alert.

Axtell's visit to Lincoln was brief but damaging for the McSween forces. Accompanied by the Santa Fe Ring allies Jimmy Dolan and John Riley, the governor was in town a mere three hours before he canceled Squire Wilson's appointment as justice of the peace and revoked Rob Widenmann's appointment as deputy U.S. marshal.[44] With a single stroke of Axtell's pen, the Regulators went from lawmen to outlaws.

Over the next few weeks there were no serious confrontations except for a couple of shooting exchanges that produced no casualties. For the most part, the Regulators lay low and bided their time at their homes or hung around friendly San Patricio. Late in March the time had come to exact more revenge. Some of the Regulators, including the Kid and Fred Waite, got together with McSween, who with his wife was staying at Chisum's ranch.[45] At that meeting they hatched a plot to take out Sheriff Brady once and for all. On the night of March 31, six Regulators—Billy Bonney, Fred Waite, Frank McNab, Jim French, Henry Brown, and John Middleton—slipped into Lincoln and took up positions behind the Tunstall store in a corral hidden by a ten-foot-high adobe wall.[46] They waited for daybreak.

Around nine o'clock on the morning of April 1, Sheriff Brady left the Dolan store accompanied by deputies George Hindman, Billy Mathews, John Long, and George Peppin. They walked down the street, muddy after a recent rain, to the courthouse, where they posted legal notices, then started back to the store. After pausing to exchange a few friendly words with a woman in her yard, Brady hurried to catch up with his men. Just as the lawmen drew opposite the Tunstall corral, the six Regulators rose as one, poked their Winchesters through gunports carved in the adobe wall, and cut loose with a steady stream of fire.[47]

At least a dozen rounds tore through Brady, the main target. Sitting in the middle of the road, Brady groaned, "Oh, Lord," as he attempted to get to his feet. A second volley of shots struck him dead. The deputies rushed for cover, but one bullet hit Hindman, who lay on the street crying. Ike Stockton rushed from his saloon and tried to pull the wounded man to safety, but Hindman was struck again and died. Squire Wilson, only recently relieved of his post as justice of the peace and hoeing onions in his backyard across the road from the Tunstall store, survived a stray bullet in his buttocks.[48]

When the shooting stopped, only the barking of the village dogs could be heard. The Kid and Jim French jumped over the wall and ran to Brady's lifeless body in the road. It is not clear if the Kid was trying to find warrants or trying to recover the Winchester that Brady had taken when he'd jailed Billy in February. As the Kid bent over the lifeless Brady, a bullet fired by Billy Mathews from his position at the nearby Cisneros house ripped through the Kid's thigh and then struck French in his leg. The Kid dropped the rifle, and the two of them hobbled away. They later escaped with the other Regulators.[49]

The ambush slayings of Brady and his deputy had a devastating impact on the Regulators. The community became even more fragmented. Many people who had earlier sympathized with the Regulators viewed the killings as cold-blooded and no different from the brutal murder of Tunstall. Public opinion no longer favored the McSween faction. Both sides in the war were now considered equally nefarious and bloodthirsty.

A few days after the Brady and Hindman killings in Lincoln, the Regulators, including Bonney and French who were recovering from their gunshot wounds, picked up new recruits in the San Patricio area. They all then rode up the Ruidoso into the mountains and headed down the Tularosa Creek canyon to Blazer's Mill on the Mescalero Apache Indian Reservation.[50] Several of the men involved in Tunstall's murder were reportedly in the area. Although the arrest warrants Brewer carried as well as his commission as special constable had been ruled invalid, the Regulator captain was intent on hunting down anyone who had had anything to do with the demise of Tunstall.

Dr. Joseph Blazer, a former dentist who had started the small settlement of Blazer's Mill in 1869, leased a two-story adobe just upstream from the sawmill and gristmill to the federal government as housing for Indian agent Frederick

Godfroy and his family. Godfroy took in lodgers and his wife prepared meals for travelers.[51]

Around noon on April 4, 1878, the Regulators reined in their horses at Blazer's Mill and tramped into the big house for one of Clara Godfroy's celebrated dinners. While the posse wolfed down hot vittles, Buckshot Roberts, who sometimes went by the alias Bill Williams, arrived at Blazer's Mill astride a mule and leading a packhorse.[52] Although he had had no direct hand in Tunstall's death, Roberts had ridden with the posse that swooped down on the Tunstall ranch on the day the Englishman was killed. Unfortunately for Roberts, one of the warrants in Brewer's pocket had his name on it.

Frank Coe, who was acquainted with Roberts, tried to convince him that given the odds, the best course was to surrender. Buckshot could not be budged. He refused to give up his weapons and told Coe that he would not be taken alive.[53] A fierce gun battle ensued. "Bowdre had the drop on Roberts, as the latter had to raise his gun from his lap," recalled George Coe. "With his refusal to throw up his hands, they then fired simultaneously. Bowdre's bullet entered Roberts right through the middle, while Roberts's ball glanced off Bowdre's cartridge belt, and with my usual luck, I arrived just in time to stop the bullet with my right hand. It knocked the gun out of my hand, took off my trigger finger, and shattered my hand which still bears record of the fight. . . . I ran right in front of Roberts. He shot once at John Middleton, and the bullet entered his breast. He fired three times at me, but missed."[54]

Mortally wounded but with some fight still in him, Roberts grabbed an old Springfield rifle from the wall and used a mattress as a breastwork. The shooting continued. A frustrated and angry Brewer, with several of his Regulators wounded, dashed across a footbridge and took up a shooting position behind a pile of logs.[55] At a range of about 125 yards he got off one shot at Roberts in the doorway of the house. The bullet missed its mark and smashed into the wall. Seeing the puff of gun smoke, Roberts could tell where the shot came from. When Brewer lifted his head over the logs again, Roberts cut loose with the Springfield. The bullet crashed into Brewer's left eye and blew out the back of his head.[56]

Stunned by Brewer's death, the Regulators lost their taste for further battle that day. They knew that Buckshot Roberts, so desperate with pain that two men had to hold him down, was done for even though he did not die until the following day. In a macabre twist, Brewer and Buckshot were buried in the same grave, some said next to each other in the same coffin.[57]

The Blazer's Mill episode did not endear the McSween faction to the local populace. Despite the death of Brewer, a well-liked and sympathetic figure whom McSween called "nature's nobleman," the public generally disapproved of the circumstances of Buckshot Roberts's death. Many people, particularly those who appreciated marksmanship, admired the way Roberts put up a gutsy fight against overwhelming odds.

The rest of April brought little joy to the Regulators. The Kid and some of the others nursed their wounds in San Patricio, where the town constable Jose Chavez y Chavez, long simpatico to their cause, joined the Regulators. In Lincoln, Judge Bristol appointed John Copeland, the post butcher at Fort Stanton, as acting sheriff, and a short time later the county commissioners gave him the job permanently. Bristol had picked Copeland because he was thought to be neutral. The assumption proved wrong. Copeland was susceptible to McSween's influence and sympathetic to the cause of the Regulators. Other than the Copeland appointment, there was little else for the "iron clads" to cheer about.[58]

A few indictments, including one against Jesse Evans, were handed down in the Tunstall killing. The spring term of the grand jury also indicted William H. Bonney, John Middleton, and Henry Brown for Brady's murder and Fred Waite for Hindman's. Indictments in the slaying of Buckshot Roberts were returned against the same four, only in this instance Bonney was listed as "Henry Antrim, alias Kid."[59] Also indicted for the murder of Roberts were Charlie Bowdre, Doc Scurlock, Steve Stevens, John Scroggins, and George Coe. No one questioned the fact that Joseph Blazer, the foreman chosen from the ten men constituting the grand jury, had witnessed the shootout at Blazer's Mill and had given testimony during the grand jury proceedings.[60]

The Regulators often congregated at the home of McSween, who came back to town with his wife once the charge against him of embezzling money from the estate of Emil Fritz had been dismissed.[61] Frank McNab, a former cattle detective, was elected captain of the Regulators to take the slain Brewer's place.[62] When in town, the Regulators enjoyed carousing, often with the new sheriff, who had arrest warrants for several of them but somehow never remembered to serve them.

The Kid, never attracted to strong drink, preferred the evenings in the McSweens' parlor, where Mary Ealy, the preacher's wife, banged away on Sue McSween's piano. Those who were willing, like Billy Bonney, sang their hearts out. "And how they did sing," recalled Mary. "They stood behind me with their guns and belts full of cartridges; I suppose I was off tune as often as on it as I felt very nervous, though they were nice and polite."[63]

Meanwhile, Dolan, on the verge of shutting down his store and itching for more bloodshed, sent George W. "Dad" Peppin and Billy Mathews, former deputies under the late Sheriff Brady, to the Seven Rivers country to form yet another posse.[64] Peppin and Mathews, who went without Sheriff Copeland's approval, had little trouble rounding up recruits. Many of the Pecos ranchers were angry with the Regulators and Captain McNab, who had let it be known that any further rustling of John Chisum's cattle had to stop at once or there would be hell to pay. Among the more than twenty men, most from Seven Rivers, who signed up were William Johnson, Buck Powell, Marion Turner, Bob and John Beckwith, Wallace and Bob Olinger, Charles "Dutch Charlie" Kruling, and Manuel "Indian" Segovia.

On April 29 the freshly formed group, dubbed the Seven Rivers posse, rode off for Lincoln to bolster the Dolan forces. That afternoon they stopped for a rest at the Charles Fritz ranch on the Rio Bonito, just nine miles outside Lincoln.[65] There they learned from the Fritz family that in a few hours Frank Coe and two other Regulators would be stopping to water their horses on their way back to Coe's place on the Hondo. After taking up concealed positions, all the posse had to do was wait for their quarry to appear.

Riding with Coe was his brother-in-law Ab Saunders and Regulator Captain Frank McNab. As the trio approached the spring at the Fritz place, Coe's racing pony took the lead, putting him a hundred yards ahead of his two companions. Coe was allowed to pass unmolested, but when McNab and Saunders drew near, the hidden gunmen opened fire. In the melee that followed, McNab's horse bucked him off. McNab jumped to his feet and ran up a ravine, where several of his pursuers shot him dead. Saunders's horse was killed in the first volley of shots, and when he attempted to escape on foot, he was shot in the hip and captured.[66] That left only Coe.

"Several of them began shooting at me," Coe related many years later. "Someone shot from the Fritz house and killed my horse. A bullet hit her right in the back of the head. She stumbled along for thirty feet and fell."[67]

Unable to retrieve his Winchester and armed with just a six-gun, Coe exchanged only a few shots with the posse before he wisely surrendered. It was then that he learned that his brother-in-law was badly wounded. The Seven Rivers posse took up positions on the edge of Lincoln and in the surrounding foothills. A few of them, with Coe in custody, slipped into town and found refuge in the Dolan store.[68]

At the McSween house, some of the Regulators and Sheriff Copeland learned that the posse's mission was to assist the sheriff in arresting the Kid and the others under indictment for murder. The Regulators scattered throughout Lincoln, and gunfire erupted. While his captors were occupied, Frank Coe simply walked away and rejoined his friends. Both sides traded shots most of the day, but there were few casualties.[69]

At Sheriff Copeland's request, the army finally arrived. Lieutenant Colonel Nathan A. M. Dudley, a contentious career officer who had only recently taken command at Fort Stanton, sent a detachment of buffalo soldiers to Lincoln along with orders for the sheriff to arrest responsible parties on both sides.[70] At least thirty men surrendered to the sheriff and were taken back to Fort Stanton. After a few days Copeland asked that the detainees be released to his custody. Unable to control the unruly bunch of toughs, the sheriff soon turned them loose with their guns, and orders to return to Seven Rivers and stop fighting.[71]

That of course was not to be. The forces behind the Dolan faction had no intention of quitting the battle. As far as the Kid and his pals were concerned, the murder of another leader of their "iron clads" ensured that the war was a long way from being over. Neither side knew that in one way the conflict was rapidly concluding, and yet it was also a war that would never end, except for those who perished in it.

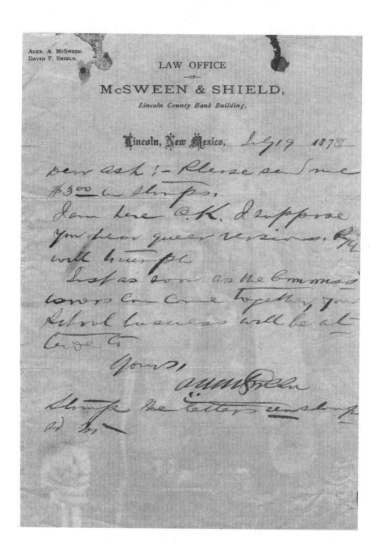

Letter written by Alexander McSween on July 19, 1878,
the day he was killed

TWENTY-TWO

FIRESTORM

*The history of Lincoln County has been one of bloodshed from
the day of its organisation.*[1]

•

—FRANK WARNER ANGEL

IN EARLY MAY 1878, as Jimmy Dolan and John Riley were formally
dissolving their troubled partnership, Billy Bonney and his fellow Regulators
elected their third captain, Josiah "Doc" Scurlock. Billy remained a rank-and-file
member. Unlike Dick Brewer and Frank McNab before him, Doc appeared to have
a somewhat better legal standing in the community, thanks to Sheriff Copeland,
who had commissioned him as a deputy with the power to issue warrants and
make arrests.[2] Lincoln had been relatively quiet once a cavalry troop from Fort
Stanton ended the squabble between the Regulators and the Seven Rivers posse.
But it was only the proverbial calmness before the storm. Both sides, including
those released from custody shortly after that battle, plotted their next moves and
bided their time.

An invigorated band of Regulators struck first. On May 14 both Hispanic and
Anglo riders, led by Captain Scurlock and Josefita Chavez, stormed into the Seven
Rivers country.[3] Mounted on swift ponies, they swept down on the Dolan-Riley

cow camp on the Pecos, not far from the Black River and just a few miles north of the Beckwith ranch. Chavez was in charge of eleven Hispanic Regulators, and the equal number of Anglo riders following Doc included Billy Bonney, Bowdre, Scroggins, Brown, and George Coe.[4]

Clearly outnumbered, the Dolan cowboys ran off. Two herders were wounded but managed to escape. A third man, the camp cook, Manuel "Indian" Segovia, was captured. Segovia had ridden with the posse that raided the Tunstall ranch as well as with the gang at the Fritz ranch ambush. He was believed to have killed Frank McNab.[5]

The Regulators scattered the herds of cattle and gathered up more than two dozen horses and mules at the cow camp and the nearby Beckwith spread before they departed. On the way back to Lincoln, Segovia was shot and killed "while attempting to escape," much the way Baker, Morton, and McCloskey had met their ends in March just after Tunstall's murder.[6]

Doc Scurlock and his Regulators came to regret ever making that raid on the Dolan camp. Returning to Lincoln, they learned that since Boss Catron had recently foreclosed on J. J. Dolan & Co., all assets, including cattle and horses, now belonged to him, not to Dolan and Riley. The Regulators now faced the full fury and force of Catron, the most powerful man in the territory. When he was told that his cattle were adrift on the plains and mixing with the Chisum herds, he erupted. He delivered a blistering letter of protest to Governor Axtell demanding immediate relief.[7] "There seems to be no authority in the county of Lincoln to compel people to keep the peace or obey the law," wrote the indignant Catron, "and there seems to be an utter disregard of the law in the county, as well as of life and private rights."[8]

Not only did Catron want Governor Axtell to disarm the gun-toting citizens, but he further requested that "the military may be instructed to see that they can keep the peace." In a reference to Copeland, Catron pointed out that the sheriff in Lincoln County "keeps with his deputies large armed posses, who are of one faction only and who take occasion at times to kill persons and take property of the other faction whenever they get an opportunity."

Whenever Catron barked, Axtell jumped. This time was no different. The governor dashed off a letter to Colonel Edward Hatch, commander of the Military District of New Mexico, in which he urged that immediate steps, such as the use of troops, be taken to assist Catron "since he is unable to deliver two thousand head of cattle to the government due to violence."[9]

Axtell was not through fulfilling his commitment to the Santa Fe Ring. In a blatant disregard for the law, he issued a proclamation removing Copeland from the office of sheriff. Axtell's handpicked replacement was George Peppin, former deputy for William Brady and ardent supporter of the Dolan-Riley side.[10]

As soon as the sheriff's badge was pinned on his shirt, Peppin, with input from Dolan and Riley, selected his deputies and brought in a slew of hired guns and thugs to form a posse and serve the sheaves of federal warrants on the Regulators. A federal investigation was under way at the same time as the result of all the letters McSween, Widenmann, and others had sent to the British Foreign Office and high-ranking officials in Washington. In response, Frank Warner Angel, a Wall Street attorney before becoming a special agent for the Justice Department, arrived in Lincoln County in mid-May and stayed for almost two months.[11] His mission was to probe the cause and circumstances of John Tunstall's death and to look into charges of official misconduct in both Colfax and Lincoln counties.

"If the iron heel of the 'ring' is to be removed from the necks of our people; if monopolies are to be broken; if the blighting, despotic, and pernicious power and influence of officials in New Mexico are to be brought to an end and authoritatively exposed, the people must come to the front,"[12] Widenmann wrote in a letter of support for Angel published in the *Cimarron News and Press*.

However, Special Agent Angel's task proved difficult, particularly when it came to obtaining affidavits from all the parties involved in the Tunstall case. The *Santa Fe New Mexican*, then a tool of many of those being investigated, berated and defamed Angel to no end. He received little, if any, cooperation from Axtell and none at all from U.S. Attorney Catron.[13] He persisted, though, and gradually collected testimony from several Dolan supporters, including Dolan himself, as well as from McSween, Widenmann, Gauss, and Billy Bonney on the other side.

The Kid's deposition was taken on June 8, 1878, in Lincoln, when some of the Regulators returned to the McSween house. Much of his testimony concerned events that ended with Tunstall's death, and the actual document was in Widenmann's handwriting. Some researchers later noted that the Kid's statement was suspiciously similar to Widenmann's deposition.[14]

Despite Frank Angel's presence, the violence between the two factions continued unabated. The skirmishes along the Ruidoso, raids on San Patricio, shootouts and ambushes, looting of ranches, and running gunfights were endless. Many of the confrontations ended in standoffs; some resulted in more casualties and wounded men. Both sides attempted to serve their warrants, and innocent citizens just tried to stay out of the crossfire or abandoned Lincoln County altogether. John Kinney and a gang of his paid mercenaries joined up with Peppin's men in hopes of snagging the illusive McSween or some of his followers.

Peppin's power increased because Nathan Dudley's soldiers were on call and at the ready at Fort Stanton. That changed, however, when Congress passed the Posse Comitatus Act, forbidding military intervention in civil disturbances except when authorized by the Constitution or an act of Congress.[15] Dudley received his new orders in late June and quickly recalled the cavalry unit that had been helping the sheriff's posse pursue the McSween band. The Regulators celebrated this development while Peppin realized he was on his own and could no longer rely on the army's support unless, of course, he could come up with a good reason.

Both sides now began building up sizable forces. One of the new Regulator recruits was the affable Thomas O'Folliard, a tall redhead about the same age as Bonney.[16] Like the Kid, Tom was the son of an Irish immigrant. He also was an orphan who had lost both his parents to smallpox in Mexico and had been raised by family back in Texas. After teaching O'Folliard how to handle a big buffalo gun, the Kid told Frank Coe that he intended to make Tom into a "real warrior." The two teenagers became fast friends.[17] "He was the Kid's inseparable companion and always went along and held his horses," Coe related in a 1927 interview. "He held the horses when the Kid would pay attention to some Mexican girl. It mattered not that he was gone thirty minutes or half the night, Tom was always there when he came out."

Shortly after O'Folliard joined their ranks, the Regulators expanded even more. They were joined by scores of local men including a good-size contingent of Hispanic fighters led by Martin Chavez from the tiny village of Picacho on the Rio Hondo.[18] Both sides were headed for a major showdown. McSween and the hardcore Regulators, especially the Kid, had grown weary of living as fugitives. They wanted to stop running around and force some kind of conclusion.

The climactic episode everyone anticipated began on the moonless night of July 14, when McSween and a force of about sixty Regulators slipped into Lincoln and took up strategic positions.[19] Under the cover of darkness, the Regulators, at the direction of Doc Scurlock and Martin Chavez, took up positions at the McSween residence, a granary behind the Tunstall store, the Montaño store, Juan Patrón's house, and the Ellis store.[20] The fighters barricaded doors and windows with sacks of flour and adobe bricks. They carved gunports in the walls and took stock of their hoard of food, water, and ammunition. Joining the McSweens and some friends at their house was a mix of a dozen local citizens.

Dolan and Peppin and about forty of their men prepared for battle at their headquarters in the Wortley Hotel, across the road from The House. Another half dozen men were posted inside the old torreón. Although at first outnumbered, Dolan breathed easier the following day when John Kinney, Jesse Evans, and a gang of other "hard cases" reined in their horses at the hotel corral and another large group of Pecos cowboys rode in from the west.[21]

By then many of the terrified citizens of Lincoln had vanished, leaving the town empty except for a few unwitting bystanders and the two opposing armies. Gunfire suddenly broke out all over Lincoln. The spectacle that came to be known as the Five-Day War had begun. The first four days brought mostly sporadic firing and no resolution. Fighters from both sides began thinking a stalemate of this sort could last for weeks. Some from the McSween faction, however, aware of their limited drinking water, had their doubts. The Dolan army had plenty of water, and time was on its side. The tide of battle turned even more in its favor. On July 15, Peppin sent word to Lieutenant Colonel Dudley requesting, of all things, the loan of a mountain howitzer. Not surprisingly, Dudley was sympathetic to Peppin, but because of the new act prohibiting the use of federal troops in civil matters, his hands were tied. A buffalo soldier was dispatched to Lincoln with a message of regret for Peppin. As the mounted trooper rode past the McSween house, someone inside opened fire on the soldier, who managed to ride away.[22]

To make matters worse, when Dudley sent a board of officers to Lincoln to look into that shooting incident, McSween partisans fired on them as they comforted a wounded man. These events, coupled with repeated pleas for help from some of the few remaining civilians, changed Dudley's mind. He believed there was now ample reason to send in the troops "for the preservation of the lives of the women and children."[23]

On the morning of July 19, Dudley with Captain George Purrington rode to Lincoln at the head of a column consisting of a cavalry company and an infantry company with three days' rations, a twelve-pound mountain howitzer, and a Gatling gun with two thousand rounds of ammunition.[24]

Dudley paraded his troops through town and established a camp. Although he claimed that the army would remain neutral in the dispute, he ordered his men to aim the cannon at the Montaño store and "blow the house away" if anyone inside fired. He also badgered the justice of the peace to swear out an arrest warrant for Alex McSween.[25] At the show of such force, many of the Regulators decided to leave. A number of them forded the Bonito and fled into the hills. In a very short time, the Regulator forces were reduced from sixty to just thirteen. All of them were stationed in the McSween house.

Peppin's men moved in for the kill. They left the Wortley Hotel and shifted their headquarters to the torreón, a better location for directing a siege on the McSween place. They surrounded the house and hollered through shattered windows for McSween to surrender at once or face the consequences. When McSween refused, Peppin ordered the house set on fire to drive out the occupants. Coal oil was splashed on the walls and a match struck, but the blaze soon went out.[26] At one point, Susan McSween bravely left the house in an effort to stop further bloodshed. She faced off with Peppin and then implored Dudley to allow her husband to surrender to him instead of the sheriff. Dudley refused, and Susan, desperate and bitter, staggered back to the house.[27] After a failed second attempt at igniting the house, the sheriff's men were finally able to get a fire started. The fire burned slowly in the U-shaped adobe, but the smoke thickened. While the flames spread, the Kid and the others, in what must have been a spectacular scene, dragged Susan's prized piano with them as they moved from room to room.[28] Late in the afternoon a keg of gunpowder in the house exploded, and the fire then became more intense, as did the exchange of gunfire. McSween appeared near collapse.

The Kid now stepped forward and took command of the situation. He had devised an escape strategy for those trapped inside. "We can stick it out, if the fire does not burn any faster than it is now," he told the others huddled around him. "Some of us are certain to get hit, but most of us can make it out and across the river. It's only a few hundred yards and, if we run fast and shoot fast, we can hold off Peppin's crowd so they can't do us much damage."[29]

The Kid then convinced Susan McSween to leave, pointing out that "a dress ain't very good to make a run in."[30] Susan obeyed and kissed her husband one last time before she fled with her sister, Elizabeth Shield, and her five terrified children, and took refuge with Reverend Ealy's family at the Patrón house.

"The boys [the Kid and other Regulators] talked to each other and McSween and I were sitting in one corner," Susan said in a 1927 interview of her final moments in the house.[31] "The boys decided I should leave. They were fighting the fire in my sister's house [the McSweens' east wing]. McSween said he guessed that was better. . . . The Kid was lively and McSween was sad. McSween sat with his head down, and the Kid shook him and told him to get up, that they were going to make a break."

Surrounded by the other dozen defenders in the kitchen, the only intact room left in the house, the Kid laid out his plan. He proposed that he and four others— Tom O'Folliard, Jim French, Chavez y Chavez, and Harvey Morris, a law student from New York—draw the gunfire of the attackers by making a dash for the Tunstall store. In the confusion, McSween and the rest could then make their break, race to the back gate, and escape to the river.[32] It was a desperate plan, but there seemed no other viable option. They waited for the mantle of darkness before they instituted the plan.

Despite its being pitch black by nine o'clock that evening, the burning house "made it almost light as day for a short distance around," the Kid later testified during an official inquiry into the incident.[33] Deciding that they could wait no more, the Kid and the four others crept outside, perhaps, as some claimed, in their stocking feet so as not to make any noise. Suddenly bolting for freedom, they were met by a barrage of gunfire from the posse. Morris, McSween's hapless law clerk, got only as far as the gate when a single rifle shot to the head killed him. The other four made it to the gate and beyond unscathed. They danced through the hail of bullets and disappeared into the darkness. During the escape the Kid managed to get off a shot that grazed John Kinney's upper lip, ripping off his mustache.[34]

As their attackers were diverted, McSween and his followers, mostly local Hispanics, should have made their move. But they waited too long, and by the time they did make a run, the shooting had stopped. They had not gotten very far before more guns exploded and drove some back inside the burning house and others into a chicken house. More precious time passed. McSween, dazed and confused, yelled that he would surrender and then changed his mind after coming out into the yard. The shooting resumed. A bullet from the McSween side struck Bob Beckwith, a Seven Rivers deputy, and instantly killed him. More guns barked, and "the big killing," as it became known, took place. One of those who died was Alex McSween, riddled with at least five bullets.[35]

Some of the McSween bunch escaped. Among the injured, badly wounded Yginio Salazar pretended he was dead. Later the fifteen-year-old crawled off to a relative's house half a mile away.[36] Salazar eventually recovered and remained one of the Kid's favorite compañeros.

The bodies of McSween and those who died with him remained untouched on the ground while the triumphant posse celebrated their success in the McSween yard. They forced two of McSween's distraught hired men, bitter tears streaming down their faces, to fetch their fiddles and play while the victors danced and got drunk and fired their guns into the night sky. Other celebrants broke into Tunstall's store and looted it, cleaning out every shelf and showcase.[37]

Colonel Dudley, one of those largely responsible for the terrible battle, shooed away chickens pecking at the eyes of McSween and the other dead men.[38] Then Dudley threw a store blanket over McSween's bloody corpse.

McSween's death marked the conclusion of the war but certainly did not halt its consequences. A reign of terror continued in Lincoln County and elsewhere in New Mexico Territory. The civil disorder, the antics of corrupt politicians, and the ineffectual lawmen who did their bidding attracted national attention. The result was even more federal scrutiny and public outcry for reform.

Boss Catron, Governor Axtell, Jimmy Dolan, and the rest of their crowd did not want to take the fall for the graft and violence. They desperately needed to sidestep the glaring light of truth that shone forth. They needed someone else to bear all the blame. It was on that night of fire and death at McSween's place in Lincoln that the prime candidate came to center stage. He had danced through a ring of flames and a hail of bullets and into the safety of the shadows. It was the Kid, and as hard as he tried, he would never get away.

Lew Wallace, governor, New Mexico Territory 1878–1881

TWENTY-THREE

DEVIL OR ANGEL

There are two Billy the Kids in legend. The first is a tough little thug, a coward, a thief, and a cold-blooded murderer. The second is a romantic and sentimental hero, the brave and likeable leader of an outnumbered band fighting for justice.[1]

•

—KENT STECKMESSER

FROM EARLY 1878 until his death in the summer of 1881, William Bonney's activities can be documented week by week and sometimes daily.[2] Nevertheless, little reliable information about the Kid during this time is known. Incidents in those years, such as the slayings of Tunstall and McSween or the Kid's nefarious activities leading up to his death, are the ones frequently explored by grassroots historians and authors and portrayed by Hollywood's most imaginative minds.

"When the legend becomes fact, print the legend." This memorable line from John Ford's 1962 western film *The Man Who Shot Liberty Valance* best describes the approach most writers and filmmakers have taken when interpreting the life and times of the Kid.[3] It was not, however, just circumstances and timing that created the myth of Billy the Kid. The young man may have been used and abused by the many duplicitous people that he encountered in the final years of his life, but he himself also played a critical role in establishing his own identity. A virtual orphan and an opportunist who out of necessity lived by his wits, the Kid had developed a keen survival instinct and was fully capable of seizing the moment. He skillfully improvised his own destiny until finally his Irish luck ran out. "Henry McCarty left the dark history of his family's Ireland, the shame of their famine and exile, and became Billy the Kid," writes Fintan O'Toole in his profile of the Kid for *The New Yorker*.[4] "He invented a new Identity, and, when the [Lincoln County] war broke out around him, he got the opportunity to live up to it."

The Kid may have lived up to that new identity, but he did not live very long. The duality of his remade persona was blurred and distorted at the end of his own lifetime and long after. He would not be referred to as Billy *the* Kid in print until just seven months before he died.[5] Yet it is by that colorful epithet and what it represents—whether truthful or not—that he will always be remembered.

With Tunstall and McSween out of the way, he became, as the notorious Billy the Kid, a convenient target for the Santa Fe Ring and the Dolan faction. The simple fact is they deliberately used him as a target bad boy in order to divert the adverse public attention coming to them. The Kid was cast in the role of avenger. He was out to get retribution for the execution deaths of Tunstall and McSween. He also was labeled an outlaw and became the most wanted man in the Southwest.

This focused legend building all started just weeks after the McSween house was burned. The Kid and several of his fellow Regulators were on the scout, looking for horses to replace those lost during the fighting in Lincoln. Along the way this band of Regulators sometimes gambled in one of the scattered villages or camps and carried on as usual, but something had changed, something new fouling the air. They began drawing a lot more notice wherever they went. Charlie Bowdre and Jim French were accused of threatening to burn the home of Captain Saturnino Baca for supporting the Dolan faction. Lieutenant Colonel Dudley called out the troops to protect the civilian, but Baca's home was never torched. A short time later the shooting death of Morris Bernstein, the clerk at the Mescalero Agency, was pinned on the Regulators despite proof to the contrary.[6]

The Kid and a few other Regulators next showed up with some purloined stock at Bosque Grande, Chisum's original ranch headquarters on the Pecos, about thirty miles south of Fort Sumner. Old John Chisum was in St. Louis at the time, and two of his brothers, Jim and Pitzer, were moving their herds out of turbulent New Mexico Territory to the grazing grounds of the Texas Panhandle. Sallie Chisum, Jim's pretty daughter, was traveling with them. She had met the Kid before at the South Spring ranch, where they rode together and enjoyed a few front porch visits. In the past the Kid had sent letters to the Texas beauty, including one he wrote during the siege of the McSween house. At Bosque Grande, and later when the Chisum herd rested along the trail at Fort Sumner, the Kid presented her with an Indian tobacco sack and some candy hearts.[7]

Miss Sallie was winsome, but Fort Sumner appealed to the Kid more. When the Chisums moved on with their cattle, he stayed and waited for the arrival of some of the other "iron clads," including the Coes. "When we got there," remembered Frank Coe, "Kid and others had a baile for us. . . . House was full, whiskey free, not a white girl in the house, all Mexican, and all good dancers. Danced all night. Boys swinging them high."[8]

Using Fort Sumner as their base of operations, the Regulators rode to Puerto de Luna, a settlement on the Pecos that had got its name when Coronado camped there. According to legend, when the full moon rose through a mountain gap, the Spaniard had exclaimed, "*Puerto de Luna!* [Gateway to the moon]."[9] Coronado and the bridge his men built across the Pecos were long gone, but the Kid found that the many dances held there were memorable, as were those the Regulators attended just upriver to the north at Anton Chico, "the best of the towns this side of Las Vegas," according to Frank Coe.

In Anton Chico the Regulators held what George Coe called a "war powwow" to talk over their future.[10] The Coe cousins announced that they had had enough of New Mexico Territory and were heading up to Colorado for a fresh start. They tried to convince the Kid to join them, but he would have none of it. They shook hands and rode off in different directions. It was the last time either of the Coes ever saw the Kid.[11] Two more of the Kid's buddies, Doc Scurlock and Charlie Bowdre, also decided to quit riding as Regulators.[12] They moved their families to Fort Sumner and took jobs with Pete Maxwell, the eldest son of Lucien Maxwell of Maxwell Land Grant fame. When his father died in 1875, Pete had taken over the ranch, headquartered at the old army post.

The Kid was the undisputed chief of the Regulators when he returned to Lincoln County with Tom O'Folliard and some others. They boldly swooped down on the Charles Fritz ranch, where Frank McNab had been bushwhacked, and made off with 15 horses from the remuda and 150 head of cattle.[13] In late September 1878, the Kid, accompanied by O'Folliard, Fred Waite, Henry Brown, and John Middleton, set off with the stolen stock. Acquiring plenty more horses along the way, they were bound for the Texas Panhandle and the town of Tascosa on the sandy north bank of the Canadian River.[14]

The settlement in a cottonwood grove had been called Atascosa, "boggy creek," for a nearby tributary that was notorious for quicksand, but eventually the A was dropped.[15] This part of the Llano Estacado (Staked Plain) had been the hunting grounds of Kiowas and Comanches. Then came buffalo hunters as well as *ganaderos*, Hispanic sheep ranchers from New Mexico Territory with their *pastores*, herders, and great flocks of sheep. Eventually Anglo cattlemen appeared and looked at the free grass plains as one gigantic cow pasture.[16] When the Kid and his crew turned up, Tascosa was becoming a roundup and trade center and a popular cattle trail stop.

In Upper Tascosa, the Exchange Hotel boasted the first wood floors in town and served as the social gathering place for the more respectable folks. Drovers and brush poppers, a common name for cowboys in Texas and New Mexico Territory, fancied Lower Tascosa, or hogtown, and its array of gambling houses, rooster fighting pits, brothels, cribs, and other carnal enticements.[17] Drinking establishments, such as the Jim East Saloon, Equity Bar, and Captain Jinks' Saloon, flourished by catering to thirsty men. Dance hall girls and fancy ladies sported colorful names like Boxcar Jane, Slippery Sue, Mustang Mae, Gizzard Lip, and Midnight Rose.[18] Life in Tascosa was cheap, as were the drinks and the harlots.

The Kid and his mates had heard that Tascosa was split-lipped and black-eyed, but they also had been told that anyone looking to trade off or sell stolen horses was welcome. There were plenty of buyers who asked very few questions.

The time that the Kid spent in Tascosa provides yet another revealing portrait of him and offers glimpses into his personal life. The best of those memories of the Kid came from Henry Hoyt, a young doctor seeking adventure before settling down to a distinguished medical career.[19] A native Minnesotan, Hoyt had completed his medical studies and before coming to Texas had doctored miners and gold hunters for a short time in Deadwood, the rough-and-tumble mining camp in Dakota Territory.[20] After moving to the Panhandle, Hoyt supplemented his doctor wages by working as a cowhand. He was twenty-four years old when he came across the Kid and his four companions riding into Tascosa for the first time. "Billy Bonney was eighteen years old, a handsome youth with smooth face, wavy brown hair, an athletic and symmetrical figure, and clear blue eyes that could look one through and through," Hoyt recounted forty-two years later. "Unless angry, he always seemed to have a pleasant expression with a ready smile. His head was well shaped, his features regular, his nose aquiline, his most noticeable characteristic a slight protrusion of his two upper front teeth."[21]

Hoyt and Bonney became instant friends. Hoyt's accounts of the Kid and their experiences are generally considered highly reliable. "Bonney's party mingled freely, sold and traded horses with anyone so inclined, varying their business dealings with drinking, gambling, horseracing, and target shooting. Billy was an expert at most Western sports, with the exception of drinking,"[22] Hoyt recalled. He shared this aversion to whiskey drinking although, he pointed out, the Kid frequented places where alcohol was served so he could play his share of three-card monte and poker.

Another popular pastime was to take part in the many bailes held on the small plazas or in the haciendas of such prominent families as Don Casimero Romero, a Castilian by birth and chief of the *pastores*.[23] His nephew Don Pedro Romero also hosted weekly dances attended by Hispanic belles in festive dresses as well as by cowboys, hunters, and other hombres scrubbed reasonably clean for the festivities.

An unwritten law made it clear that anyone attending the dances at Don Pedro's place fronting the east side of the Tascosa plaza had to leave his weapons checked at a nearby store. "One beautiful moonlight night a Romero *baile* was in full swing," remembered Hoyt. "The Kid and I stepped out to enjoy [the evening]."[24] They had strolled about a hundred yards away when Hoyt challenged the Kid to a race back to the dance. The Kid was fast, but Hoyt led all the way until they reached the door, when he "slacked up" and the Kid, running full speed, tripped on the doorsill and tumbled full length in the middle of the dance floor.

"Quicker than a flash," wrote Hoyt, "his prostrate body was surrounded by his four pals, back to back, with a Colt's [sic] forty-five in each hand, cocked and ready for business." When the Kid crashed inside, they immediately thought something was amiss and sprang into action. How they had hidden their guns was never explained, and although they were repentant, the Kid and his boys were barred from future dances at that home.[25]

One evening Hoyt won a gold watch in a draw poker game. For some reason, the Kid wanted that watch, and it was through his "wanting" that Hoyt figured out that the "little New Mexican beauty" the Kid constantly talked about had to be Paulita Maxwell, Pete Maxwell's young sister back in Fort Sumner. As the story goes, Hoyt too had been somewhat smitten by the fourteen-year-old when he stopped at Fort Sumner in 1877 to aid William Maxwell, Paulita and Pete's adopted brother, who was dying of smallpox. When the Kid admired the watch with its long chain of braided hair, Hoyt suspected he wanted to present it to Paulita, so he gave it to the Kid.[26]

In late October 1878, Hoyt decided to leave the Panhandle, and on the day he departed the Kid rode into Tascosa leading Dandy Dick, an Arabian sorrel branded BB on the left hip. He handed the reins of the racehorse to a surprised Hoyt. No money changed hands, but the Kid wrote out a bill of sale for seventy-five dollars to make it look like an actual purchase. He signed the paper W. H. Bonney and had it witnessed so there would be no question about ownership. It was more than forty years later before Hoyt learned that Dandy Dick was the same horse Sheriff William Brady had ridden into Lincoln on April 1, 1878, the day he was gunned down and died. The horse had been a gift to Brady from none other than Major L. G. Murphy, the old political boss of Lincoln County.[27]

As he had many times, Hoyt again advised the Kid to quit his outlaw ways. "I often urged him, while he was free and the going good, to leave the country, settle in Mexico or South America, and begin all over again. He spoke Spanish like a native, and although only a beardless boy, he was nevertheless a natural leader of men. With his poise, iron nerve, and all-round efficiency properly applied, the Kid could have been a success anywhere."[28]

The Kid nonetheless did not heed Hoyt's good advice, nor did he agree with Waite, Middleton, and Brown when they urged him and O'Folliard to follow their suit and never return to New Mexico Territory. When the Kid refused, the last of the hard-core Regulators went their separate ways.

Fred Waite, who at one time had dreamed of ranching with the Kid, returned to Indian Territory, became a tax collector, and held many prestigious offices in the Chickasaw Nation. John Middleton went on to punch cows in Kansas, wed a wealthy woman, and died in 1885 from the effects of the gunshot wound at Blazer's Mill. Henry Brown served as a deputy sheriff in Texas and in 1884, while marshal at Caldwell, Kansas, was gunned down by a lynch mob after he killed a bank president during an aborted robbery.[29]

The Kid and the ever-loyal Tom O'Folliard headed right back to New Mexico, where, except for more jaunts either to steal or to sell stock in Texas, they stayed. At Fort Sumner, the Kid and Tom resumed their social life. They attended bailes, gambled at Beaver Smith's saloon, and visited with Charlie Bowdre, Doc Scurlock, and their families and friends.

During the Kid's absence from Lincoln County, there had been a dramatic increase in lawlessness, mostly perpetrated by former elements of the Dolan faction. By far the worst of the lot was Selman's Scouts, sometimes called the Rustlers or the Wrestlers. They were led by John Henry Selman, a Texas deputy turned desperado. True to their name, the Rustlers raided cattle herds and horse remudas across the county. They also committed murder and rape, burned down ranches, and pillaged homes and businesses in Lincoln and elsewhere. One of Selman's gang members told a bystander, "We are devils come from Hell!"[30] Of that there was no doubt.

The high crimes committed by Selman and his gang in Lincoln County did not go unnoticed. Even before most of those outrages took place, federal investigator Frank Angel's final report blasting Governor Samuel Axtell and his administration prompted President Rutherford Hayes to take action.[31] Heads rolled throughout the territory. Although he retained much of his power as head of the Santa Fe Ring, Tom Catron was forced to resign as U.S. attorney, while Axtell was removed from the office of governor.[32] His replacement was Lew Wallace, the noted Civil War general who had served on the court-martial of Lincoln's assassins and presided at the proceedings that convicted Henry Wirtz, the commander of the infamous Andersonville prison camp. Back in Indiana, Wallace had pursued a legal and literary career and in 1873 published *Fair God*, his first novel.[33] President Hayes figured Wallace was just the man to tame the renegades in New Mexico Territory.

After sizing up the situation, Wallace called for an immediate halt to the violence. To back this up, he issued a proclamation of amnesty for all parties that had taken took part in the Lincoln County War, except for those already under criminal indictment.[34] The Kid predictably failed the amnesty test. He had previously been indicted by the territory for the murder of Sheriff Brady and faced a federal indictment in the killing of Buckshot Roberts. Still, like others from the old McSween faction, the Kid remained hopeful about his future. His spirits were further buoyed when George Kimbrell, a former government scout, replaced George Peppin as sheriff.[35] It was that optimism and a desire to clear the air once and for all that perhaps prompted the Kid to offer an olive branch to his enemies.

On February 18, 1879, exactly one year after the murder of Tunstall, the Kid rode into Lincoln to meet with his nemesis, Jimmy Dolan. With the Kid standing behind a low adobe wall on one side of the road were O'Folliard, Doc Scurlock, Joe Bowers, and Jose Salazar. Across the road behind another wall, Jesse Evans, Billy Mathews, Edgar Walz, and Billy Campbell backed Dolan.[36] The parley nearly turned into a gunfight when Evans suggested killing the Kid where he stood, but cooler minds prevailed. In due course both sides gathered in the center of the road to shake hands and sign an agreement that called for them to stop killing or testifying against each other. Furthermore, if anyone failed to comply with the compact, "he should be killed on sight."[37]

To seal the treaty properly, the signatories, except for the Kid, downed large quantities of whiskey. At one point, as they were making the rounds, the intoxicated mob encountered Houston Chapman, an outspoken and highly strung one-armed lawyer who was representing Susan McSween in her fight to find justice for her dead husband. The drunks demanded that Chapman do a jig for them, and when he refused, Dolan and Campbell fired their guns at the same time. "My God, I am killed," yelped Chapman as he fell, his clothing on fire from the powder flash.[38]

The Kid now became anxious to put some distance between himself and the drunken killers. He found his chance at the next saloon stop. Dolan tried to get Walz, Catron's brother-in-law, to return to the smoldering body and plant a gun in the unarmed Chapman's hand so it would appear to be a case of self-defense. When Walz balked, the Kid volunteered. He grabbed the gun but instead of going to Chapman, the Kid hooked up with O'Folliard, who had managed to slip away from the others. They quickly saddled their mounts and skinned out for San Patricio.[39] Not only had the peace been extremely short-lived, but now the Kid was implicated in yet another killing. The words of the Irish proverb rang true: "Those who shake hands with the devil often have trouble getting their hand back."

The Chapman murder outraged the citizens of Lincoln, and in response Sheriff Kimbrell and the troops went back on the hunt. The killing also convinced Governor Wallace to go to Lincoln County and investigate the unrest there for himself. In truth, Wallace had been putting off the journey. He was content to stay in El Palacio, the Palace of the Governors on the Santa Fe Plaza and complete his next novel, *Ben-Hur: A Tale of the Christ*.[40] Set in the New Testament, it told the classic story of betrayal, revenge, and redemption involving a young man whose life combined both good and bad fortune.

After reaching Lincoln in early March, Wallace at once engineered the suspension of the incompetent Lieutenant Colonel Dudley as commander of Fort Stanton and his eventual transfer to Fort Union. Next he ordered the arrest of anyone involved in Chapman's death. Posses and troopers crisscrossed the county in search of culprits, sometimes even making arrests without warrants.[41]

On March 13, 1879, Wallace received the first of several letters from the Kid. Delivered by one of Billy's San Patricio friends, it was an explanation of the events surrounding Chapman's murder. The Kid expressed his willingness to testify against those responsible in exchange for a pardon. He explained that he was afraid to surrender because of his enemies and asked to meet with Wallace. He concluded by saying: "I have no wish to fight any more. Indeed I have not raised an arm since your proclamation, As to my character, I refer to any of the citizens, for the majority of them are my friends and have been helping me all they could. I am called Kid Antrim but Antrim is my stepfather's name. Waiting for an answer I remain your obedient servant."[42]

Two days later Wallace replied. He told the Kid to appear at Squire Wilson's house in Lincoln at a prescribed date and time. The governor then wrote: "I have the authority to exempt you from prosecution, if you will testify to what you know. The object of the meeting at Squire Wilson's is to arrange the matter in a way to make your life safe. To do that the utmost secrecy is to be used. So come alone. Don't tell anybody—not a living soul—where you are coming or the object. If you could trust Jesse Evans, you can trust me."[43]

On the evening of March 17, St. Patrick's Day, Wallace and Squire Wilson waited for the Kid to appear. Several years later Wallace described the meeting to a newspaper reporter. "At the time designated, I heard a knock at the door, and I called out, 'Come in.' The door opened somewhat slowly and carefully, and there stood the young fellow generally known as the Kid, his Winchester in his right hand, his revolver in his left."[44]

The meeting was brief and to the point. Wallace, a former army general who had led troops at bloody Shiloh and faced off with the killers of Lincoln, was not particularly concerned about negotiating with a teenage boy. The plan Wallace unfolded that night called for a "fake arrest" of the Kid, a sort of protective custody, followed by a court appearance at which time he would testify to all he knew about the murder of Chapman. "In return for you doing this," Wallace told the Kid, "I will let you go scot free with a pardon in your pockets for all your misdeeds."[45] The Kid liked what he heard. After making sure his friend O'Folliard was included in the deal, the Kid said he would give the governor a decision in a few days and slipped, as was his want, into the dark night.

A few days later the governor received another note penned by the Kid from his San Patricio digs. Bonney agreed to Wallace's scheme but had an additional request: "I will keep the appointment I made but be sure and have men come [to make the "fake arrest"] that you can depend on. I am not afraid to die like a man fighting but I would not like to be killed like a dog unarmed."[46]

Sheriff Kimbrell and a posse rode into San Patricio the next afternoon and took the Kid and O'Folliard into custody. They were brought back to Lincoln and placed under house arrest in the home of Juan Patrón. While waiting to testify, the Kid and O'Folliard played cards with their guards and were furnished with ample food and comforts by their many friends. Wallace, who stayed next door at the Montaño store, was mystified by the Kid's popularity. "A precious specimen named 'The Kid' whom the sheriff is holding here in the Plaza, as it is called, is the object of tender regard," Wallace wrote to Secretary of the Interior Carl Schurz. "I heard singing and music the other night; going to the door I found the minstrels of the village actually serenading the fellow in his prison."[47]

As he had promised, the Kid appeared as a witness before the April term of the grand jury and testified that Jimmy Dolan and Billy Campbell had killed Chapman with help from Jesse Evans. Tom O'Folliard took the stand and told the grand jurors the same thing. As a result, Dolan and Campbell were indicted for murder, and Evans named an accessory. In all, more than two hundred criminal indictments were returned against fifty men, the largest number for the murders of Alex McSween and Frank McNab, the burning of McSween's house, and the various offenses committed by Selman and his Rustlers.[48]

Only a very few of those indicted ever came close to going to trial. Many of them took advantage of the governor's generous amnesty or were released on writs of habeas corpus. Others just disappeared and were never heard of again. Some with strong ties to the Santa Fe Ring, such as Dolan, Peppin, and Dudley, won acquittals in friendly courts or had the charges dropped altogether.[49]

The Kid was not so fortunate. District Attorney William Rynerson, a ruthless prosecutor remembered for his own acquittal in the killing of a New Mexico chief justice back in 1867, wanted him punished to the full extent of the law.[50] A solid member of the Santa Fe Ring and Dolan's close friend, Rynerson had no intention of honoring Governor Wallace's promise of immunity for Billy Bonney.

"I tell you[,] governor," attorney Ira Leonard wrote to Wallace back in Santa Fe, "the District Attorney here is no friend of law enforcement. He is bent on going after the Kid. He proposes to distroy [sic] his evidence and influence and is bent on pushing him to the wall. He is a Dolan man and is defending him in every manner possible."[51]

A week after the grand jury adjourned, the military board of inquiry convened at Fort Stanton to look into the conduct of Lieutenant Colonel Dudley during the attack on the McSween residence. More than one hundred witnesses, including Lew Wallace, the Kid, and Susan McSween, testified during the eight-week hearing. Dudley's formidable legal counsel, Henry Waldo, a former attorney general and member of the Catron and Elkins law firm, discounted the testimony of the prosecution's witnesses, especially the Kid.[52] In his closing argument Waldo attacked the Kid's veracity and called him "a precocious criminal of the worst type, although hardly up to his majority, murderer by profession, as records of this court connect him with two atrocious murders."[53]

The three officers presiding at the hearing took little time in coming back with a decision that surprised no one: Dudley was fully exonerated. When the verdict was announced, the Kid and O'Folliard took their leave from the guards at the Patrón house and quietly rode away on horses supplied by friends.

The Kid realized that his hatred of Dolan and his allies was matched only by *their* hatred for him. What's more, he knew that Rynerson would not rest until he was swinging from a hemp rope. Most of all, he was certain that the promises of Lew Wallace were as empty and meaningless as a withered teat. He was dead sure of that.

The Kid did what he knew best. He ran away and lived by his wits. He headed to Las Vegas, the old Santa Fe Trail stop, where it was said there were so many public hangings on the old windmill in the plaza that the little boys all over town started hanging their dogs in imitation.[54] The Kid did not go to Las Vegas to witness a hanging but to pick up some income from the busy gaming tables. In 1879 Las Vegas, too often confused today with its Nevada counterpart, had become a big draw ever since the Fourth of July, when the first train of the Atchison, Topeka, and Santa Fe Railroad chugged into the depot, setting off a wild celebration.[55]

While the Kid visited the new gambling halls and hotels, he supposedly shared a Sabbath dinner with Jesse James, the Missouri bandit. Henry Hoyt, the itinerant doctor from Tascosa, was working as a bartender at one of the hotels when he by chance came across the Kid at the hot springs resort north of town.[56]

"We were chatting away of old times in Texas as if we were a couple of cowboy friends," Hoyt explained many years later, "when the man on Bonney's left made a comment on something he said. Whereupon Billy said, 'Hoyt, meet my friend Mr. Howard from Tennessee.' " Later that day the Kid pledged Hoyt to secrecy and admitted "Mr. Howard was no other than the bandit and train robber, Jesse James."[57]

Whether Hoyt's facts and memory were correct or not, the story only adds to the thick veneer of myth surrounding Billy Bonney.[58] What is not conjecture is that about the same time as the supposed Jesse James meeting, the Kid turned to John Chisum and requested back pay for his services during the Lincoln County War. When Chisum turned him down, the Kid found another way to get his money: He stole Chisum's cattle and sold them.[59]

The Kid spent more and more of his time at Fort Sumner. Although Doc Scurlock had grown tried of cattle rustling and moved his family to Texas, the Kid still had a wide circle of friends at Fort Sumner. Besides Tom O'Folliard and Charlie Bowdre there were some new pals, Dave Rudabaugh, Billy Wilson, and Tom Pickett.

And then there were the Kid's female companions. As Paulita Maxwell put it, "Billy the Kid, I may tell you, fascinated many women. . . . Like a sailor he had a sweetheart in every port of call. In every *placita* [small plaza] in the Pecos some little señorita was proud to be known as his *querida* [lover]."[60]

Although she later denied it, there is little doubt that Paulita was one of the Kid's favorite queridas. The Kid was linked romantically to other young women—Nasaria Yerby, Abrana Garcia, and Celsa Gutierrez, the sister of Pat Garrett's second wife—and supposedly fathered children with at least two of them. Yet many who knew Billy Bonney believed it was his love for Paulita that kept him in Fort Sumner and ultimately lured him to his death.[61]

Reward notice published May 3, 1881

THE BOB BOZE BELL COLLECTION,

TRUE WEST MAGAZINE

TWENTY-FOUR

EL CHIVATO

The Americans are certainly hero-worshippers and always take their
heroes from the outlaw classes.[1]

•

—OSCAR WILDE

THE KID STARTED off 1880 with a wallop. As he was buying drinks for some Chisum cowboys at Bob Hargrove's saloon in the old quartermaster's building at Fort Sumner ten days into the new year, a staggering drunk named Joe "Texas Red" Grant started making threats. He removed a pistol from the holster of one of the cowboys and put his own gun in its place.[2] When the Kid asked if he could take a look at the pearl-handled pistol, Grant handed it over. The Kid saw that three shots had been fired. He spun the cylinder so that the hammer would strike an empty chamber the next time it was fired, then gave the gun back to the drunk.

A little while later Grant got into an argument with Billy and made the mistake of drawing the gun when the Kid turned his back to leave. The Kid heard the hammer click on the empty chamber and whirled around. Quicker than a jackrabbit, Texas Red lay dead on the barroom floor with three bullets in his chin. One of the witnesses said a silver dollar would have covered the tight bullet pattern.

Grant's death was only the second murder that the Kid had unquestionably committed.[3] Unlike the aftermath of his first killing, that of Windy Cahill back in Arizona, the Kid was not worried about retribution. Most people chalked it up as just another saloon shooting. Asked about the incident, the Kid replied, "It was a game of two and I got there first."[4]

At this point, the Kid was spending a lot of his time in and around Fort Sumner. When he was not rustling cattle, dancing, or courting Paulita Maxwell, he often showed up to deal some monte or play a bit of poker at Beaver Smith's, the most popular drinking and gambling establishment in town. That is where he most likely first encountered Patrick Garrett, a trail driver and buffalo hunter from Texas who had moved to Fort Sumner in 1878.[5]

Almost six and a half feet tall in an age when men were typically a full foot shorter, Pat Garrett turned heads wherever he went. Women were drawn to the handsome mustachioed fellow with southern manners reflective of his native Alabama roots and upbringing on a Louisiana plantation. The Hispanics dubbed him Juan Largo, or Long John. Garrett loved all the attention.

In Fort Sumner he worked as a cowhand for Pete Maxwell long enough to have a disagreement with him and get fired. When Beaver Smith needed a barkeep at his place, Garrett took the job. Besides serving hard drinks and maintaining order at the saloon, he raised hogs on the side and partnered with Thomas "Kip" McKinney, a native Texan who had run with the Seven Rivers posse down in Lincoln County.

Controversy dogged Garrett most of his life. The story of his shooting another buffalo hunter named Joe Briscoe to death over a campfire argument made the rounds of Fort Sumner. So did rumors that Garrett was a fugitive from justice wanted in an earlier killing and that he had abandoned a wife and family in Texas.[6]

At some point, Garrett married Juanita Gutierrez, although the exact date and circumstances remain unclear, as does her death, which supposedly occurred only months after they wed.[7] If so, Garrett was a widower when he wed Apolonaria Gutierrez, presumably his late wife's sister, on January 14, 1880, just four days after the Kid plugged Joe Grant. The Garretts' nuptials in Anton Chico were a double ceremony that also joined Pat's trusted friend Barney Mason and his betrothed, Juanita Madril.[8]

In Fort Sumner, Garrett quietly took the stage as yet another actor in the ongoing drama of Billy the Kid. Depending on the audience, he functioned as both protagonist and antagonist. To this day that is how he is viewed. To some, Garrett was a hero, and for others he played the role of villain. Perhaps he was a combination of the two.

Neither Billy nor Garrett has been well served by books and films depicting them as bosom buddies. While Garrett, who rubbed shoulders with several law-breakers at the saloon, undoubtedly knew the Kid, stories that they rode together and stole cattle have never been proved, even by Garrett's diligent biographer.[9]

Certainly both of them frequented the same haunts in Fort Sumner and elsewhere, but the Kid ran with his closest chums, O'Folliard and Bowdre. In fact, the 1880 census for Fort Sumner, San Miguel County, records a William Bonny (*sic*) living under the same roof as Charles and Manuela Bowdre.[10] Besides the misspelled surname, some of the data given to the census taker appear to have come from someone other than the Kid. His age is given as twenty-five, his place of birth Missouri, and his parents are listed as Missouri natives. Next to occupation are the three words "working in cattle," which of course was at least partially true.[11]

In early 1880 (or late 1879) the Kid posed in Fort Sumner for what remains the only documented photographic image of him. More than likely, an itinerant photographer took it, using a multilens camera that simultaneously produced four two-by-three-inch ferrotypes, popularly called tintypes. Ferrotypes were easy to prepare. The photographer could have set up the shot, taken the image, developed it, varnished a ferrotype plate, and handed it to the Kid in only minutes at a cost of probably twenty-five cents.[12]

Like so much else about Billy Bonney, the faded and abused image is an icon that cannot be understood or explained. "I never liked the picture," Paulita Maxwell said in later years. "I don't think it does Billy justice."[13] The young man standing with head slightly tilted, Winchester at his side and gun belt riding high on his hip, is, despite Maxwell's misgivings, forever frozen in time.

While Billy stood for his portrait, Garrett, no longer content to slop hogs and tend bar for the rest of his life, considered his options. By 1880 he had caught the attention of the all-powerful cattle interests that were weary of losing their stock to thieves like the Kid and his lot. At the urging of John Chisum and Joseph Lea, a former Quantrill raider who had become a respectable citizen and huge land-owner, Garrett took on George Kimbrell and ran for sheriff of Lincoln County.[14] Dolan, by that time owner of both the Tunstall store and the ranch on the Rio Feliz, backed Garrett all the way, as did Boss Catron up in Santa Fe.

Garrett moved to Roswell so he would be eligible to run for office in Lincoln County. Both he and Kimbrell worked hard at courting voters, especially from the Hispanic community since both candidates were married to Hispanic women. Naturally, the Kid campaigned for Kimbrell because it was believed that the sheriff generally "turned a blind eye to the Kid's movements."[15]

On November 2, 1880, the citizens of Lincoln County turned out in big numbers, and as a result, they elected the striking Garrett. Although he would not officially take office until January 1881, Kimbrell straightaway made Garrett a deputy and Catron appointed him U.S. deputy marshal.[16] Later in November the Kid and some of his riders stole horses from Alexander Grzelachowski, a Polish merchant in Puerto de Luna and former Catholic priest, called Padre Polaco by everyone who traded at his store.[17] The Kid, Dave Rudabaugh, Billy Wilson, and other members of the gang sold some of the horses to Jim Greathouse at the ranch he owned with Fred Kuch on the road connecting Las Vegas and White Oaks.

Newly elected Deputy Sheriff Garrett assembled bands of armed men who went on the hunt throughout the county for the thieves. On November 27, a posse from White Oaks tracked the Kid and his boys back to the Greathouse-Kuch ranch, and a gun battle broke out. During a pause in the action an unarmed Jim Carlyle, a popular White Oaks blacksmith riding with the posse, voluntarily entered the house to discuss terms of surrender with the Kid. Nothing came of the talks, and when Carlyle leaped from a window in an escape attempt, he was shot and killed.[18] The standoff ended in a stalemate with each side blaming the other for his death. Most fingers pointed at the Kid, who vehemently denied shooting Carlyle.

The Kid's protest did not matter. Public sentiment, at least from the Anglo population, had begun to turn against Bonney and his men. As a result, the Kid was on the run, with Garrett posses numbering close to two hundred men in hot pursuit. But even more deadly than the armed riders chasing the Kid was the attack waged by J. H. Koogler, the indignant editor and publisher of the *Las Vegas Gazette*. In a stinging editorial on December 3, 1880, Koogler took the Kid and his men to task in no uncertain terms: "There's a powerful gang of outlaws harassing the stockmen of the Pecos and Panhandle country, and terrorizing the people of Fort Sumner and vicinity. The gang includes forty or fifty men, all hard characters, the off-scourings of society, fugitives from justice, and desperadoes by profession. . . . The gang is under the leadership of 'Billy *the* Kid,' a desperate cuss, who is eligible for the post of captain of any crowd, no matter how mean or lawless."[19]

What made this editorial exceptional was that it was the first time ever that Billy Bonney was referred to in print not just as the Kid but as Billy *the* Kid. The impact of inserting "the" between "Billy" and "Kid" was surprisingly powerful. Now people had a descriptive name that made Billy unique. Beyond the colorful nom de guerre, Koogler's steady stream of editorials exaggerated the Kid's activities and fabricated a reputation that he did not deserve. Also, the editorial broadsides, along with the letters Koogler wrote to Governor Wallace pushing for decisive action, had the effect of erasing any thoughts of amnesty for the Kid.

In hope of resurrecting his relationship with the governor, the Kid sent Wallace a letter protesting the bad publicity. "I noticed in the Las Vegas *Gazette* a piece which stated that Billy the Kid, the name by which I am known in the county, was the Captain of a Band of Outlaws who hold Forth on the Portales. There is no such organization in existence."[20]

The Kid went on to plead his case in a lengthy explanation of the Greathouse shoot-out. He explained that the posse shot and killed Carlyle when they mistook him for the Kid trying to escape. He also stated that Chisum was "the man who got me into trouble" and that Deputy Sheriff Garrett took his orders from Chisum.[21]

The Kid's words had no effect. Wallace had other thoughts on his mind. On November 12, Harper Brothers, a publishing house in New York, released Wallace's *Ben Hur: The Story of the Christ*. The novel was acclaimed by reviewers and the public and became an instant bestseller.[22] Content to hold forth at the Palace of the Governors and read his piles of fan mail, Wallace had given up on the Kid. He was not moved. Two days after getting the Kid's letter, Governor Wallace published a reward notice to be printed in newspapers throughout New Mexico Territory:

BILLY THE KID.
$500 REWARD.

I will pay $500 reward to any person or persons
who will capture William Bonny, alias The Kid, and
deliver him to any sheriff of New Mexico.
Satisfactory proofs of identity will be required.

LEW. WALLACE,
Governor of New Mexico.

The manhunt, sweetened by the promise of cash money, was now on in earnest. Garrett pulled together a posse composed of his best men and some Texas stock detectives and cowboys sent by the Panhandle Cattlemen's Association. They rummaged through the villages and ranches in search of the Kid. When information gathered by scouts and spies led the Garrett posse to Fort Sumner, they took over the old Indian hospital on the eastern side of the fort. Living in one of the many rooms was Charlie Bowdre's wife, Manuela, and her mother.

Word was that the Kid and his amigos were in hiding out at the Wilcox-Brazil Ranch east of town. Garrett figured if he could lure the Kid, Bowdre, and the others into Fort Sumner, they would head directly to check on Manuela, where the posse waited. He was right.

Garrett sent a local boy to the Kid with news that all was clear in Fort Sumner, that the Texans had gone home and the other posse men had ridden off for Roswell. Garrett's men, their horses out of sight in Pete Maxwell's stable, more than likely bound and gagged Manuela, built a fire, checked their weapons, and waited.

On the evening of December 19 there was a big moon, but a thick fog hung over the deep snow that covered the ground.[23] Posse lookouts spied dark figures in the distance and then heard horses' hooves muffled by the snow. Garrett and his men crept outside and took up firing positions.

Six riders approached: the Kid, Tom O'Folliard, Charlie Bowdre, Dave Rudabaugh, Billy Wilson, and Tom Pickett. When they drew closer, Garrett yelled, "Halt!" O'Folliard went for his sidearm, and a barrage of gunfire broke out.[24] The surprised riders wheeled about and dashed away through the snow into the darkness, but one horse lingered and came back at a slow walk. Hanging on the saddle was a badly wounded O'Folliard, shot through the chest. Garrett barked for him to throw up his hands, but he was only able to whisper, "Don't shoot[,] Garrett, I'm killed."[25]

They carried O'Folliard inside, laid him near the fire, and went back to playing poker. It was too dark and icy to pursue the other renegades until the morning.

Jim East, a member of the posse, later recalled that O'Folliard remained conscious and managed a few words. "God damn you[,] Garrett, I hope to meet you in hell," O'Folliard said.

"I wouldn't talk that way, Tom," Garrett replied, "you are going to die in a few minutes."

O'Folliard replied, "Go to hell, you long-legged son-of-a-bitch."

Shortly after the last exchange, O'Folliard groaned and asked East for some water. He took a sip, fell back on the blanket, shuddered some, and died.[26]

Garrett paid for a coffin, and the next day some villagers and members of the posse buried O'Folliard in the old military cemetery where Lucien Maxwell and other civilians had been laid to rest near the many soldiers' graves.

Garrett waited for a break after another heavy snowfall. The Kid and his four men back at the Wilcox-Brazil Ranch plotted their next move. The Kid, devastated by the loss of his best friend Tom O'Folliard, pleaded with Manuel Brazil to ride into Fort Sumner to find out Garrett's plans. A fearful Brazil complied, but instead of helping the Kid, he reported directly to Garrett and told him where the outlaws were hiding.[27]

In the early hours of December 23, Garrett's men surrounded an abandoned one-room stone house at Stinking Springs on Taiban Creek about five miles east of the Wilcox-Brazil house. Garrett told the posse that the Kid often wore a Mexican sugarloaf hat and that if they saw him, they should "cut down and kill him."[28]

They dug in and waited for daybreak, and when first light broke, a man wearing a sombrero came outside, carrying feed for the tethered horses. Garrett was convinced it was the Kid. He ordered his men to open fire, and a ring of Winchesters exploded. The man, mortally wounded, staggered inside. It was not the Kid but Charlie Bowdre. The dying Bowdre then staggered outside (some posse members said he was pushed by the Kid) and fell over dead. Garrett later checked the body and found a bloodstained ferrotype of a heavily armed Bowdre and his wife that had been taken a short time before in Las Vegas.[29]

The four men trapped inside the rock cabin had no place to hide or run. When he saw the Kid trying to pull one of the horses inside, probably for a breakout, Garrett shot the animal, and it fell, blocking the entrance. For most of the day the Kid and Garrett bantered back and forth and exchanged a few slurs. Finally the aroma of cooked bacon and beans that Brazil brought the posse did the trick. The Kid and the others surrendered.[30]

The four outlaws were taken to Brazil's ranch house for the night. The next morning, Christmas Eve, the lawmen with their captives and the dead Bowdre in a wagon struck out for Fort Sumner. There they were met by what was described as "a deranged and lamenting" Manuela Bowdre, who "kicked and pummeled Pat Garrett until she had to be pulled away."[31] Jim East and another man carried Bowdre into her room in the old hospital, and as they did, Manuela bashed East over the head with a branding iron. Garrett ponied up for a new suit of clothes for Bowdre, as he had done with O'Folliard, and he also picked up the burial cost.[32]

Deluvina Maxwell, a Navajo servant who had been taken captive by Apaches as a girl and traded to Lucien Maxwell for ten horses, was especially fond of the

Kid. She requested that Garrett allow the Kid to say his farewell to Paulita Maxwell.[33] He agreed—it was Christmas Eve after all—and told East and Lee Hall to accompany the Kid to the old officers' quarters that served as the Maxwell family home. Dave Rudabaugh, who was shackled to the Kid, had no choice but to go along.

Doña Luz Maxwell, Paulita's mother, asked the deputies to remove the shackles so the Kid and her daughter could have a private moment, but her request was denied. East later described how the Kid and his querida embraced, and "she gave Billy one of those soul kisses the novelists tell us about, till it was time to hit the road for Vegas, we had to pull them apart, much against our wishes, for you know, all the world loves a lover."[34]

That afternoon the party, including a wagonload of shackled prisoners, left Fort Sumner for Las Vegas. After spending the night on the road at John Gerhardt's ranch, they got to Puerto de Luna on Christmas Day in time for a festive roast wild turkey dinner at the Grzelachowski store and home.[35] The men ate in two shifts, and Padre Polaco made sure everyone, including the shackled diners who recently had stolen horses from him, had plenty to eat.

When they arrived in Las Vegas on December 26, both Pat Garrett and the Kid were the talk of the town. Many people wanted to buy Garrett and his men drinks, but the Kid, now that he had a price on his head, was also big news. Crowds clamored to catch a glimpse of him being transported to jail. The Kid relished all the attention. The next morning, just after he and the other prisoners were presented with new suits of clothes, the Kid obliged a reporter from the Las Vegas Gazette with a jailhouse interview.[36]

"You appear to be taking it easy," the reporter told the Kid.

"What's the use of looking on the gloomy side of everything?" responded the Kid. "The laugh's on me this time." Then, looking around, he asked if the jail at Santa Fe was better than the one at Las Vegas. He also spoke of the big crowd "gazing at me" and suggested that "perhaps some of them will think me half man now; everyone seemed to think I was some kind of animal."

The reporter agreed that the Kid was no animal and described him as "quite a handsome looking fellow" who looked "human, indeed, but there was nothing very mannish about his appearance, for he looked and acted like a mere boy."

The following day the reporter showed up again at the train depot before the prisoners departed for Santa Fe. A crowd of onlookers had turned menacing. They wanted the blood of Dave Rudabaugh, often called Dirty Dave because of his poor hygiene. Earlier in 1880, before he hooked up with the Kid, Rudabaugh had killed

Las Vegas Deputy Lino Valdez while trying to break a convicted killer out of jail.[37] The local sheriff wanted Garrett to surrender Rudabaugh to him for trial, and the angry mob was ready to march him to the windmill in the plaza for a neck stretching.

Garrett finally was able to appease all sides and leave town with all his prisoners, but before that happened, the Kid leaned out of the window of his train car and casually visited with the reporter. "I don't blame you for writing of me as you have," the Kid said. "You had to believe other stories; but then I don't know as any one would believe anything good of me anyway. I wasn't the leader of any gang— I was for Billy all the time."[38]

The *Santa Fe New Mexican* warmly welcomed the newest residents upon their arrival, which the newspaper explained "created a good deal of excitement and Sheriff Garrett is the hero of the hour."[39]

On New Year's Day 1881, the Kid sent a letter to Governor Wallace from the Santa Fe jail on Water Street, just a short distance from the Plaza and the Palace of the Governors. The one-sentence letter read: "I would like to see you for a few moments if you can spare the time."[40]

Wallace could not spare any time. He was not even in town. He was back East, basking in his literary glory. Just before Christmas the first edition of *Ben Hur* sold out and Harper Brothers scrambled to get more books in print.[41] The Kid's request went unanswered. So did the other three letters he sent Wallace asking for his help over the course of three months before being taken to Mesilla to stand trial for the murders of Buckshot Roberts and Sheriff Brady. The Kid became desperate. He looked for good legal counsel and in a more drastic move planned a jail escape. He started digging a tunnel beneath the cell wall, but it was quickly discovered, and the Kid and his mates ended up in irons and under constant guard.[42]

On March 4, the day the Kid sent his third letter to Governor Wallace, the inauguration of President James Garfield took place in the nation's capital. Just five days later Wallace tendered his letter of resignation to Garfield, who formally accepted it on March 17 and appointed Lionel A. Shelton of Ohio as the new governor of New Mexico Territory. Several weeks later, when a reporter told him that the Kid "appears to look to you to save his neck," Wallace said, smiling, "Yes, but I can't see how a fellow like him should expect any clemency from me."[43]

On March 28, the day after sending his fourth and final plea for help to Wallace, the Kid and Billy Wilson, who was charged with counterfeiting, robbery, and rape, were escorted under heavy guard from the jail to the train depot. When the tracks stopped at the settlement of Rincon, the prisoners were locked in a saloon overnight and the next day spent nine hours with their guards in a cramped stage bound for Mesilla.[44]

Presiding at the court proceedings in the Third Territorial District Court was Judge Warren Bristol, an ardent foe of everyone the Kid ever respected, especially Tunstall and McSween. The Kid was arraigned in Mesilla on March 30 before Judge Bristol in the murder of Buckshot Roberts at Blazer's Mill. The Kid entered a plea of not guilty. All others named in the killing, such as Charlie Bowdre, had either been killed or could not be found. When the Kid told the judge he did not have a red cent to hire a lawyer, Ira Leonard was appointed his defense counsel. Leonard did a decent job of proving that Roberts was not killed on federal land as charged and therefore there was no federal jurisdiction. On April 6 the indictment was quashed, and Bristol had to dismiss the charge.[45]

Two days later the Kid's trial for the Brady murder commenced. The prosecuting attorney was Simon Newcomb, who had succeeded his good friend William Rynerson as district attorney.[46] The actual trial was a mere formality since the Kid had already been tried and found guilty in most of the newspapers that served the Santa Fe Ring and its network.

For this proceeding, Leonard was replaced, and Bristol appointed John Bail and Albert Jennings Fountain as the Kid's new legal representatives.[47] Fountain was a well-known and respected figure dating back to his days as a newspaper editor when he crusaded against Jesse Evans and the infamous banditti. However, neither of the two lawyers was acquainted with the Kid, nor did they know very much about Lincoln County.

On April 9, after just two days of testimony from a few prosecution witnesses and hearing arguments, both sides rested. Judge Bristol gave such narrow instructions in his charge to the jury that they had no choice but to return a predictable verdict. After a short deliberation, the jury came back with a verdict of guilty in the first-degree murder of William Brady and assessed the death penalty as the Kid's punishment.[48]

For the very first time in his brief but violent life the Kid had been tried and found guilty. Among the more than fifty individuals indicted for crimes in the Lincoln County War, only the Kid was ever convicted.[49]

On April 13, the now-notorious young man was brought back to the courtroom for formal sentencing. The Kid knew that the judge would show no mercy. The Kid offered no words to the court. He stood before the bench and listened to Bristol proclaim that "the said William Bonney, alias Kid, alias William Antrim, be hanged by the neck until his body be dead."[50] Sheriff Garrett in Lincoln was to carry out the sentence in May on Friday the thirteenth. "I expect to be lynched in going to Lincoln," the Kid told a reporter after his sentence was pronounced. "Advise person never to engage in killing."[51]

Concerned that some of the Kid's friends might try a rescue attempt, seven heavily armed guards were assigned the task of returning the condemned man to Lincoln. The Kid, shackled and handcuffed, was placed in a wagon. He was escorted by Deputy U.S. Marshal Robert Olinger, Deputy Sheriff Dave Woods, and five other special deputies, including Billy Mathews and John Kinney, the territory's most successful cattle rustler.[52]

After an uneventful journey to Lincoln, the Kid was housed in a northeast corner room on the second story of the old Murphy-Dolan store known as The House.[53] It had since been sold by Boss Catron and converted into the county courthouse with jail facilities on the top floor. Garrett made sure that the Kid was housed away from the other prisoners. He assigned Bob Olinger and Deputy James W. Bell to guard the Kid around the clock and keep him handcuffed and his legs shackled. Bell was a pleasant man and treated the Kid with respect. Olinger was a different story. He was a bully described as "two hundred pounds of bone and muscle, six feet tall, round as a huge tree trunk, with a regular gorilla-like chest that bulged out so far his chin seemed to set back on his chest."[54] It was no secret that he hated the Kid and blamed him for the death of Olinger's friend Bob Beckwith at the McSween shoot-out. Every chance he got, Olinger prodded and tormented the Kid.

After just a week of confinement in Lincoln, a routine had developed. Sam Wortley sent the Kid's meals to the courthouse while the five other prisoners were taken to the hotel to eat. The Kid carefully observed the habits of his guards and on April 28 he made his move. That day Garrett had ridden over to White Oaks to collect some taxes or, as some believe, to buy lumber for a gallows.[55]

At about five o'clock in the evening, Olinger walked the five prisoners to the hotel for supper, leaving Bell to watch over the Kid. There are many theories about what happened next, but it seems likely that the Kid asked Bell to take him out back to use the privy. The Kid either found a gun concealed for him inside the privy or had somehow procured a weapon by the time the two men returned to the courthouse.[56] However he had become armed, once the Kid got to the top of the sixteen stairs leading to the second floor, he turned on Bell and struck him in the head with the heavy handcuffs. When the stunned Bell tried to escape, the Kid fired twice. One of the bullets smashed into the wall and the other struck Bell, who staggered out into the yard and fell dead at the feet of Gottfried Gauss, the old ranch cook who now lived behind the courthouse where he worked as a caretaker.[57]

Gauss ran screaming for help. The Kid dashed into Garrett's office and grabbed Olinger's ten-gauge shotgun. He hopped in his shackles to the room in the northeast corner and threw open a window. Olinger, who had heard the gunshots, ran from the hotel across the road to the courthouse. As Olinger approached the building, the Kid took aim with the shotgun cocked. "Hello, Bob," the Kid said, firing both barrels just as Olinger looked up at the window.[58] Thirty-six buckshot found their mark and the bullying Olinger was dead before his body slammed to the ground.

The Kid did not take flight right away. He had Gauss fetch a pickax, which he used to knock the shackles off one of his legs. Out on the balcony overlooking the road, the Kid addressed the crowd below and explained that he had not meant to kill Bell, or for that matter anyone else, but that he would kill anyone who tried to prevent his escape. He grabbed several weapons and ordered Gauss to bring him a horse. The old man went to the corral and saddled a horse owned by Billy Burt, the deputy court clerk.[59]

Billy mounted the spirited pony, but it spooked and bucked him off. He ordered one of the prisoners to get the horse back and he remounted. He promised to send back the pony. Some people in Lincoln that evening said that as the Kid rode off, he was singing.[60]

"Billy the Kid's defining moment was when, against all odds, he escaped from the Lincoln County jail," writes author and artist Bob Boze Bell. "That was the event that really catapulted him into history and folklore."[61]

The Kid's escape spawned hundreds of news stories and pulp articles recounting his bloodthirsty exploits and criminal outrages. Although the slain Olinger and Bell brought the Kid's proven murder count to four, most people believed he had killed at least twenty or more white men and an untold number of Mexicans and Indians. The Las Vegas Daily Optic called him "the daredevil desperado" and a "young demon" whose name "has long been the synonym of all that is malignant and cruel."[62]

While the Anglo establishment and power brokers aided and abetted by sensationalist journalists and dime novelists propagated the demonic Billy the Kid, many in the Hispanic community cheered him as their hero. To them he was not a ruthless killer. He was their El Chivato, their little Billy, a champion of the poor and oppressed. He became both the ultimate underdog and a true social bandit, a Robin Hood of the West. He was a freedom fighter out to halt manifest destiny. He was not afraid to tangle with the big cattle ranchers and politicians in Santa Fe who, in their quest for statehood and more power, had to bring El Chivato to justice to show that law and order had come to New Mexico Territory.

His many Hispanic friends did not view him as a ruthless killer but rather as a defender of the people who was forced to kill in self-defense. In the time that the Kid roamed the land he chided Hispanic villagers who were fearful of standing up against the big ranchers who stole their land, water, and way of life. It was said that El Chivato told them:

> *Oh timid Mexicans don't be afraid.*
> *Listen to the sound of the bullets,*
> *The bullets of those gringos say:*
> *chee chee cha ree*
> *If you don't kill me, I shall kill thee*[63]

"He connected with the people, it's just that simple," explained James Sanchez, a local citizen, almost 125 years after the Kid died.[64] "The people trusted him and invited him into their homes. He was one of us." Sanchez, born in 1941 into an old Lincoln County family, grew up in a household where stories of El Chivato were told. "He was against the big guys, the outsiders who tried to take our property, our rights, and everything we had. Mostly there was a fear of losing the land. That's a fear that is still very real today. You have to put your life on the line. People still die protecting their land."

The Kid appeared to show no fear when, instead of heading for old Mexico after he escaped from the Lincoln County jail, he remained in familiar New Mexico Territory. Pat Garrett was more surprised than anyone that the Kid did not leave. Just a day after he headed west out of Lincoln, the horse he had borrowed for his getaway returned to Lincoln, dragging a rope halter.

The Kid rode over the Capitan Mountains and stayed with several Hispanic friends including Yginio Salazar, one of his oldest compadres in Lincoln County. Salazar and all the others the Kid encountered as he rode tried to convince him to leave the territory. The Kid chose not to leave. He stayed even after Wallace posted another five-hundred-dollar reward for the Kid's capture before departing to take a new job as U.S. ambassador to Turkey.[65]

May soon passed into June, and then July, and still the Kid remained on the lam. Pat Garrett heard rumors that the Kid was back in Fort Sumner, but he wrote it off as hearsay. Finally some reliable tips were passed on that the Kid was indeed living in the Fort Sumner area once again, moving between sheepherder camps and spending time in town at the Maxwell house with Paulita or one of his other girlfriends. Garrett and his two best deputies, John W. Poe, a former lawman from Texas, and Thomas "Kip" McKinney, discussed paying a visit to Fort Sumner.[66] Even the shocking news of the July 2 shooting of President Garfield did not derail the lawmen.

A week later, as President Garfield fought for his life in far-off Washington, Pat Garrett and his deputies departed Roswell and rode north. They made camp near Fort Sumner on July 13, unaware that newspapers had been reporting sightings of Billy the Kid as far away as Denver and on the Red River between Texas and Indian Territory.[67]

On July 14, 1881, John Poe was snooping around the plaza in Fort Sumner, but learned nothing about the Kid or his whereabouts. At moonrise Poe rendezvoused with Garrett and McKinney, and they slipped into Fort Sumner to have yet another unsuccessful look for the Kid. Then Garrett had a hunch, perhaps based on gossip from his wife, Apolonaria, that had been passed on by her sister Celsa, one of the Kid's girlfriends. If the women's whispers were true, Paulita Maxwell was pregnant with the Kid's child.[68]

As historian Frederick Nolan later theorized, the Kid would have been told or maybe guessed about Paulita's condition during their Christmas meeting after he was captured at Stinking Springs. If true, according to Nolan, "this was the reason the Kid had gone to Sumner, this the reason he was still there."[69]

A little after nine o'clock on a warm July evening, the three lawmen made their way on foot to a peach orchard near the Maxwell house. They stayed put for a long time, in hopes that the Kid would show up to pay a visit to Paulita. After a while the trio slowly moved toward the building when they heard voices speaking in Spanish and realized they were not alone in the orchard.

"Soon a man rose from the ground in full view, but too far away to recognize," Garrett later recalled. "He wore a broad-brimmed hat, a dark vest and pants, and was in his shirt sleeves."[70] The figure jumped over the picket fence and disappeared inside the compound.

It was almost midnight when the lawmen slowly crept out of the orchard and edged their way through the shadows to the white picket fence that encircled the

Maxwell house. They entered through the gate and stood on the porch near Pete Maxwell's bedroom at the southeastern corner of the big adobe. Garrett told the two deputies to wait while he went inside to ask Maxwell if he had seen the Kid. Poe sat on the edge of the steps and McKinney squatted nearby. Garrett entered Maxwell's room and sat near the head of Pete's bed.

As Garrett sat on the bed, waiting in Maxwell's room, the Kid gave in to his hunger pangs. He picked up a butcher knife in Celsa's kitchen and walked outside to cut some meat from a freshly slaughtered yearling hanging from a beam on Maxwell's porch. The Kid had taken off his sombrero and boots and as he shuffled down the porch in his stocking feet, the two deputies saw him. Poe later said The Kid was bareheaded and seemed to be buttoning his trousers as he walked. In the dark, Poe thought it was either Maxwell or one of his guests.[71]

Suddenly the Kid spotted Poe and McKinney and was startled. He pulled the .41-caliber Colt Thunderer from his waistband and covered the deputies, hissing at them, "*¿Quién es?* [Who is it?]" As he backed toward Maxwell's door, he repeated, "*¿Quién es? ¿Quién es?*"

Poe rose to his feet and began walking toward Billy with the idea of keeping him occupied, but the Kid backed into Maxwell's room. Garrett who had been in the room for a while had just managed to awaken Maxwell and was asking about the Kid when they were interrupted by a voice. "*¿Pedro, quiénes son esos hombres afuera?* [Pete, who are those men outside?]" At the same time, the Kid must have suddenly realized someone else was in the room. "*¿Quién es?*" he asked, and then in English, "Who is it?"

Maxwell whispered, "*El es* [It's him]," to Garrett.

Garrett yanked out his gun and fired twice. He was ready to fire a third time when he heard a groan and knew his first shots had hit their mark.

Henry McCarty lay dead on the floor. The endless ride of Billy the Kid had just begun.

Painting by Buckeye Blake

EPILOGUE
BILLY'S NEVER-ENDING RIDE

Billy the Kid just keeps riding across the dreamscape of our minds—
silhouetted against a starlit Western sky, handsome, laughing, deadly.
Shrewd as the coyote. Free as the hawk. The outlaw of our dreams, forever
free, forever free, forever riding.[1]

•

—PAUL HUTTON

As SOON AS Pat Garrett fired the second bullet from his .44 Colt, he and Pete Maxwell, uncertain who had been shot, rushed from the bedroom. All was silent and gun smoke hung in the dark room as Maxwell fetched a lighted candle and placed it on the windowsill. Garrett and his deputies peered in the window at a body lying on the floor. They went inside and saw that it was the Kid, felled by the first shot, which had struck him just above his heart.

A crowd quickly gathered outside the Maxwell house. It was said that a distraught Deluvina Maxwell, the servant woman who ministered to the Kid, sobbed uncontrollably. She hit Garrett's chest with her fists and snarled, "You pisspot! You son of a bitch!"[2] Some of the women consoled Paulita Maxwell, the Kid's best sweetheart and the primary reason he had remained in New Mexico. Fearful of reprisal, Garrett and the deputies took refuge inside the house for the rest of the night. The Kid's friends kept vigil over his body while they recited prayers.

The next morning a coroner's jury convened and ruled that the Kid's death was justifiable homicide. His body was carried to a carpenter shop in the old quartermaster's building and laid on a workbench. The women carefully washed the corpse, combed the Kid's hair, and stuffed a rag into the exit wound in his back. A white shirt Pete Maxwell donated for a shroud was too large and had to be pinned up before the Kid could be laid in the coffin surrounded by lit candles.[3] In the afternoon, a somber procession followed the wagon carrying the coffin to nearby Fort Sumner cemetery and a freshly dug grave. There the Kid was laid to rest near his compadres Tom O'Folliard and Charlie Bowdre.

News of the Kid's death flashed around the world. Even the *Illustrated London News* ran a summary of his life and times. The *New York Daily Graphic* reported that the Kid "had built up a criminal organization worthy of the underworld in any of the European capitals." One of the more sensational obituaries appeared in the *Santa Fe Weekly Democrat*: "No sooner had the floor caught the descending form, which had a pistol in one hand and a knife in the other, than there was a strong odor of brimstone in the air, and a dark figure with the wings of a dragon, claws like a tiger, eyes like balls of fire, and horns like a bison, hovered over the corpse for a moment, and with a fiendish laugh said. 'Ha! Ha! This is my meat!' and then sailed off through the window. He did not leave his card, but he is a gentleman well known by reputation, and there by hangs a 'tail.' "[4]

Dime novels about the Kid, including Garrett's ghostwritten book, began sprouting in 1881. Since then hundreds of books about the Kid have been published, and it seems a safe wager that hundreds more are yet to come. Sometimes the Kid is presented as a hero and sometimes as a villain.

No matter how the story is told, Billy the Kid lives on. Whether he is described as El Chivato, champion of the oppressed, or a Satanic psychopath, he remains irrepressible, mysterious, and lethal.

His ride across our popular imagination will never end.

NOTES

ONE • ONCE UPON A TIME

1. Frederick Nolan, *The West of Billy the Kid* (Norman: University of Oklahoma Press, 1998), p. 3.
2. Robert M. Utley, *Billy the Kid: A Short and Violent Life* (Lincoln and London: University of Nebraska Press, 1989), p. 1.
3. Nolan, pp. 3–4.
4. Utley, p. 2.
5. Ibid.
6. Philip J. Rasch, with Allan Radbourne, *Trailing Billy the Kid* (Laramie: National Association for Outlaw and Lawman History, Inc., in affiliation with the University of Wyoming, 1995), p. 153. Prior to 1855 and the opening of the Castle Garden center on the southwestern tip of Manhattan Island in Battery Park, passengers, including immigrants, simply got off the ship at whichever wharf they had landed.
7. Terry Golway, *The Irish in America* (New York: Hyperion, 1997), p. 4.
8. Ibid., p. 21.
9. Source information: Ancestry.com, *Irish Immigrants: New York Port Arrival Records, 1846–1851* (database online). Provo, Utah: Ancestry.com, 2001. Original data: *Famine Irish Entry Project, 1845–1851.* Electronic database from the National Archives and Records Administration, Washington, D.C.
10. Source information: Ancestry.com, *1850 United States Federal Census* (database online). Provo, Utah: MyFamily.com, Inc., 2004. Original data: *1850 United States Federal Census.* M432, 1009 rolls. National Archives and Records Administration, Washington, D.C.
11. Utley, p. 2.
12. Bob Boze Bell, interview by author in Cave Creek, Arizona, November 4, 2004. Bell points out that November 23 became the preferred date because Pat Garrett's ghostwriter, Marshall Ashmun Upson, chose his own birth date (same day but different year) as the day Billy was born in New York City. Many researchers conclude that November 23 is highly suspect.
13. Source information: Ancestry.com, *Irish Immigrants: New York Port Arrival Records, 1846–1851* (database online). Provo, Utah: Ancestry.com, 2001. Original data: *Famine Irish Entry Project, 1845–1851.* Electronic database from the National Archives and Records Administration, Washington, D.C.

14. Ancestry.com, *1850 United States Federal Census* (database online). Provo, Utah: MyFamily .com, Inc., 2004. Original data: *1850 United States Federal Census.* M432, 1009 rolls. National Archives and Records Administration, Washington, D.C.

15. Rasch, pp. 154, 159, 162.

16. Herbert Asbury, *The Gangs of New York: An Informal History of the Underworld* (New York: Alfred A. Knopf, 1927, 1928), p. 158. The term "the modern Gomorrah" was used by the Reverend T. DeWitt Talmage in a sermon delivered in the Brooklyn Tabernacle in the mid-1870s.

17. Ibid., p. 110.

18. Ibid., p. 9.

19. Ibid., pp. 96–97.

20. Alfred Connable and Edward Silberfarb, *Tigers of Tammany: Nine Men Who Ran New York* (New York: Holt, Rinehart and Winston, 1967), p. 139.

21. Howard Zinn, *A People's History of the United States: 1492 to Present,* rev. and updated (New York: Harper Perennial, 1995), p. 230.

22. Connable and Silberfarb, p. 142.

23. Asbury, p. 154. Some historians have challenged these figures while others contend they are conservative estimates.

24. Eric Foner and John A. Garraty, eds., *The Reader's Companion to American History* (Boston: Houghton Mifflin Company, 1991), p. 1091. Tweed was born and bred in a Fourth Ward tenement.

25. Ibid., p. 171. The Tweed Ring reportedly spent $13 million to construct a courthouse originally estimated to cost $250,000, prompting a prominent reformer to observe that the building's cornerstone "was conceived in sin, and its dome, if ever finished, will be glazed over with iniquity."

26. Ibid., p. 238.

27. The sordid nature of life in the New York tenements was exposed by Jacob A. Riis in the 1890 tome *How the Other Half Lives,* published by Charles Scribner's Sons.

28. Asbury, p. 208.

Two • On the Trail

1. Quoted in Stan Steiner, *The Waning of the West* (New York: St. Martin's Press, 1989), p. 253. Not to be confused with Frederick Jackson Turner, the noted nineteenth-century historian, Frederick W. Turner is a southwestern author and essayist. His testimonial about the American West appears in Steiner's book.

2. Frederick Nolan, a careful researcher, points out in the endnotes of his *The West of Billy the Kid* (Norman: University of Oklahoma Press, 1998) that within days of the Kid's death in 1881 several newspapers across the nation reported that he was born in New York. According to Nolan, "It is hardly surprising, then, that so many people 'knew' the kid was born in New York. . . ."

3. Nora Henn, interview with author, Lincoln, New Mexico, November 20, 2004. A longtime resident of Lincoln, New Mexico, Nora and her late husband, Walter Henn, a distinguished artist, were charter members of the Lincoln County Historical Society. They were also instrumental in the success of many important Lincoln County historic preservation projects.

4. Philip J. Rasch, with Allan Radbourne, *Trailing Billy the Kid* (Laramie: National Association for Outlaw and Lawman History, Inc., in affiliation with the University of Wyoming, 1995), p. 155.

5. Waldo E. Koop, *Billy the Kid: The Trail of a Kansas Legend* (Wichita: Kansas City Posse of the Westerners, 1965), p. 9.

6. Ibid., p. 10.

7. Ibid.

8. Ibid.

9. Ibid.

Stephen Tatum, *Inventing Billy the Kid* (Tucson: University of Arizona Press, 1997), p. 18.

10. Koop, p. 10.

Private Michael McCarty's service records.

S. P. Kaler and R. H. Manning, *History of Whitley County, Indiana* (Indianapolis: B. F. Bowen & Co., 1907), p. 218.

11. Koop, p. 10.

12. Ibid.

13. Ibid.

14. Don Cline, *Antrim & Billy* (College Station, Texas: Creative Publishing Company, 1990), pp. 14–17.

15. Ibid., p. 19.

Source information: United States National Archives, *Civil War Compiled Military Service Records* (database online). Provo, Utah: Ancestry.com, 1999.

16. Cline, p. 19.

Source information: Hoosiersoldiers.com.

17. Cline, p. 19.

18. Koop, p. 9.

19. Ibid., p. 8.

20. Ibid., p. 9.

21. Ibid.

22. Ibid.

23. Ibid., p. 6.

Three · Wichita

1. William G. Cutler, *History of the State of Kansas* (Chicago: A. T. Andreas' Western Historical Publishing Co., 1882–1883).

2. Frederick Nolan, *The West of Billy the Kid* (Norman: University of Oklahoma Press, 1998), p. 9. The federal census for Sedgwick County was completed on June 27, 1870.

3. Cutler. This book, originally published by subscription, is available online because of the efforts of Early Kansas Imprint Scanners (EKIS) and Kansas Collection (KanColl) volunteers. Cutler's text appeared in *Voices*, KanColl's Online magazine, vol. 3, no. 1 (Spring 1999).

   The Empire House opened in May 1870 on the corner of Third and Lane streets. Other hotels soon followed.

4. Cutler. The murder of John Ross, along with that of an unnamed hired man, occurred in October 1860.

5. John Rossel, "The Chisholm Trail," *Kansas Historical Quarterly*, vol. 5, no. 1 (February 1936), pp. 3–14. The trail did not become known as the Chisholm Trail until after its extensive use by cattlemen. Rossel points out that Chisholm laid out a trail not for the cattle trade but for his own private business. However, the cattle trade made it famous.

6. Stan Hoig, *Jesse Chisholm: Ambassador of the Plains* (Niwot: University Press of Colorado, 1991), p. 159.

7. Genevieve Yost, "History of Lynchings in Kansas," *Kansas Historical Quarterly*, vol. 2, no. 2 (May 1933), pp. 182–219. The thieves were hanged on May 19, 1870.

8. George A. Root, "Ferries in Kansas, Part IX—Arkansas River: Concluded," *Kansas Historical Quarterly*, vol. 5, no. 2 (May 1936), pp. 180–90. By 1871 work had begun on a river bridge that became operational in the spring of 1872.

9. Data provided by the Historic Preservation Alliance of Wichita and Sedgwick County and the Kansas State Historical Society, Topeka. Greiffenstein was mayor of Wichita in 1878 and again from 1880 to 1884. He earned the title Father of Wichita.

10. Cutler. A herd of bison grazing southwest of what became Dodge City, Kansas, in 1871 was estimated to number more than four million.

11. Ibid. Further information about early Wichita schools can be found in a book compiled by Kansas educators and published under the auspices of the Kansas State Historical Society: *The Columbian History of Education in Kansas* (Topeka: Hamilton Printing Company, 1893), pp. 199–203.

12. Cutler. The first school in Sedgwick County was a subscription school held in the winter of 1869–1870. The first school building was not erected until 1871, when voters passed a five-thousand-dollar bond issue. Neither Henry nor Joseph McCarty is listed among the scholars to attend the first school. More than likely, Catherine McCarty home-schooled her sons.

13. *Wichita Weekly Eagle*, August 18, 1881.

14. Nolan, pp. 10–11.

15. Ibid.

16. Ibid.

17. Waldo E. Koop, *Billy the Kid: The Trail of a Kansas Legend* (Wichita: Kansas City Posse of the Westerners, 1965), pp. 7–8.

18. Ibid., pp. 6–7.

19. Ibid.

20. *Wichita Tribune*, March 15, 1871.

21. Koop, p. 7.

22. Ibid., p. 8.

23. Ibid.

24. Ibid., pp. 7–8.

25. Ibid.

26. Becky Tanner, "Early Wichita Helped Put 'Wild' in the Old West," *Wichita Eagle*, June 19, 2004. This article was one of a yearlong series of historical vignettes entitled "To the Stars: The Story of Kansas." The series marked the 150 years since Kansas became a U.S. territory.

27. Ibid.

Four • Brotherhood of the Gun

1. W. Eugene Hollon, *Frontier Violence: Another Look* (New York: Oxford University Press, 1974), p. x.

2. Waldo E. Koop, *Billy the Kid: The Trail of a Kansas Legend* (Wichita: Kansas City Posse of the Westerners, 1965), p. 12.

    Wichita Vidette, October 13, 1870.

3. Ibid.

    Sources include Report of the Adjutant General of the State of Kansas, 1861–65, transcribed and published online by the Museum of the Kansas National Guard.

4. Wichita got a new jail, paid for with poll and dog taxes, the following year. The *Wichita Tribune* of June 22, 1871, noted: "Our saloon keepers sell the drinks, and the next week Marshal Megher will be ready to cell the drinker—in the new calaboose."

5. Koop, p. 12.

6. Ibid.

7. Volney P. Mooney, *History of Butler County* (Lawrence, Kan.: Standard Printing Co., 1916), pp. 250–61, transcribed by Carolyn Ward, Columbus, Kansas. The killings in Butler County took place in November 1870.

8. Koop, p. 12.

9. *Walnut Valley Times*, March 3, 1871. The article was titled "Horrible Affair at Wichita."

10. Ibid.

11. Ibid.

12. Ibid. Ledford did not have his own pistols with him when the posse arrived. He was forced to grab two pistols described as "old and rusty" as he ran through the saloon to hide in the privy.

13. Nyle H. Miller and Joseph W. Snell, *Why the West Was Wild: A Contemporary Look at the*

Antics of Some Highly Publicized Kansas Cowtown Personalities (Norman: University of Oklahoma Press, 1963), p. 45.

14. Ibid., pp. 44–47.

15. Ibid., p. 47. This story was also printed in the *Ford County Globe* on July 25, 1882. The *Dodge City Times* published a vigorous defense of Bridges on July 27 and branded as "scurrilous" the *Caldwell Commercial* editorial by W. B. Hutchison.

16. Koop, pp. 12–13.

17. Hollon, p. 109.

18. Russ A. Pritchard, Jr., *Civil War Weapons and Equipment* (Guilford, Conn.: Lyons Press, 2003), pp. 52–54.

19. Geoffrey Ward, with Ric Burns and Ken Burns, *The Civil War* (New York: Vintage Books, 1994), p. xii. More than three million Americans fought in the war, and 2 percent of the population died.

20. Ibid.

21. Michael Bellesiles, *Arming America: The Origins of a National Gun Culture* (Brooklyn, N.Y.: Soft Skull Press, 2003), p. 429.

22. Ibid., p. 434.

23. Eric T. Dean, Jr., *Shook over Hell: Post-Traumatic Stress, Vietnam, and the Civil War* (Cambridge, Mass., and London: Harvard University Press, 1997), pp. 98, 102.

24. Ibid., p. 99.

25. Hollon, pp. 115–16.

26. Garry Wills, *A Necessary Evil: A History of American Distrust of Government* (New York: Simon & Schuster, 2002), p. 243.

27. Ibid., p. 247.

28. Ibid.

29. Bellesiles, p. 437.

   Hollon, p. 106.

   Joseph G. Rosa, *The Gunfighter: Man or Myth?* (Norman: University of Oklahoma Press, 1969), p. 5.

30. Edward W. Wood, Jr., *Beyond the Weapons of Our Fathers* (Golden, Colo.: Fulcrum Publishing, 2002), p. 12.

31. Rosa, p. 5.

32. According to Rosa, the origin of the word "gunfighter" is obscure. Some sources state the term was not commonly used until the late 1890s. The legendary Bat Masterson used the word in articles he wrote in 1908.

Five • Contagious War

1. Dale Keiger, "Why Metaphor Matters," *Johns Hopkins Magazine* (February 1998).

2. Waldo E. Koop, *Billy the Kid: The Trail of a Kansas Legend* (Wichita: Kansas City Posse of the Westerners, 1965), p. 13.

3. Keith Wheeler, *The Townsmen* (New York: Time-Life Books, 1975), p. 32.

4. Ibid.

5. Old Cowtown Museum, Wichita; Kansas State Historical Society, Topeka; Historic Preservation Alliance of Wichita and Sedgwick County.

   E. B. Allen, who started his medical practice in 1870, is considered Wichita's first physician. He also served two terms as coroner and two terms as mayor.

   Andrew Fabrique served with the Union army. In May 1862 he was taken prisoner by Confederates but escaped in less than one hour. Fabrique later received a gunshot wound at the Battle of Shiloh. His medical practice in Wichita ranged from the cattle trail town of Newton to the north to Indian Territory to the south.

6. Ibid.

   Thomas J. Schlereth, *Victorian America: Transformations in Everyday Life* (New York: HarperCollins, 1991), p. 288.

7. Ibid.

   Another excellent source of information about the disease is Katherine Ott, *Fevered Lives: Tuberculosis in American Culture since 1870* (Cambridge, Mass.: Harvard University Press, 1996).

8. Ibid.

9. Dr. Samuel J. Crumbine, who later wrote *Frontier Doctor*, which describes his medical experiences during the "wild years" in Dodge City, Kansas, became one of the leading figures in the field of public health in Kansas. Crumbine became alarmed when he saw tuberculosis patients spitting on the floor of a train and drinking from public water glasses. Many years later, when he was secretary of the Kansas State Board of Health, he came up with an ingenious way to curb tuberculosis and other diseases. He banned common drinking vessels and spitting in public places. He also promoted health campaigns with such slogans as "Swat the Fly" and "Bat the Rat." He even convinced a brick company to imprint "Don't Spit on the Sidewalk" on every fourth brick manufactured.

10. Koop, p. 13.

11. Frederick Nolan, *The West of Billy the Kid* (Norman: University of Oklahoma Press, 1998), p. 16.

12. Ibid.

13. Ibid.

Six · Pulp Fiction

1. Kent Ladd Steckmesser, *The Western Hero in History and Legend* (Norman: University of Oklahoma Press, 1965), p. xi.

2. Stephen Tatum, *Inventing Billy the Kid* (Tucson: University of Arizona Press, 1997), pp. 18–19.

3. Colorado Territory was organized by an act of Congress in 1861. Colorado became the

thirty-eighth state on August 1, 1876, America's 100th birthday year, giving it the nickname Centennial State.

4. Edwin S. Hooker, *Denver Post*, April 1, 1928, p. 15.

Waldo E. Koop, *Billy the Kid: The Trail of a Kansas Legend* (Wichita: Kansas City Posse of the Westerners, 1965), p. 16.

5. Tatum, pp. 3, 210. Tatum also cites an *El Paso Times* story from September 16, 1923, in which Coe mentions McCarty's brief residence in Denver.

6. Koop, p. 9.

7. Historic photographs collection and accompanying material, from Western History/ Genealogy Department, Denver Public Library; Colorado Historical Society; Denver Art Museum; and Denver Metro Convention and Visitors Bureau.

8. Ibid.

9. Ibid. Other sources include www.denvergov.org.

10. Isabella Bird, *A Lady's Life in the Rocky Mountains* (Norman: University of Oklahoma Press, 1999), p. 41.

Isabella Bird ascended Long's Peak in the company of mountain man Jim Nugent, also known as Rocky Mountain Jim. Bird's book was a critical success when originally published in 1879.

11. Robert Antheam, *The Coloradans* (Albuquerque: University of New Mexico Press, 1976), p. 93.

12. W. H. Buchtel, "A Paradise for Dyspeptics and Consumptives: The Climate of Colorado," February 1873, Western History Photography Collection of Denver Public Library, Call Number: C362.196995 B854par 1873.

13. Ibid.

14. Ibid.

A source of additional information about Barnum in Colorado is Uchill Ida Libert, *Howdy, Sucker! What P. T. Barnum Did in Colorado* (Denver: Pioneer Peddler Press, 2001).

15. Irving Wallace, *The Fabulous Showman: The Life and Times of P. T. Barnum* (New York: Alfred A. Knopf, 1959), pp. 170–71.

In this cited work and in several other books about Barnum, his son-in-law's surname appears as Buchtel, which this author uses. Barnum family genealogists, however, contend that the physician's name was spelled Butchell.

16. Ibid., p. 172.

17. Michael Wallis, *The Real Wild West: The 101 Ranch and the Making of the American West* (New York: St. Martin's Press, 1999), p. 20.

18. Ibid.

19. Ibid., p. 21.

20. Ibid.

21. *Handbook of Texas Online*, s.v. "MOODY, ROBERT," www.tsha.utexas.edu/handbook/ online/articles/MM/fmo20.html (accessed May 1, 2005).

A native of England, Moody first met Barnum in New York in 1857. Barnum hired him to manage the Dipper Ranch in 1871 and Moody later bought an interest in the enterprise that he sold in 1876.

22. *Daily Kansas State Record*, Topeka, October 26, 1870.

23. Ibid.

24. Wallace, p. 225.

25. Ibid.

26. Wallis, pp. 20–22.
    Wallace, p. 106.

27. Ibid., pp. 176–77.

28. William H. Goetzmann and William N. Goetzmann, *The West of the Imagination* (New York and London: W. W. Norton, 1986), pp. 287–88.

29. Wallis, pp. 45–47.

30. Larry McMurtry, "Inventing the West," *New York Review of Books*, vol. 47. no. 130 (August 10, 2000).

31. *Harper's Weekly* (January 11, 1868), p. 18.

32. Ibid. (September 23, 1871), p. 897.

33. Robert V. Hine and John Mack Faragher, *The American West: A New Interpretive History* (New Haven and London: Yale University Press, 2000), p. 478.

34. Ibid.

35. Thomas J. Lyon, "The Literary West," *The Oxford History of the American West*, ed. Clyde A. Milner II, Carol A. O'Conner, and Martha A. Sandweiss (New York and Oxford, U.K.: Oxford University Press, 1994).

36. Richard Slotkin, *Gunfighter Nation: The Myth of the Frontier in Twentieth-Century America* (Norman: University of Oklahoma Press, 1998), p. 127.

Seven • Silver Threads Among the Gold

1. From Carol Muske-Dukes, "Howdy, Pardner," review of *Cowboy*, by Sara Davidson, in *Washington Post*, June 14, 1999, Style section.

2. From August 25, 1871, to March 1, 1873, the exact whereabouts of the McCarty-Antrim party are unknown.

3. Michael Wallis and Suzanne Fitzgerald Wallis, *Songdog Diary: 66 Stories from the Road* (Tulsa: Council Oak Books, 1996), pp. 173–74.
    Russian thistle, also called rolling brush, white man's plant, prickly glasswort, Russian cactus, saltwort, and wind witch, can be found throughout the western United States. Old-time cowboys in the Southwest claimed tumbleweeds were put on earth to show folks the way the wind is blowing.

4. Scott Bidstrup, "A Shameful Legacy: The Shocking Mismanagement of America's Public Lands," 2000, 2002, an essay in hypertext, www.bidstrup.com/publiclands.htm.

5. Robert Leonard Reid, *America, New Mexico* (Tucson: University of Arizona Press, 1998), p. 18.

6. Philip J. Rasch and R. N. Mullin, "New Light on the Legend of Billy the Kid," *New Mexico Folklore Record,* vol. 7 (1952–1953), pp. 1–5.

7. Richard Harris, *National Trust Guide Santa Fe* (New York: John Wiley & Sons, 1997), pp. 82–84.

8. Rasch and Mullin, p. 4.

9. Ibid.

   Both the Book of Marriages of Santa Fe County and First Presbyterian Church of Santa Fe's records misspelled Antrim. The county records listed it as Antrum, the church as Antram.

10. Frederick Nolan, *The West of Billy the Kid* (Norman: University of Oklahoma Press, 1998), p. 17.

    Bob Boze Bell, *The Illustrated Life and Times of Billy the Kid* (Phoenix: Tri Star-Boze Publications, 1992, 1996), p. 18.

11. A fonda, or inn, first appeared on La Plaza de Armas in Santa Fe shortly after the Spanish arrived in the early 1600s. Through the centuries several different hotels have stood on this site, making it the oldest hotel corner in the United States. The current hotel, La Fonda, was built in the 1920s. Hotel brochures still boast that Billy the Kid once worked there.

12. Stephen Tatum, *Inventing Billy the Kid* (Tucson: University of Arizona Press, 1997), p. 19.

13. Billy the Kid Historic Preservation Society (BTKHPS), www.billythekidhistoricpreservation .com.

    Marcelle Brothers, cofounder of BTKHPS, maintains a carefully researched Web site, www.aboutbillythekid.com.

14. Charles W. Harris, New York, published "Silver Threads Among the Gold" in 1873, with music by Hart Pease Danks and words by Eben Eugene Rexford. The song sold more than three million copies, but Danks, having sold all rights to the song, never profited from the sales.

    Henry McCarty's other favorite tune, "Turkey in the Straw," was an early American minstrel song and a fiddle tune, titled "Natchez under the Hill," before it was published with words in 1834 as "Old Zip Coon." It was a popular song during Andrew Jackson's presidency. The tune was derived from the ballad "My Grandmother Lived on Yonder Little Green," derived in turn from the Irish ballad "The Old Rose Tree." Barbershop Harmonic Society, Kenosha, Wisconsin, Files.

15. Willa Cather, *Death Comes for the Archbishop* (New York: Alfred A. Knopf, 1926), pp. 275–76.

16. Ralph Emerson Twitchell, *The Leading Facts of New Mexico* (1912; Albuquerque: Horn & Wallace, 1963), vol. 2, p. 157.

17. Ibid., pp. 157–58.

18. Ibid., p. 159.

19. Ibid., p. 160.

20. Michael Wallis, *Heaven's Window: A Journey through Northern New Mexico* (Portland, Ore.: Graphic Arts Center Publishing, 2001), p. 25.

21. Twitchell, p. 147.

22. Donald Cline, *Alias Billy the Kid: The Man behind the Legend* (Santa Fe: Sunstone Press, 1986), p. 26.

23. Robert Julyan, *The Place Names of New Mexico* (Albuquerque: University of New Mexico Press, 1996, 1998), pp. 153–54.

24. Bell, p. 19.

Eight · Land of Little Time

1. John DeWitt McKee, "The Unrelenting Land," in *The Spell of New Mexico*, ed. Tony Hillerman (Albuquerque: University of New Mexico Press, 1976), p. 71. The essay was reprinted from the *New Mexico Quarterly*, vol. 27, no. 3 (Autumn 1957), by permission of the author.

2. Susan Berry and Sharman Apt Russell, *Built to Last: An Architectural History of Silver City, New Mexico* (Silver City: Silver City Museum Society, 1995), p. 18.

3. Jerry Weddle, *Antrim Is My Stepfather's Name* (Phoenix: Arizona Historical Society, 1993), p. 4.

   John Swisshelm, one of the town founders, probably built the Antrim cabin. It was enlarged to include a dining room and rooms for boarders but not until after the Antrims lived there. Later the residence became a shoe store. It was demolished in 1894.

4. Ibid., pp. 4–5.

5. Ibid., p. 6.

6. Robert Julyan, *The Place Names of New Mexico* (Albuquerque: University of New Mexico Press, 1996, 1998), p. 335.

   The Spanish cherished their martyred saints as well as such folk heroes as the legendary El Cid, who, like St. Vincent, was associated with the port city of Valencia.

7. From accounts furnished by Oscar Waldo Williams, a frontier lawyer and surveyor, Silver City Museum files. Williams describes Apaches parading single file through Silver City, "marked with a red cotton band tied around each copper-colored forehead to show that they were army scouts."

8. Library of Congress, Manuscript Division, WPA Federal Writers' Project Collection. Manuscripts from the Federal Writers' Project, "WPA Life Histories from New Mexico," Interview of Robert Golden, June 22, 1938, collected by Frances E. Totty.

9. Julyan, p. 335.

   Berry and Russell, p. 12.

   John Bullard was leading a force of volunteers against the Apaches when he was "shot straight through the heart," according to an early settler. Historian Ralph Emerson Twitchell later wrote that the early settlers of Silver City never forgave the Apaches for killing Bullard.

10. Ibid., p. 11.

11. Ibid., pp. 11–12.

12. *Las Cruces Borderer*, March 16, 1871.

13. Berry and Russell, p. 13.

14. Ibid., pp. 13–14.

   Silver City Mining Life, May 31, 1873. According to this newspaper story, which promoted the virtues of Silver City, such as a climate "beneficial to invalids," there were more Anglos than Hispanics living there. "Silver City is a town of about 1,200 inhabitants, romantically situated in the mountains, and populated by about 300 Mexicans and 900 Americans, the very larger part of whom are engaged in mining."

15. Ibid., January 17, 1874. The editorial under the headline A TRIP TO SANTA FE also stated that in the writer's opinion there was nothing in Santa Fe that "would cause one to wish it as a permanent residence."

16. Frederick Nolan, *The West of Billy the Kid* (Norman: University of Oklahoma Press, 1998), p. 21.

17. *Silver City Mining Life*, March 21, 1874.

18. Winfred Blevins, *Dictionary of the American West* (New York: Facts on File, 1993), p. 131.

19. *Silver City Mining Life*, December 27, 1873.

   Bob Boze Bell, *The Illustrated Life and Times of Billy the Kid* (Phoenix: Tri Star-Boze Publications, 1992, 1996), p. 19.

20. Bell, p. 19.

   Nolan, p. 23.

   Bell, p. 19.

   Chauncey O. Truesdell, a classmate of Henry Antrim's in Silver City, was one of several people who said he had no knowledge of Catherine Antrim's ever taking in boarders.

21. "WPA Life Histories from New Mexico," interview of Louis Abraham, 1937.

22. Ibid.

23. Weddle, p. 7.

24. "WPA Life Histories from New Mexico," interview of Louis Abraham, 1937.

25. Nolan, p. 29.

26. American Guide Series, Compiled by Workers of the Writers' Program of the Works Projects Administration, *New Mexico: A Guide to the Colorful State* (New York: Hastings House, 1940), p. 127.

27. Calvin Horn, *New Mexico's Troubled years: The Story of the Early Territorial Governors* (Albuquerque: Horn & Wallace, 1963), pp. 152–53.

   Giddings, who had been appointed by President Ulysses Grant, made his remarks about education during his first address to the territorial legislature, December 7, 1871.

28. P. R. Burchard, "Our Educational Outlook," *Scribner's Monthly*, vol. 4, no. 1 (May 1872), p. 98.

29. Richard Melzer, *When We Were Young in the West: True Stories of Childhood* (Santa Fe: Sunstone Press, 2003), p. 301.

30. *Silver City Mining Life*, August 9, 1873.

   Peter Ott's lot in life improved when he quit teaching and became the proprietor of the

Keystone House, a popular hotel later known as the Tremont House. In October 1874 a disgruntled former employee wielding a navy Colt six-shooter wounded Ott. He survived and became known as the prince of caterers.

31. *Silver City Mining Life*, January 3, 1874

32. Ibid., February 21, 1874.

33. Ibid.

34. Ibid., January 17, 1874.

35. Ibid., January 24, 1874.

36. Nora Henn, interview with author, Lincoln, New Mexico, November 20, 2004.

NINE · ONE STEP OVER THE LINE

1. Library of Congress, Manuscript Division, WPA Federal Writers' Project Collection. Manuscripts from the Federal Writers' Project, "WPA Life Histories from New Mexico," interview of Louis Abraham, 1937, collected by Frances E. Totty.

2. The contemptuous term "greaser" dates to at least 1836 in Texas. The origin of the word is uncertain, but through the years it came to be a demeaning term just like "bean-eater," "pepper-eater," and "never-sweats." Derisive Anglo cowboys occasionally called New Mexico greaserdom. Hispanics, for their part, used the word "gringo" as their derogatory name for Anglos or someone who did not speak Spanish. The etymology of this word also remains unclear.

3. Jerry Weddle, *Antrim Is My Stepfather's Name* (Phoenix: Arizona Historical Society, 1993), p. 8.

   As pointed out in the book's foreword by historian Robert Utley, many gaps in Billy the Kid's early life were filled in, thanks to Weddle's tenacious research. Weddle's detailed description of the young Henry Antrim in Silver City came from a variety of credible sources, published works, interviews, and historical records.

4. *Silver City Independent*, March 22, 1932.

5. Weddle, p. 8.

6. Frederick Nolan, *The West of Billy the Kid* (Norman: University of Oklahoma Press, 1998), p. 24.

7. Data imaged from National Archives and Records Administration, 1870 Federal Population Census; 1880 Federal Population Census; and Fort Selden State Monument, Radium Springs, New Mexico.

   Established thirteen miles north of Las Cruces in 1865, the fort was active for a quarter century. A young Douglas MacArthur (1880–1964) called it home in 1884, when his father, Captain Arthur MacArthur, became the post commander. Douglas, the World War II general, spent several years of his childhood at Fort Selden in the company of officers and soldiers including units of African-American troops called buffalo soldiers. The fort was decommissioned in 1891.

8. Nolan, p. 24.

Sometimes the mostly motherless children were referred to as street rats or the dangerous classes, because they formed gangs that fought against law officers.

9. *Wichita Weekly Eagle*, August 11, 1881.

Editor Marsh Murdock's reference to Henry as a street gamin did not appear in print until ten years after he made the statement.

10. Weddle, p. 9.

11. *Silver City Mining Life*, February 7, 1874.

12. Weddle, pp. 12–13.

13. Ibid., p. 13.

As mining flourished in the Silver City area, the watersheds were heavily logged and overgrazed, resulting in an enormous increase in runoff. Main Street became the principal floodway, and the road eroded down to bedrock, well below the original street grade. Main Street became known as the Big Ditch.

14. Ibid., pp. 6–7.

15. Ralph Emerson Twitchell, *The Leading Facts of New Mexico* (1912; Albuquerque: Horn & Wallace, 1963), vol. 2, p. 160.

16. Ibid., pp. 160–61.

17. Ibid., p. 162.

18. "WPA Life Histories from New Mexico," interview of Louis Abraham, 1937.

19. Weddle, pp. 14–15.

20. Robert Julyan, *The Place Names of New Mexico* (Albuquerque: University of New Mexico Press, 1996, 1998), p. 130.

21. "WPA Life Histories from New Mexico," June 16, 1937.

22. Weddle, pp. 14–15.

23. Ibid.

24. Nolan, p. 27.

Author Don Cline, in *Antrim & Billy*, claims that one Emma Norris succeeded Webster in May 1874. Most other sources, including Nolan, Bob Boze Bell, and Jerry Weddle, maintain that Mrs. Pratt was Henry's second schoolteacher.

25. Nolan, p. 27.

26. Ibid.

27. Weddle, p. 17.

28. Ibid.

29. January 9, 1952, interview with Chauncey O. Truesdell, Phoenix, Arizona, from Silver City Museum files.

30. Ibid.

31. *Silver City Mining Life*, September 19, 1874.

32. "WPA Life Histories from New Mexico," interview of Louis Abraham, 1937.

33. First verse and refrain, "Silver Threads Among the Gold," 1873, music by Hart Pease Danks, words by Eben Eugene Rexford.

Ten · Gone on the Scout

1. Robert Utley, *Billy the Kid: A Short and Violent Life* (Lincoln and London: University of Nebraska Press, 1989), p. 9.

2. Geoffrey C. Ward, "Henry the Kid," *American Heritage*, vol. 41, no. 3 (April 1990), p. 14.

3. Lou Blachly, "I'll Never Forget," *Silver City Enterprise*, November 3, 1949, quoting from Wayne Whitehill's memories of Silver City: "Mama made all our clothes. Most all the people, especially the youngsters, wore moccasins just like the Indians."

4. Frederick Nolan, *The West of Billy the Kid* (Norman: University of Oklahoma Press, 1998), p. 27.

5. Ibid., p. 28.
   Some authors use Patience as Mary Richards's middle name, but according to several documents, including federal census records, her name was Mary Phillipa Richards. She was born in Southampton, England, in 1846.

6. Joan Nunn, *Fashion in Costume, 1200–2000* (Chicago: New Amsterdam Books, A&C Black Ltd., 2000).
   During this period large quantities of false hair were used for braids and curls or worn in a chignon, a knot of hair at the back of the head. Much of the hair was obtained in Catholic countries, from novices entering convents, peasant girls in Europe, or prisoners or paupers in workhouses. By 1876 some fashion influences declared that the use of false hair was passé.

7. Nolan, p. 29.

8. Bob Boze Bell, *The Illustrated Life and Times of Billy the Kid* (Phoenix: Tri Star-Boze Publications, 1992, 1996), p. 24.

9. Nolan, p. 30.

10. Ibid., p. 28.

11. Library of Congress, Manuscript Division, WPA Federal Writers' Project Collection. Manuscripts from the Federal Writers' Project, "WPA Life Histories from New Mexico," interview of Augusta Abraham, 1937, collected by Frances E. Totty.

12. Ibid., interview of Dick Clark, 1937.

13. *Silver City Enterprise*, January 3, 1902.
    Whitehill gave this interview after the eastern press once more focused its attention on Billy the Kid, following the appointment of Pat Garrett as collector of customs at the port of El Paso, Texas.

14. Nolan, p. 32.

15. Jerry Weddle, *Antrim Is My Stepfather's Name* (Phoenix: Arizona Historical Society, 1993), p. 19.

16. January 9, 1952, interview with Chauncey O. Truesdell, Phoenix, Arizona, from Silver City Museum files.

17. Ibid.

Truesdell was eighty-eight years old at the time of his interview. He was deaf but mentally alert, living with his cat in a comfortable cottage on North 37th Street, where he enjoyed watching his new television. He is considered one of the more credible sources of those who actually knew Henry Antrim before he became Billy the Kid.

18. *Silver City Mining Life*, November 5, 1874.

19. Nolan, p. 31.

20. Ibid.

21. Ibid.

22. Ibid.

23. Donald Cline, *Alias Billy the Kid: The Man behind the Legend* (Santa Fe: Sunstone Press, 1986), p. 31.

24. Pat Garrett, *The Authentic Life of Billy, the Kid, the Noted Desperado of the Southwest, Whose Deeds of Daring and Blood Made His Name a Terror in New Mexico, Arizona and Northern Mexico* (Norman: University of Oklahoma Press, 1954), p. 10.

25. Unpublished manuscript in the files of the New Mexico Writers' Project, Museum of New Mexico, Santa Fe, interview of Jim Blair, 1937, compiled by Frances E. Totty.

26. *Silver City Independent*, March 22, 1932.

Anthony Connor was interviewed while in Silver City to which he returned to attend the funeral of his sister, Sara Knight, wife of Richard Knight.

Ward, p. 14.

27. *Silver City Enterprise*, January 3, 1902.

28. Weddle, p. 22.

29. Ibid., p. 24.

30. Nolan, p. 33.

31. *Silver City Herald*, September 5, 1875.

Other news items that day included word of Indians stealing twenty-eight head of horses from a ranch near Augustin Springs and of George Potten's being attacked and severely bitten by a dog in front of Ward's Saloon in Silver City. The newspaper noted the dog was a repeat offender and went on to report: "He has ceased to bite—he's a dead dog now."

32. Weddle, p. 58.

33. Maurice Kildare, "Saga of the Gallant Sheriff," *The West: True Stories of the Old West*, vol. 9, no. 3 (August 1968), p. 53.

34. Weddle, p. 26.

35. *Silver City Mining Life*, February 14, 1874.

The story about the jail went on to say, "Black Bros., the builders, will receive many an inverted blessing from future inmates, for the thoroughness with which they did their work."

36. Weddle, pp. 26–27.

37. *Silver City Independent*, March 22, 1932.

38. *Silver City Enterprise*, January 3, 1902.

39. *Silver City Herald*, September 26, 1875.

The translation of "sans cue [queue], sans joss sticks" is "without a braid of hair, without incense." Joss sticks were slender sticks of incense burned before a Chinese idol or image.

40. "On the scout" meant "on the lam from the law." "Among the willows" had the same meaning, but it also described a couple making love.

Eleven • Saddle Tramp

1. Lee Priestley, with Marquita Peterson, *Billy the Kid: The Good Side of a Bad Man* (Las Cruces, N.M.: Yucca Tree Press, 1993), p. 14.
2. Frederick Nolan, *The West of Billy the Kid* (Norman: University of Oklahoma Press, 1998), p. 34.
3. Will C. Barnes, *Arizona Place Names* (Tucson: University of Arizona Press, 1988), p. 442.
    Camp Thomas was established on August 12, 1876, on the south bank of the Gila River, San Carlos Apache Indian reservation, just above Old Camp Goodwin. The camp was moved up the Gila two years later and in 1883 was renamed Fort Thomas.
4. Nolan, p. 34.
5. Ibid.
6. January 9, 1952, interview with Chauncey O. Truesdell, Phoenix, Arizona, from Silver City Museum files.
7. Note: "Hoosegow," also "hoosgow," was adapted from the Spanish word *juzgado* for courthouse or court of justice.
8. Jerry Weddle, *Antrim Is My Stepfather's Name* (Phoenix: Arizona Historical Society, 1993), p. 28.
9. Ibid., p. 29.
10. Ibid., p. 30.
11. Ibid.
12. Robert A. Tennert, "A Different Perspective: Victorian Travelers in Arizona, 1860–1900," *Journal of Arizona History*, vol. 29, no. 4 (Winter 1988), p. 352.
13. E. Conklin, *Picturesque Arizona* (New York: Continent Stereoscopic Co., 1878), p. 369.
14. Tennert, p. 353.
15. Barnes, p. 99.
16. Ibid., p. 288.
17. Lowell Parker, *Arizona Towns and Tales* (Phoenix: Phoenix Newspapers, 1975), p. 55.
18. Joseph F. Park, "The 1903 'Mexican Affair' at Clifton," *Journal of Arizona History*, vol. 18 (Summer 1977), pp. 119–48.
19. Weddle, p. 31.
20. Ibid., pp. 30–31.
21. From files and information provided by Round Valley Public Library, the Casa Malpais Museum, Springerville, Arizona.

22. Joseph A. Munk, *Arizona Sketches* (New York: Grafton Press, 1905).

In 1884 Dr. Munk (1847–1927) came to Arizona Territory, where he and two brothers operated the Munk Cattle Ranch near Wilcox. Prompted by his abiding love of Arizona, Munk amassed an extensive library of books, maps, prints, and other material about what became the forty-eighth state. He donated his collection to the Southwest Museum in Los Angeles in 1908. He also wrote several books.

23. Weddle, p. 31.

24. Ibid., p. 32.

TWELVE · KID ANTRIM

1. Robert N. Mullin, *The Boyhood of Billy the Kid*. Southwestern Studies, vol. 5, no. 1, Monograph No. 17 (El Paso: Texas Western Press, 1967).

2. Vincent dePaul Lupiano and Ken W. Sayers, *It Was a Very Good Year: A Cultural History of the United States from 1776 to the Present* (Holbrook, Mass.: Bob Adams, 1994), pp. 154–55.

Thomas J. Schlereth, *Victorian America: Transformations in Everyday Life* (New York: HarperCollins, 1991), p. 5.

3. Schlereth, p. 5.

4. Ibid., p. 4.

5. Joseph A. Munk, *Arizona Sketches* (New York: Grafton Press, 1905).

6. John S. Bowman, gen. ed., *The World Almanac of the American West* (New York: World Almanac, imprint of Pharos Books, 1986), pp. 208–10.

7. Ibid., p. 211.

8. Ibid.

9. Jerry Weddle, *Antrim Is My Stepfather's Name* (Phoenix: Arizona Historical Society, 1993), p. 32.

10. Fintan O'Toole, "The Many Stories of Billy the Kid," *New Yorker* (December 28, 1998–January 4, 1999), p. 97.

11. Will C. Barnes, *Arizona Place Names* (Tucson: University of Arizona Press, 1988), p. 188.

12. Marshall Trimble, *Arizona: A Cavalcade of History* (Tucson: Rio Nuevo Publishers, 2003), pp. 114–15.

Chip Colwell-Chanthaphonh, Center for Desert Archaeology, Tucson, Arizona, "The 'Camp Grant Massacre' in the Historical Imagination," a paper presented April 25–26, 2003, at the Arizona History Convention, Tempe, Arizona.

13. Ibid.

According to Trimble, "No jury in the Arizona Territory would find anyone guilty of killing an Apache."

14. Fort Grant historical material provided by Arizona Department of Corrections, Phoenix, Arizona.

In 1912 the federal government turned over Fort Grant to the newly created state of Arizona to be used as a state industrial school for wayward boys and girls. In 1968 the school was made part of the state's Department of Corrections, and in 1973 it became an adult male prison.

15. From biographical information supplied by the Historical Society of Oak Park and River Forest, Oak Park, Illinois.

16. L. R. Arms, *A Short History of the Noncommissioned Officer* (El Paso, Tex.: U.S. Army Museum of the Noncommissioned Officer, Fort Bliss, Texas, 1989).

17. John Bourke, *On the Border with Crook* (New York: Charles Scribner's Sons, 1891), pp. 12–13.

John Gregory Bourke was first and foremost a soldier. At sixteen he ran away from his comfortable Philadelphia home to enlist in the Union cavalry, and he served with distinction during the Civil War, receiving the Congressional Medal of Honor for his gallantry at Stone River, Tennessee. Mustered out in 1865, he received an appointment to West Point and was commissioned second lieutenant in 1869. He went on to serve with distinction in Indian campaigns in the West. He also was a first-rate anthropologist and historian with a particular interest in Native American culture. He mastered the Apache tongue. He left behind fascinating accounts of military life on the hard frontier before he died from an aneurysm of the aorta in 1896, just two weeks before his fiftieth birthday. He was buried at Arlington National Cemetery, as was his wife, Mary.

18. Barnes, p. 57.

Some years later, the settlement became known as Bonita (Spanish for "pretty") after the Sierra Bonita, a name often given the Graham Range. Bonita Creek, a dry wash for most of its course to the Gila River, also was nearby.

19. Ibid.

Barnes was a cowman and a prolific writer, best known for his compendium *Arizona Place Names,* one of the earliest of such dictionaries.

20. Weddle, p. 33.

21. Herbert M. Hart, *Old Forts of the Far West* (New York: Bonanza Books, 1965), p. 155.

A sutler was a civilian who traded goods to soldiers on or near a military post. With the approval of the commanding officer, he carried such necessities as knives, tobacco, cloth, buttons, and whiskey.

22. Anne M. Butler, *Daughters of Joy, Sisters of Misery: Prostitutes in the American West, 1865–90* (Urbana and Chicago: University of Illinois Press, 1987), p. 8.

The hog ranches described by Bourke were about three miles from Fort Laramie, Wyoming Territory. His choice of the term "Cyprian," or a woman of the night, derives from Cyprus, the birthplace of Aphrodite, the goddess of love.

23. Weddle, pp. 33–34.

24. Frederick Nolan, *The West of Billy the Kid* (Norman: University of Oklahoma Press, 1998), p. 49.

25. Ibid.

26. Gertrude Hill, "Henry Clay Hooker: King of the Sierra Bonita," *Arizoniana: The Journal of Arizona History,* vol. 2, no. 4 (Winter 1961), pp. 12–13.

27. Ibid.

28. Earle R. Forrest, "The Fabulous Sierra Bonita," *Journal of Arizona History*, vol. 6, no. 3 (Autumn 1965), pp. 137–38, 140.

29. Munk, p. 98.

30. Weddle, pp. 34–35.

31. Ibid., p. 35.

A logbook and other material pertaining to William Whelan (1843–1908), noted sheriff and rancher, as well as the reminiscences of his son, William Whelan, Jr. (1872–1975), describing ranch life and family are at the Arizona State Library, Archives and Public records, Phoenix, Arizona.

32. Mullin, p. 14.

33. J. Cabell Brown, *Calabazas or Amusing Recollections of an Arizona City* (San Francisco: Valleau & Peterson, 1892), pp. 25–26.

The town of Calabazas, from the Spanish for "pumpkin" or "gourd," was founded and named by the Calabasas Land and Mining Company in 1865. The spelling changed to Calabasas in 1882. Found just north of the Mexican border, the town was a sanctuary for tough hombres from all over the West.

34. Richard Erdoes, *Saloons of the Old West* (Salt Lake City and Chicago: Howe Brothers, 1985), p. 219.

35. Weddle, p. 32.

36. Nolan, p. 51.

37. Ibid.

38. Ibid., pp. 51, 306, fn 7.

Born in Glasgow, Scotland, in 1849, Mackie was actually named McAckey. According to records, after Mackie and Henry Antrim parted company, he roamed the West until 1894, when he entered an old soldiers' home in Milwaukee. He died there on July 21, 1920, his seventy-first birthday.

39. *Silver City Herald*, October 17, 1875.

Thirteen • First Blood

1. From the transcription of Frank Cahill's deathbed statement, taken on August 18, 1877, by notary public Miles Wood at the post hospital, Camp Grant, Arizona Territory.

2. Winfred Blevins, *Dictionary of the American West* (New York: Facts on File, 1993), p. 211.

The precise derivation of the words "lynching" and "lynch law" remains open for debate. Most scholars credit Captain William Lynch (1742–1820), who, with some followers, known as lynch-men, seized a band of ruffians in Pennsylvania in 1780 and promptly lynched them. Almost a century later in the American West, the word "lynchy" came into usage, as in "The mob had a lynchy look."

3. F. R. Casey, *The Western Peace Officer: A Legacy of Law and Order* (Norman: University of Oklahoma Press, 1972), p. 12.

4. Casey Tefertiller, *Wyatt Earp: The Life behind the Legend* (New York: John Wiley & Sons, 1997), p. 5.

Earp was indicted for horse theft but never stood trial.

5. Jerry Weddle, *Antrim Is My Stepfather's Name* (Phoenix: Arizona Historical Society, 1993), p. 35.

6. Frederick Nolan, *The West of Billy the Kid* (Norman: University of Oklahoma Press, 1998), p. 52.

7. Ibid., pp. 52–53.

8. Weddle, p. 36.

9. Ibid.

10. W. A. Haak, *Copper Bottom Tales: Historic Sketches from Gila County* (Globe, Ariz.: Gila County Historical Society, 1991), p. 10.

11. Weddle, p. 37.

12. Ibid., p. 38.

13. Nolan, p. 54.

14. *Grant County Herald*, February 24, 1877, Silver City Museum files.

15. Nolan, p. 55.

16. In his book *The West of Billy the Kid*, Nolan identifies Caleb Martin as a "local rancher."

17. Weddle, pp. 40–41.

18. Ibid., p. 40.

19. Bob Boze Bell, *The Illustrated Life and Times of Billy the Kid* (Phoenix: Tri Star-Boze Publications, 1992, 1996), p. 36.

20. Weddle, p. 41.

21. From an interview with Wood, *Tucson Citizen*, December 23, 1901.

22. Weddle, p. 42.

Smith got his colorful nickname because he was known for raising bumper crops of sorghum for cattle feed.

23. Ibid.

24. J. Marvin Hunter, *The Trail Drivers of Texas* (Austin: University of Texas Press, 1985), pp. 975–78.

Gildea at one time considered becoming a doctor, but after a year of studying medicine he returned to the cattle trails. "I got lonesome and wanted to hear the wolves howl and the owls hoot back in the West. . . ."

25. Weddle, p. 42.

26. Philip J. Rasch, with Allan Radbourne, *Trailing Billy the Kid* (Laramie: The National Association for Outlaw and Lawman History, Inc., in affilliation with the University of Wyoming, 1995), pp. 184–85.

This reference originally appeared in an article entitled "The Story of Windy Cahill," *Real West*, vol. 28 (August 1985), pp. 22–27.

27. Weddle, p. 34.

28. Rasch and Radbourne, p. 184.

Francis Cahill enlisted in the Thirty-second Infantry, U.S. Army in New York on July 25, 1868. "He was described as 5′ 4¾″ tall, dark hair, blue eyes, dark complexion, aged 22 years, born in Dublin, Ireland, occupation: horseshoer." On his deathbed, however, Cahill stated that he was born in Galway, Ireland.

29. Weddle, p. 42.

30. Ibid., p. 43.

31. Ibid.

32. Nolan, p. 60.

33. Ibid.

Ainsworth, born in Vermont in 1852, graduated from the University of the City of New York (later New York University) in 1874, the same year he enlisted in the U.S. Army Medical Corps. After serving at frontier posts, he returned to Washington, D.C., and rose through the ranks. He retired from the army in 1912 and died in 1934. He is buried at Arlington National Cemetery.

34. *Arizona Weekly Star,* August 23, 1877.

35. Rasch and Radbourne, p. 187.

36. Ibid.

37. Robert N. Mullin, *The Boyhood of Billy the Kid* (El Paso: Texas Western Press, 1967), p 16.

The term "equalizer" means a revolver and comes from the expression "A Colt makes all men equal."

FOURTEEN · AT LARGE

1. Major Charles Compton's reply to the telegram sent on August 23, 1877, by Pima County Sheriff William Osborn, who read about the shooting in a Tucson newspaper and apparently wired Compton in order to determine jurisdiction.

2. Robert N. Mullin, *The Boyhood of Billy the Kid* (El Paso: Texas Western Press, 1967), p 18.

3. Ibid.

4. Jerry Weddle, *Antrim Is My Stepfather's Name* (Phoenix: Arizona Historical Society, 1993), p. 44.

5. Mullin, p. 18.

6. J. Cabell Brown, *Calabazas or Amusing Recollections of an Arizona City* (San Francisco: Valleau & Peterson, 1892), p. 25.

"Cayuse," sometimes spelled *kiuse,* was the term for an Indian pony or a mount that had not been properly trained by white men and was still a bit wild.

7. Richard Maxwell Brown, "Violence," in *The Oxford History of the American West,* ed. Clyde A. Milner II, Carol A. O'Connor, and Martha A. Sandweiss (New York and Oxford, U.K.: Oxford University Press, 1994), p. 393.

8. Ibid.

9. Ibid., p. 394.

The case Brown makes for the rise in murder rates is well taken. Throughout the twentieth century and into the twenty-first, the concept of no duty to retreat, sometimes known as the castle doctrine, has continued to be championed by politicians and by lobbyists for the gun industry and by the National Rifle Association. In 2005, Florida Governor Jeb Bush signed a law that decreed that a person under attack "has no duty to retreat and has the right to stand his or her ground and meet force with force, including deadly force if he or she reasonably believes it is necessary to do so to prevent death or other bodily harm to himself or herself or to prevent the commission of a forcible felony."

10. Robert Weisberg, "Values, Violence, and the Second Amendment: American Character, Constitutionalism, and Crime," Stanford Law School, Public Law Research Paper No. 37, *Houston Law Review*, 2002, http:ssm.com/abstract=311082.

11. Peter Lyon, "The Wild, Wild West," *American Heritage*, vol. 11, no. 5 (August 1960), p. 34.

12. Brown, p. 393.

13. Ibid., p. 398.

14. Garry Wills, *A Necessary Evil: A History of American Distrust of Government* (New York: Simon & Schuster, 2002), pp. 248–49.

15. Frederick Nolan, *The West of Billy the Kid* (Norman: University of Oklahoma Press, 1998), p. 68.

16. Thomas Edwin Farish, *History of Arizona* (San Francisco: Filmer Brothers Electrotype Co., 1915), vol. 2, pp. 143–48.

When the surgeon removed Mangus Colorado's head, it was found to measure larger than Daniel Webster's; the brain was of corresponding weight.

Following the death of Mangus Colorado, the Apaches elected Cochise as their new chief.

17. Nolan, p. 68.

Some historians question whether Henry ever actually joined the gang of outlaws called the Boys, or simply met some of the gang members. However, such respected Billy the Kid scholars as Frederick Nolan and Jerry Weddle have stated they believe that Henry did ride with the gang for a short time.

FIFTEEN • BANDITTI

1. W. Eugene Hollon, *Frontier Violence: Another Look* (New York: Oxford University Press, 1974), p. 183.

2. *Mesilla Valley Independent*, July 21, 1877.

3. Maurice Fulton, *History of the Lincoln County War* (Tucson: University of Arizona Press, 1968), pp. 66–67.

4. Frederick Nolan, *The West of Billy the Kid* (Norman: University of Oklahoma Press, 1998), p. 64.

5. Ibid., pp. 64, 66.

6. Robert M. Utley, *Billy the Kid: A Short and Violent Life* (Lincoln and London: University of Nebraska Press, 1989), p. 14.

7. Ibid., p. 15.

8. Records indicate that when Jesse Evans entered the Rusk Prison in Texas on December 1, 1880, to serve a ten-year term for second-degree murder, he stood five feet five and three-fourths inches and weighed 150 pounds.

9. Ibid.

10. Ibid.

11. Library of Congress, Manuscript Division, WPA Federal Writers' Project Collection. Manuscripts from the Federal Writers' Project, "WPA Life Histories from New Mexico," interview of Louis Abraham, 1937, collected by Frances E. Totty.

12. Nolan, p. 68.

13. *Grant County Independent*, October 6, 1877; *Mesilla Valley Independent*, October 13, 1877.

14. Ibid.

Robert Julyan, *The Place Names of New Mexico*, rev. ed. (Albuquerque: University of New Mexico Press, 1998), p. 94.

The infamous canyon took its name from Cooke's Peak, named for Philip St. George Cooke, leader of the Mormon Battalion, which passed through the area in 1846 and 1847. Once part of the Butterfield Overland Mail stage line, the four-mile-long canyon road also was known as the Gauntlet of Death, because by 1862 an estimated four hundred travelers and soldiers had been killed there by Apaches.

15. *Mesilla Valley Independent*, October 13, 1877.

16. Ibid.

17. Ibid.

18. Ibid.

19. Ralph Emerson Twitchell, *The Leading Facts of New Mexico* (Albuquerque: Horn & Wallace, 1963), vol. 2, pp. 495–96.

20. Ibid.

21. Ibid.

22. Ibid.

23. Ibid.

24. William A. Keleher, *Violence in Lincoln County, 1869–1881* (Albuquerque: University of New Mexico Press, 1957), p. 129.

25. *Mesilla Valley Independent*, October 13, 1877.

26. Ibid.

27. Ibid., October 6, 1877.

28. Ibid.

29. Keleher, p. 52.

30. *Mesilla Valley Independent*, October 13, 1877.

31. Ibid.

32. Utley, pp. 25–26.

33. Maurice Fulton, *History of the Lincoln County War* (Tucson: University of Arizona Press, 1968), p. 51.
34. *Mesilla Valley Independent*, October 13, 1877.
35. Ibid.

Sixteen • Seven Rivers

1. Quoted in Ralph Emerson Twitchell, *The Leading Facts of New Mexico History* (1912; Albuquerque: Horn and Wallace Publishers, 1963), vol. 2, p. 418.
2. New Mexico in 1877 was also stricken by severe drought, an infestation of grasshoppers, and an epidemic of black pox, the hemorrhagic variety of smallpox that turned the skin black.
3. Ibid.
4. *Handbook of Texas Online*, s.v. "SALT WAR OF SAN ELIZARIO," www.tsha.utexas.edu/handbook/online/articles/SS/jcs1.html.
5. T. C. Bass to Hubbard, October 9, 1877, Records of Richard Hubbard, Texas Office of the Governor, Archives and Information Services Division, Texas State Library and Archives Commission, Austin, Texas.
   During the Civil War Colonel Bass commanded the Twentieth Texas Cavalry Regiment. He and his unit saw action in Arkansas, Indian Territory, and Texas.
6. Ibid.
7. William H. Leckie, *The Buffalo Soldiers: A Narrative of the Negro Cavalry in the West* (Norman: University of Oklahoma Press, 1967), pp. 25–26, 186–90.
   Called Brunettes, niggers, and Moacs by many white people, the buffalo soldiers were proud of the name given them by Indians.
8. William A. Keleher, *Violence In Lincoln County* (Albuquerque: University of New Mexico Press), p. 156.
9. Ibid., p. 158.
   Kinney was no doubt aware that his chief nemesis, Albert Fountain, was an original member of the Salt Ring but had since turned against the gang and joined an anti–Salt Ring movement.
10. Ibid.
11. Three scouts serving under Bullis were awarded the Congressional Medal of Honor after they rescued him during a skirmish with Comanches in Texas. Bullis went on to a distinguished career, including service in the Spanish-American War. In 1904 President Theodore Roosevelt promoted him to the rank of brigadier general, and the following day Bullis retired.
12. Ibid., p. 159.
13. David J. Weber, ed., *Foreigners in Their Native Land: Historical Roots of the Mexican Americans* (Albuquerque: University of New Mexico Press, 1973), p. 208.

14. Robert N. Mullin, *The Boyhood of Billy the Kid*. Southwestern Studies 5, No. 1 (El Paso: University of Texas at El Paso, 1967), p. 19.

This account of Van Patten's meeting with the Kid comes from a letter Griggs sent to historian Robert N. Mullin, dated September 4, 1922. Griggs was the son of James Edgar Griggs, whose mining and mercantile interests led him to settle in Mesilla, and Eugenia Ascarte, from one of the most prominent Mexican families in the territory. Van Patten was the nephew of John Butterfield, founder of the famed Butterfield Overland Mail stage line. In 1896, Van Patten, an army veteran, led a posse to investigate the murders of Albert Fountain and his young son in southeastern New Mexico Territory. The bodies were never found. In 1908, Van Patten led another posse to the place where Pat Garrett, the former law officer known for killing Billy the Kid, was shot and killed. No one was ever found guilty for that murder.

15. T. M. Pearce, ed., *New Mexico Place Names* (Albuquerque: University of New Mexico Press, 1965), pp. 153–54.

In the 1880s the town was moved farther north and called Henpeck, for reasons unknown. Still later it was briefly named White City, after a local rancher. By 1900 the old Seven Rivers was essentially a ghost town, and the new settlement assumed the Seven Rivers name.

16. Hal K. Rothman, *Promise Beheld and the Limits of Place: A Historic Resource Study of Carlsbad Caverns and Guadalupe Mountains National Parks and the Surrounding Areas* (Washington, D.C.: U.S. Government Printing Office, 1998), p. 100.

17. T. Dudley Cramer, *The Pecos Ranchers in the Lincoln County War* (Oakland, Calif.: Branding Iron Press, 1996), p. 50.

18. Frederick Nolan, *The West of Billy the Kid* (Norman: University of Oklahoma Press, 1998), p. 71.

19. Cramer, p. 19.

Refugia Rascón y Piño was the daughter of José María Rascón, a native of Andalusia, Spain, who became a sheep rancher in northern New Mexico. Beckwith and Refugia wed in Santa Fe on December 22, 1849.

20. Ibid., p. 23.

21. Ibid., p. 92.

22. Nolan, p. 77.

23. Eve Ball (1887–1976) taught at all levels of education, including college, and also authored several award-winning books. She served as president of the New Mexico Folklore Society and in 1982 was inducted into the National Cowgirl Hall of Fame. At the time of her death she was honored by the U.S. Senate for her life's work.

24. Eve Ball, *Ma'am Jones of the Pecos* (Tucson: University of Arizona Press, 1969), pp. 116–17.

25. Ibid., p. 117.

26. Ibid., p. 118.

27. Robert M. Utley, *Billy the Kid: A Short and Violent Life* (Lincoln and London: University of Nebraska Press, 1989), p. 217, fn 19.

28. Frederick Nolan, *Bad Blood: The Life and Times of the Horrell Brothers* (Stillwater, Okla.: Barbed Wire Press, 1994), p. 164.

29. Maurice G. Fulton, *History of the Lincoln County War* (Tucson: University of Arizona Press, 1968), p. 27.

30. Ibid., pp. 27–28.

31. Ibid., p. 28.

In Lincoln County the bungled execution was commonly called the double hanging. Many suspected that it had actually been a clever ruse, plotted by the Murphy-Dolan faction, that went wrong. They contended the plan to fake Wilson's death and then spirit him away backfired because an onlooker saw his body move in the coffin and alerted the others that he was still alive and needed to be hanged yet again.

32. *Santa Fe New Mexican*, December 15, 1875.

33. Lily Klasner, *My Girlhood among Outlaws* (Tucson: University of Arizona Press, 1972), p. 169.

34. Ibid., p. 174.

35. Utley, p. 28.

36. Klasner, p. 170.

37. Nolan, *The West of Billy the Kid*, p. 83.

38. Ibid.

39. Cramer, p. 91.

40. Nolan, *The West of Billy the Kid*, p. 84.

41. Utley, p. 31.

42. Klasner, p. 174.

Although widely attributed to Oliver Goldsmith, the line was derived from the original version by the Athenian orator and statesman Demosthenes, who in 338 B.C. said, "The man who runs away may fight again."

Seventeen • Billy Bonney

1. Jerry Weddle, *Antrim Is My Stepfather's Name* (Phoenix: Arizona Historical Society, 1993), p. 47.

2. A search for the Bonney name on several of the more popular online genealogy databases, such as RootsWeb.com and Ancestry.com, provides many references to William H. Bonney, also known as Billy the Kid.

3. Ibid.

4. Ibid.

Frank Richard Prassel, *The Great American Outlaw: A Legacy of Fact and Fiction* (Norman: University of Oklahoma Press, 1993), pp. 220–21.

5. Ibid.

6. Ibid., pp. 81–82.

7. Ibid.
8. From Frederick Nolan e-mail to the author, February 13, 2005.
9. Ellen Bradbury-Reid, executive director, Recursos de Santa Fe, interview with author, September 26, 2005.

Recursos de Santa Fe, an educational, nonprofit organization specializing in symposiums and tours, was one of the Billy the Kid conference sponsors. Ms. Reid attended all the activities in both Ruidoso and Lincoln.
10. *El Paso Times*, September 14, 1991.
11. Bradbury-Reid interview.
12. *Lincoln County News*, October 10, 1991.
13. *El Paso Times*, September 14, 1991.
14. Ibid.
15. Jan Girand, ed., *Roswell Web Magazine*, www.roswellwebmag.com/main.htm, Roswell, New Mexico, April 21, 2004.

Ms. Girand is a long-active member of the Billy the Kid Outlaw Gang, Inc., a nonprofit organization the purpose of which is to preserve, protect, and promote Billy the Kid and Pat Garrett history. In September 2004 she was appointed editor of the *B.T.K.O.G. Gazette*, the organization's publication for members.
16. Ibid.
17. Ibid.
18. Ibid.
19. Ibid.
20. Ibid.
21. Ibid.
22. *El Paso Times*, September 14, 1991.
23. Ibid.
24. Nolan correspondence, February 13, 2005.
25. Frederick Nolan, *The West of Billy the Kid* (Norman: University of Oklahoma Press, 1998), p. 6.

Eighteen • Eye of the Storm

1. William A. Keleher, *Violence in Lincoln County 1869–1881* (Albuquerque: University of New Mexico Press, 1957), p. xii.
2. T. M. Pearce, ed., *New Mexico Place Names* (Albuquerque: University of New Mexico Press, 1965), p. 88.
3. Maurice G. Fulton, *History of the Lincoln County War* (Tucson: University of Arizona Press, 1968).

Today Lincoln County is less than one-fifth of its original size, and either all or parts of six other counties have been created within its original borders.

4. Keleher, pp. viii–ix.

Warren A. Beck, *New Mexico: A History of Four Centuries* (Norman: University of Oklahoma Press, 1962), pp. 6–8.

Randolph B. Campbell, *Gone to Texas: A History of the Lone Star State* (New York and Oxford, U.K.: Oxford University Press, 2003), p. 33.

5. The term "mescalero," or mescal maker, was used by the Spanish to refer to one of the largest Apache groups in New Mexico because of the tribe's extensive use of the mescal plant.

6. Pearce, p. 88.

7. Ibid., p. 96.

8. Walter R. Henn, *A Stroll thru Old Lincolntown* (Lincoln, N.M.: Lincoln County Historical Publications, 1996), p. 30.

El Torreón was restored in 1935 by the Works Progress Administration under the sponsorship of the Chaves County Historical Society and deeded to the state of New Mexico.

9. Pearce, p. 88.

10. John P. Ryan, *Fort Stanton and Its Community 1855–1896* (Las Cruces, N.M.: Yucca Tree Press, 1998), p. 6.

11. Fulton, p. 14.

Lee Myers, *Fort Stanton, New Mexico: The Military Years 1855–1896* (Lincoln, N.M.: Lincoln County Historical Society Publications, 1988), pp. 1–2.

At the time of his death Captain Stanton was a newlywed whose bride had arrived in New Mexico Territory just a month before he rode into the ambush. Only Stanton's bones were recovered and along with the remains of two other slain soldiers returned to the post for burial with full military honors.

12. Myers, pp. 38–41.

13. Ryan, pp. 41–43.

14. Jim Broeck, *El Defensor Chieftain*, Internet ed., Socorro, New Mexico, July 16, 2005.

In August 1862 alone, Apaches killed forty-six settlers, kidnapped scores of children, and stole thousands of head of cattle.

15. Neal W. Ackerly, Ph.D., "A Navajo Diaspora: The Long Walk to Hwéedi," Dos Rios Consultants, Silver City, New Mexico, 1998.

Dos Rios Consultants provides consulting services in the social and natural sciences across the greater Southwest.

16. Ibid.

17. Ibid.

18. Broeck, *El Defensor Chieftain*.

19. Hubert Howe Bancroft, *History of Arizona and New Mexico, 1530–1888* (San Francisco: History Company, 1889), p. 661.

Bancroft collected and published thirty-nine volumes on the history and peoples of western North America. Bancroft wrote very little himself. Some of his many assistants did the actual writing although they were never properly credited.

20. Pearce, pp. 19–20.

21. Records, files, and documentation provided by Scott Smith, manager, Fort Sumner State Monument, New Mexico State Monuments, Fort Sumner, New Mexico.

22. Ibid.

23. Ibid.

24. Ibid.

25. David Roberts, *A Newer World: Kit Carson, John C. Frémont, and the Claiming of the American West* (New York: Simon & Schuster, 2000), pp. 273–76.

26. Ibid.

27. Ibid., p. 281.

   Bancroft, p. 731. Bancroft wrote that "the Bosque Redondo as a reservation had no merits whatsoever; and as a means of civilizing the Indians, the project proved a total failure."

28. Roberts, p. 277.

   On November 3, 1865, every Mescalero Apache fit to travel left the confines of Bosque Redondo. Shortly afterward even the sick and injured Apaches were able to flee and return to their native home.

29. Dale F. Giese, *Forts of New Mexico* (Silver City, N.M.: Privately printed, 1991), p. 28.

30. Ryan, p. 26.

31. Ibid., pp. 25–26.

32. Ibid., pp. 23–24.

33. Dan Scurlock, *From the Rio to the Sierra: An Environmental History of the Middle Rio Grande Basin* (Fort Collins, Colo.: Rocky Mountain Research Station, U.S. Department of Agriculture, May 1998), pp. 165–67.

   In the 1870s army horses usually received a daily ration of fourteen pounds of hay and twelve pounds of grain.

34. Ryan, p. 24.

35. Fulton, p. 14.

Nineteen • Dream Killers

1. John Tunstall, from an April 1877 letter to his father, John Partridge Tunstall, in London.

2. Paul Kooistra, *Criminals as Heroes: Structure, Power & Identity* (Bowling Green, Ohio: Bowling Green State University Popular Press, 1989), p. 75.

3. John P. Wilson, *Merchants, Guns, and Money: The Story of Lincoln County and Its Wars* (Santa Fe: Museum of New Mexico Press, 1987), p. 41.

4. Warren A. Beck, *New Mexico: A History of Four Centuries* (Norman: University of Oklahoma Press, 1962), p. 162.

5. Interview with Jack Rigney, former monument manager, Lincoln State Monument, Museum of New Mexico, Lincoln, New Mexico, November 20, 2004.

   Rigney served as the Lincoln Monument manager for seventeen years. Previously he managed the Fort Sumner State Monument for eight years.

6. Richard Erodes, *Saloons of the Old West* (Salt Lake City and Chicago: Howe Brothers, 1985), pp. 84–85.

7. Ibid.

Prior to the advent of commercially bottled distillates, the various whiskeys served in cantinas and saloons were given colorful names, including Apache Tears, Tongue Oil, Tarantula Juice, Nockum Stiff, Red Dog, Stagger Soup, Popskull, Phlegm Cutter, and White Mare's Milk, described as "the fightingest liquor ever to come out of a bottle."

8. William A. Keleher, *Violence in Lincoln County 1869–1881* (Albuquerque: University of New Mexico Press, 1957), p. 15.

9. Erodes, p. 84.

Peter Watts, *A Dictionary of the Old West* (New York: Alfred A. Knopf, 1877), p. 162.

Although "heeled" meant to be armed with a gun, it was also said that a man's heels were armed when they were spurred. The usage probably derived from the practice of arming the heels of fighting roosters with metal spurs.

10. Lily Klasner, *My Girlhood among Outlaws* (Tucson: University of Arizona Press, 1972), p. 216.

11. Winfred Blevins, *Dictionary of the American West* (New York: Facts on File, 1993), p. 291.

"Roostered" was one of many frontier words for drunkenness. Other expressions included "bottle fever," "cuts his wolf loose," or "ties on a bear." In New Mexico, and throughout the Southwest, a drunk was often called by the Spanish word *borracho*. A great drunkard was a *borrachón*.

12. Klasner, p. 100.

In her description of the Horrell War, Lily Casey Klasner admits that some of the Horrells' followers were "very desperate men," but she also offers a defense for the family's violent acts: "It is true that several in the Horrell crowd were wanted for killings back in Texas, but those were killings that were more generally approved of than condemned under the code of the time."

13. Ibid., p. 102.

14. Keleher, p. 13.

15. Wilson, p. 44.

16. Philip J. Rasch, *Warriors of Lincoln County* (Laramie, Wyo.: National Association for Outlaw and Lawman History, in affiliation with the University of Wyoming, 1998), p. 120.

17. *Santa Fe New Mexican*, January 2, 1874, and January 27, 1874.

"Guerrilla" means a "little war" in Spanish. The word first became popular when Napoleon Bonaparte invaded Spain in 1808 and was bested by small bands of Spanish peasants fighting in unconventional ways.

18. Frederick Nolan, *Bad Blood: The Life and Times of the Horrell Brothers* (Stillwater, Okla.: Barbed Wire Press, 1994), p. 90.

19. Rigney interview.

20. Klasner, p. 161.

21. Ibid.

22. Ibid., p. 162.

23. Ibid.

24. Ibid.

25. Dan Scurlock, *From the Rio to the Sierra: An Environmental History of the Middle Rio Grande Basin* (Fort Collins, Colo.: Rocky Mountain Research Station, U.S. Department of Agriculture, May 1998), pp. 167–68.

26. William A. Keleher, *The Fabulous Frontier* (Santa Fe: Rydal Press, 1945), p. 52.

27. Klasner, p. 162.

28. Ibid.

29. Maurice G. Fulton, *History of the Lincoln County War* (Tucson: University of Arizona Press, 1968), p. 95.

30. Keleher, *Violence in Lincoln County 1869–1881*, p. 250.

31. Ibid., pp. 249–50.

Patrón made his remarks about Murphy in a sworn affidavit dated July 1, 1878.

32. Ibid., p. 51.

33. Philip J. Rasch, *Gunsmoke in Lincoln County* (Laramie, Wyo.: National Association for Outlaw and Lawman History, Inc., in affiliation with the University of Wyoming, 1997), p. 4.

34. Ibid.

35. Keleher, *Violence in Lincoln County*, p. 32.

36. Ibid.

37. Ibid.

38. Wilson, p. 30.

In 1868 L. G. Murphy & Co. was awarded a $9,390 contract to furnish lumber for rebuilding Fort Stanton.

39. Rasch, *Gunsmoke in Lincoln County*, p. 6.

40. Ibid., p. 9.

John Ryan, *Fort Stanton and Its Community, 1855–1896* (Las Cruces, N.M.: Yucca Tree Press, 1998), p. 84.

41. Ibid.

42. Keleher, *Violence in Lincoln County*, p. 33.

43. Rasch, *Gunsmoke in Lincoln County*, p. 13.

44. Keleher, *Violence in Lincoln County*, pp. 53–54.

In 1863 Dolan enlisted in Company K, Seventeenth Regiment, New York Zouaves. He was discharged in 1865.

45. Fulton, p. 47.

46. Bob Boze Bell, *The Illustrated Life and Times of Billy the Kid* (Phoenix: Tri Star-Boze Publications, 1992), p. 16.

47. Frederick Nolan, *The West of Billy the Kid* (Norman: University of Oklahoma Press, 1998), pp. 41–42.

Dolan stood only five feet two and one-half inches in his stocking feet.

48. Klasner, pp. 94–95.

49. Rasch, *Gunsmoke in Lincoln County*, p. 7.

50. Ibid., p. 8.

51. Wilson, p. 30.

52. Fulton, p. 48.

53. Ibid.

54. Klasner, p. 95.

55. William J. Parish, *The Charles Ilfeld Company: A Study of the Rise and Decline of Mercantile Capitalism in New Mexico* (Cambridge, Mass.: Harvard University Press, 1961), p. 44.

56. Klasner, pp. 95–96.

57. Nolan, *The West of Billy the Kid*, p. 43.

58. Klasner, p. 95.

59. Nolan, *The West of Billy the Kid*, p. 41.

60. Robert M. Utley, *High Noon in Lincoln: Violence on the Western Frontier* (Albuquerque: University of New Mexico Press, 1987), p. 16.

61. George W. Coe, *Frontier Fighter* (Chicago: Lakeside Press, 1984), p. 34.

62. Ibid.

63. Fulton, p. 48.
   Nolan, *The West of Billy the Kid*, p. 41.

64. Coe, p. 30.
   When the Civil War ended, at least 345 veterans of the California Column elected to remain in New Mexico Territory.

65. Robert M. Utley, *Billy the Kid: A Short and Violent Life* (Lincoln and London: University of Nebraska Press, 1989), p. 25.
   Frank Coe gave an interview to historian J. Evetts Haley at San Patricio, New Mexico, on August 14, 1927. Coe died in 1931, a couple of weeks shy of turning eighty years old.

66. *Mesilla News*, September 18, 1875; *Grant County Herald*, September 26, 1875.

67. Nolan, *Bad Blood*, pp. 173–74.

68. Ibid.

69. *Mesilla Valley Independent*, October 13, 1877.

70. Ibid.

71. Utley, *High Noon in Lincoln*, p. 29.

72. Nolan, *The West of Billy the Kid*, p. 118.

73. Ibid.
   Brady's wife was pregnant with her ninth child when Brady was shot and killed in Lincoln on April 1, 1878.

74. Utley, *Billy the Kid*, p. 61.

75. Ibid., p. 62.

76. Ibid., pp. 61–62.

77. Rasch, *Gunsmoke in Lincoln County*, p. 83.

78. Nolan, *The West of Billy the Kid*, pp. 38, 46.

79. Ibid., p. 38.

80. T. Dudley Cramer, *The Pecos Ranchers in the Lincoln County War* (Oakland, Calif.: Branding Iron Press, 1996), p. 87.

81. Wilson, p. 58.

McSween and Chisum were arrested and jailed at Las Vegas on December 27, 1877. McSween quickly posted bond, but Chisum was held in other unrelated lawsuits and remained jailed until March 1878.

82. Wilson, p. 63.

83. Frederick W. Nolan, *The Life & Death of John Henry Tunstall* (Albuquerque: University of New Mexico Press, 1965), p. 213.

Twenty • The Unfortunate War Spawns the Myth

1. Robert M. Utley, *High Noon in Lincoln: Violence of the Western Frontier* (Albuquerque: University of New Mexico Press, 1987), p. 165.

2. Robert N. Mullin, *The Boyhood of Billy the Kid* (El Paso: Texas Western Press, 1967), p. 20.

3. Frederick Nolan, *The West of Billy the Kid* (Norman: University of Oklahoma Press, 1998), pp. 87–88.

4. Ibid.

5. Ibid., p. 92.

Robert Julyan, *The Place Names of New Mexico* (Albuquerque: University of New Mexico Press, 1998), pp. 148–49.

Glencoe, a Lincoln County settlement in the Ruidoso Valley, combines a synonym for "valley" with the Coe family surname. The Coes were among the early pioneers of Lincoln and Otero counties. They came from Missouri, worked along the Santa Fe Trail, and moved into southern New Mexico Territory in the mid–1870s.

6. Miguel Antonio Otero, Jr., *The Real Billy the Kid: With New Light on the Lincoln County War* (Houston: Arte Público Press, 1998), p. 110.

Otero's two-hundred-page book was first published in 1936 by Rufus Rockwell Wilson, Inc., New York.

7. Ibid.

8. Otero, p. 133.

9. Ibid.

10. Ibid., p. xvi.

11. Frederick Nolan e-mail to the author, February 13, 2005.

12. Otero, pp. xi.

Rivera acted as editor and wrote the critical introduction for the 1998 reissue of Otero's book.

13. Ibid., p. xiii.

14. Ibid., p. 45.

15. William A. Keleher, *The Fabulous Frontier* (Santa Fe: Rydal Press, 1945), p. 97.

16. Victor Westphall, *Thomas Benton Catron and His Era* (Tucson: University of Arizona Press, 1973), p. 6.

Like Steve Elkins's father, Catron's father so admired Missouri Senator Thomas Hart Benton, the "grand old man" of the Democratic Party, that he also named his son Thomas Benton in his honor.

17. Ibid.

Catron and Elkins were in a class of nine students who graduated from the law school on July 4, 1860.

18. Ibid., p. 8.

Catron taught at a country school near his father's farm outside Lexington. Elkins was a teacher in Harrisonville, where it was said he became acquainted with Cole Younger and Jesse James before they launched their notorious outlaw careers.

19. Ibid., p. 11.

20. Ibid., p. 22.

21. Ralph Emerson Twitchell, *The Leading Facts of New Mexico* (1912; Albuquerque: Horn & Wallace, 1963), vol. 2, pp. 519–20.

22. Ibid., pp. 401–02.

23. Ibid., p. 520.

24. Howard Roberts Lamar, *The Far Southwest 1846–1912: A Territorial History* (New Haven and London: Yale University Press, 1966), p. 147.

25. *Handbook of Texas Online*, s.v. "NEWMAN, SIMEON HARRISON," www.tsha.utexas .edu/handbook/online/articles/view/NN/fne41.html.

26. Ibid.

Newman moved to Texas, renamed the newspaper *The Lone Star*, and continued his fight against lawbreakers and political scalawags. The newspaper went out of business in 1886, when Newman lost the support of business leaders who were involved in the vice he was exposing. He spent the rest of his life working for an insurance firm and for the betterment of his adopted city. He died in El Paso in 1915.

27. Westphall, p. 99.

Westphall contends that Catron's personal role in the Maxwell Land Grant controversy was minor, yet he points out that litigation over the land grant brought the Santa Fe Ring into notoriety and established Catron as the ringleader.

28. Ibid., p. 100.

29. Lamar, p. 153.

30. Ibid.

31. Ibid.

32. Richard Maxwell Brown, "Violence," *The Oxford History of the American West*, ed. Clyde A. Milner II, Carol A. O'Connor, and Martha A. Sandweiss (New York and Oxford, U.K.: Oxford University Press, 1994), p. 404.

Known to be violent when drinking, the clubfooted Allison served in the Confederate army, joined the Ku Klux Klan, and was responsible for many deaths in knife or gun duels. Unlike many shootists, Allison did not die at age forty-seven dangling from a hangman's noose or in a gunfight. On July 3, 1887, he fell from a freight wagon he was driving and one of the wheels rolled over his head.

33. Lamar, pp. 149–50.

34. Ibid., p. 147.

35. Ralph Dunlap, *Masons in Early Lincoln County prior to 1900* (Lincoln, N.M.: Lincoln Masonic Foundation, 1994), p. 5.

36. History files, Masonic Grand Lodge of New Mexico, Albuquerque, New Mexico.

Carson died in 1868 in Colorado. The following year his remains and those of his wife were removed to Taos, New Mexico, and laid to rest in the Kit Carson Cemetery. Although rarely displayed, Carson's rifle is in the possession of the Montezuma Lodge in Santa Fe, and a Masonic apron bearing his name may be viewed in the collection at the Grand Lodge Building in Albuquerque.

37. Chris Wilson, *The Myth of Santa Fe: Creating a Modern Regional Tradition* (Albuquerque: University of New Mexico Press, 1997), p. 185.

38. Matt S. Hughes, Grand Orator, "A Triad of Masonic Ideals," delivered 1914, California Grand Oration, Grand Lodge, F & A. M. of California

39. Dunlap, pp. 5–7.

40. Philip J. Rasch, *Gunsmoke in Lincoln County* (Laramie: National Association for Outlaw and Lawman History, Inc., in affiliation with the University of Wyoming, 1997), p. 11.

41. Gwendolyn Rogers, interview by author in Lincoln, New Mexico, November 19, 2004.

42. Rasch, p. 60.

Twenty-one • Endless War

1. Godfrey Gauss letter to J. P. Tunstall, dated April 19, 1882.

2. Lincoln declared the first national Thanksgiving for Thursday, November 26, 1863, in recognition of a long-standing New England tradition. The holiday date was changed from the last Thursday in November to the fourth Thursday every November by President Franklin Roosevelt in 1939 with the approval of Congress in 1941.

3. George W. Coe, *Frontier Fighter* (Chicago: Lakeside Press, 1984), p. 49–50.

4. Philip J. Rasch, with Allan Radbourne, *Trailing Billy the Kid* (Laramie: National Association for Outlaw and Lawman History, Inc., in affiliation with the University of Wyoming, 1995), pp. 89–90.

5. Ibid., pp. 90–91.

6. Coe, p. 50.

7. Robert M. Utley, *Billy the Kid: A Short and Violent Life* (Lincoln and London: University of Nebraska Press, 1989), p. 35.

Although in Spanish *gallina* means "chicken," in this instance it also means "turkey hen," as in *gallina de la tierra*, or "wild turkey."

8. T. M. Pearce, *New Mexico Place Names* (Albuquerque: University of New Mexico Press, 1965), pp. 149–50.

9. Robert M. Utley, *Four Fighters of Lincoln County* (Albuquerque: University of New Mexico Press, 1986), p. 23.

10. Ibid., p. 33.
   The Kid was also known to carry and use the .38-caliber Colt revolver called the Lightning.

11. Robert M. Utley, *High Noon in Lincoln County: Violence on the Western Frontier* (Albuquerque: University of New Mexico Press, 1987), p. 43.

12. Library of Congress, Manuscript Division, WPA Federal Writers' Project Collection. Manuscripts from the Federal Writers' Project, "WPA Life Histories from New Mexico," interview of Francisco Gomez, August 15, 1938, collected by Edith L. Crawford.

13. Frederick W. Nolan, *The Life & Death of John Henry Tunstall* (Albuquerque: University of New Mexico Press, 1965), pp. 182, 205, 238.

14. William A. Keleher, *Violence in Lincoln County 1869–1881* (Albuquerque: University of New Mexico Press, 1957), p. 252.
   According to the Lincoln County Historical Society, Gottfried Georg (Godfrey) Gauss was born in Germany in 1824 and died possibly in Kansas in 1902.

15. Frederick Nolan, *The West of Billy the Kid* (Norman: University of Oklahoma Press, 1998), p. 92.

16. Keleher, p. 325.

17. Ibid., pp. 133–34.

18. Utley, *Billy the Kid*, p. 39.

19. Nolan, *The West of Billy the Kid*, p. 95.

20. Utley, *Four Fighters of Lincoln County*, p. 23.

21. Jack Rigney, interview by author in Lincoln, New Mexico, November 16, 2004.

22. Nolan, *The West of Billy the Kid*, p. 103.

23. Nolan, *The Life and Death of John Tunstall*, p. 272.

24. Ibid.

25. Ibid.

26. Ibid., p. 273.

27. Ibid., p. 272.

28. Ibid., p. 274.

29. Paul Kooistra, *Criminals as Heroes: Structure, Power & Identity* (Bowling Green, Ohio: Bowling Green State University Popular Press, 1989), p. 82.

30. Utley, *High Noon in Lincoln County*, pp. ix–x.

31. Nolan, *The West of Billy the Kid*, p. 108.

32. Ibid.

33. Ibid.

34. Ibid., pp. 108–09.

35. Utley, *Billy the Kid*, p. 53.

36. Bob Boze Bell, *The Illustrated Life and Times of Billy the Kid* (Phoenix: Tri Star-Boze Publications, 1992, 1996), p. 56.
37. Ibid.
38. Ibid., p. 65.
39. Nolan, *The West of Billy the Kid*, p. 111.
40. Utley, *Billy the Kid*, pp. 54–55.
41. Bell, pp. 56–58.
42. Ibid., p. 58.
43. Nolan, *The West of Billy the Kid*, p. 115.
44. Bell, p. 58.
45. Utley, *Billy the Kid*, p. 63.
46. Bell, pp. 60–63.
47. Ibid.
48. Ibid.
49. Ibid.
50. Ibid., p. 65.
51. Ibid.
52. Coe, p. 94.
53. Ibid.
54. Ibid., pp. 97–98.
55. Bell, p. 67.
56. Ibid.
57. Emerson Hough, *The Story of the Outlaw* (New York: Grosset & Dunlap, 1905), p. 290.
    Johnny Patten, a sawyer and carpenter at Blazer's Mill, told Hough that he built the large coffin that held the bodies of both Brewer and Roberts. According to Emil Blazer, Dr. Blazer's son, the two men were buried in separate coffins but side by side.
58. Nolan, *The West of Billy the Kid*, pp. 134–36.
59. Keleher, pp. 119–20.
60. Ibid.
61. Ibid., p. 122.
62. T. Dudley Cramer, *The Pecos Ranchers in the Lincoln County War* (Oakland, Calif.: Branding Iron Press, 1996), pp. 116–17.
63. Utley, *Billy the Kid*, p. 78.
    The McSweens had not only a piano but also an organ and a set of bagpipes.
64. Cramer, p. 117.
65. Ibid., p. 118.
66. Ibid.
67. Nolan, *The West of Billy the Kid*, p. 139.
68. Utley, *Billy the Kid*, p. 79.
69. Ibid.

70. Cramer, p. 119.

71. Ibid., pp. 119–20.

Twenty-two • Firestorm

1. Frederick W. Nolan, *The Life and Death of John Henry Tunstall* (Albuquerque: University of New Mexico Press, 1965), p. 366.

2. John P. Wilson, *Merchants, Guns, and Money: The Story of Lincoln County and Its Wars* (Santa Fe: Museum of New Mexico Press, 1987), pp. 90–91.

3. T. Dudley Cramer, *The Pecos Ranchers in the Lincoln County War* (Oakland, Calif.: Branding Iron Press, 1996), p. 120.

4. Ibid.

5. Ibid.

6. Ibid.

7. Maurice C. Fulton, *History of the Lincoln County War* (Tucson: University of Arizona Press, 1968), p. 236.

8. Ibid., p. 237.

9. Ibid.

10. Ibid.

11. Wilson, p. 92.

12. Fulton, p. 236.

13. Howard Roberts Lamar, *The Far Southwest 1846–1912: A Territorial History* (New Haven and London: Yale University Press, 1966), p. 159.

14. Robert M. Utley, *Billy the Kid: A Short and Violent Life* (Lincoln and London: University of Nebraska Press, 1989), p. 83.

15. Wilson, p. 93.

16. Utley, p. 89.

17. Ibid.

18. Ibid., p. 90.

19. Frederick Nolan, *The West of Billy the Kid* (Norman: University of Oklahoma Press, 1998), p. 151.

20. Nolan, *The West of Billy the Kid*, p. 151.

21. Cramer, p. 129.

22. Ibid.

23. Nolan, *The West of Billy the Kid*, pp. 158–59.

24. Cramer, pp. 130–31.

25. Ibid., p. 131.

26. Ibid., p. 132.

27. Ibid.

28. George W. Coe, *Frontier Fighter* (Chicago: Lakeside Press, 1984), p. 165.

29. Fulton, p. 267.

30. Ibid., pp. 267–68.

31. Nolan, *The West of Billy the Kid*, p. 162.

32. Ibid., p. 163.

33. Ibid.

34. Ibid., p. 164.

35. Cramer, pp. 133–34.

36. Ibid., p. 134.

37. Fulton, pp. 273–74.

38. Nolan, *The Life and Death of John Henry Tunstall*, pp. 378–79.

Twenty-three • Devil or Angel

1. Kent Steckmesser, *The Western Hero in History and Legend* (Norman: University of Oklahoma Press, 1965), p. 70.

2. Philip J. Rasch and R. N. Mullin, "Dim Trails: The Pursuit of the McCarty Family," *New Mexico Folklore Record*, vol. 8 (1953–54), p. 11.

3. Actor Carleton Young in his role as newspaper editor Maxwell Scott delivers the memorable line to Jimmy Stewart playing Ransom Stoddard. Ironically, director John Ford was himself famous for embellishing reality in many of his films about the Old West.

4. Fintan O'Toole, "The Many Stories of Billy the Kid," *The New Yorker* (December 28, 1998–January 4, 1999), p. 97.

5. *Las Vegas Gazette*, December 3, 1880.

6. Bob Boze Bell, *The Illustrated Life and Times of Billy the Kid* (Phoenix: Tri Star-Boze Publications, 1992, 1996), p. 79.

7. Robert W. Utley, *Billy the Kid: A Short and Violent Life* (Lincoln and London: University of Nebraska Press, 1989), p. 105.

   Sallie Chisum married twice; both marriages ended in divorce. She became a successful rancher in her own right and died in 1934 in Roswell, New Mexico.

8. Ibid., pp. 105–06.

9. Robert Julyan, *The Place Names of New Mexico* (Albuquerque: University of New Mexico Press, 1998), p. 278.

   There is also a story that the town's name came from the Luna family, which settled near the gap, and actually refers to Lunas Gap.

10. Frederick Nolan, *The West of Billy the Kid* (Norman: University of Oklahoma Press, 1998), pp. 170–71.

11. George W. Coe, *Frontier Fighter* (Chicago: Lakeside Press, 1984), pp. 200–03.

12. Nolan, p. 171.

13. Ibid., p. 174.

14. Ibid.

15. Ibid., p. 26.

16. Pauline Durrett Robinson and R. L. Robertson, *Tascosa: Historic Site in the Texas Panhandle* (Amarillo: Paramount Publishing Company, n.d.), pp. 7–8, 26.

17. Bill Russell and Delbert Trew, *Twice Told Tales of the Llano Estacado* (Lubbock, Tex.: Hurricane Printing, 2003), p. 181.

    Cowboys, or "brush poppers," out on the llano had their own language. A hat was "a lid, a warbonnet, or a hair case"; beans were "Pecos strawberries"; sourdough biscuits were "wading"; flour gravy was "Texas butter"; onions were "skunk eggs"; and the common name for a phosphorus match was "lucifer."

18. Robinson and Robertson, pp. 29–30.

19. Dr. Henry F. Hoyt's *A Frontier Doctor*, published in 1929, was edited by Doyce B. Nunis, Jr., and reprinted in 1979 by R. R. Donnelley & Sons Co.

20. F. Hoyt, p. 39.

    Hoyt went on to achieve fame as the chief surgeon of the U.S. Volunteers in the Philippines during the Spanish-American War. He participated in twenty-five battles, was wounded, and received the Silver Star for gallantry. Following a long and illustrious career, Hoyt died on January 30, 1930, shortly after the publication of *A Frontier Doctor*.

21. Ibid., p. 147.

22. Ibid., pp. 148–49.

23. Robinson and Robertson, p. 13.

24. Hoyt, pp. 150–53.

25. Ibid., p. 153.

26. Ibid., pp. 153–54.

27. Ibid., pp. 154–56.

    The bill of sale the Kid wrote out for Hoyt was dated October 24, 1878. The document, bearing the signature of W. H. Bonney is in the Panhandle-Plains Historical Museum, Canyon, Texas.

28. Ibid., p. 154.

29. Nolan, p. 92.

    Utley, p. 244, n 19.

30. Nolan, p. 180.

    After being driven out of New Mexico, Selman resumed his life of crime in Texas until he was forced to hide in Mexico. When charges against him were dropped, he moved to El Paso, where he worked as a gambler and city constable. In 1894 he shot and killed a former Texas Ranger during a brothel brawl. On August 19, 1895, Selman killed the infamous shootist John Wesley Hardin as he rolled dice in the Acme Saloon. The following year Selman was killed in a gun duel with a law officer outside the Wigwam Saloon.

31. Utley, p. 112.

32. Paul Kooistra, *Criminals as Heroes: Structure, Power & Identity* (Bowling Green, Ohio: Bowling Green State University Popular Press, 1989), pp. 88–89.

33. Nolan, p. 180.

34. Utley, p. 112.

35. Ibid.

36. Nolan, p. 185.

37. Bell, p. 91.

38. Ibid., pp. 91–92.

39. Utley, p. 115.

40. Ibid.

41. Ibid., pp. 115–16.

42. Bell, p. 96.

43. Ibid.

44. Ibid., p. 98.

45. Ibid.

46. William A. Keleher, *Violence in Lincoln County 1869–1881* (Albuquerque: University of New Mexico Press, 1957), pp. 214–15.

47. Ibid., pp. 215–16.

48. Ibid., pp. 222–24.

49. Utley, p. 121.

50. Nolan, p. 90.

On December 15, 1867, Rynerson shot and killed Chief Justice John P. Slough during a dispute at the Exchange Hotel in Santa Fe. Rynerson, represented by Smooth Steve Elkins, was acquitted on grounds of self-defense.

51. Ibid., p. 200.

52. Ibid., p. 201.

53. Ibid.

54. Howard Bryan, *Wildest of the Wild West: True Tales of a Frontier Town on the Santa Fe Trail* (Santa Fe: Clear Light Publishers, 1988), p. xii.

55. Ibid., pp. 98–99.

56. Ibid., p. 101.

57. Hoyt, pp. 183–84.

58. Ibid., pp. 481–86.

59. Kooistra, pp. 91–92.

60. Walter Noble Burns, *The Saga of Billy the Kid* (Garden City, N.Y.: Doubleday, Page & Co., 1926), p. 185.

61. Utley, p. 127.

Twenty-four • El Chivato

1. Oscar Wilde letter dated April 19, 1882. The Irish poet and playwright wrote this letter nine months after the death of Billy the Kid and just sixteen days after Jesse James was shot and

killed. It was written in Leavenworth, Kansas, during Wilde's one-year lecture tour of America.

2. Robert Utley, *Billy the Kid: A Short and Violent Life* (Lincoln and London: University of Nebraska Press, 1989), p. 131.

3. Ibid.

4. Ibid., p. 132.

5. Frederick Nolan, *The West of Billy the Kid* (Norman: University of Oklahoma Press, 1998), p. 230.

6. Leon G. Metz, *Pat Garrett: The Story of a Western Lawman* (Norman: University of Oklahoma Press, 1974), pp. 17, 39–40.

7. Ibid., p. 40.

8. Nolan, p. 230.

9. Metz, p. 53.

10. Bob Boze Bell, *The Illustrated Life and Times of Billy the Kid* (Phoenix: Tri Star-Boze Publications, 1992, 1996), p. 118.

11. Ibid.

12. Ibid., pp. 118–19.

13. Ibid.

14. Nolan, pp. 228–29.

15. Ibid.

16. Ibid., p. 229.

17. Bell, p. 122.

18. Ibid., p. 126.

19. *Las Vegas Gazette*, December 3, 1880.

20. Bell, pp. 130–31.

21. Ibid.

22. Ibid., p. 122.

23. Ibid., p. 133.

24. Ibid., p. 134.

25. Ibid.

26. Ibid., p. 135.

27. T. Dudley Cramer, *The Pecos Ranchers in the Lincoln County War* (Oakland, Calif.: Branding Iron Press, 1996), p. 165.

28. Bell, p. 137.

29. Ibid., pp. 138–39.

30. Cramer, p. 166.

31. Nolan, p. 248.

32. Ibid.

33. Ibid.

34. Bell, pp. 140–41.

Bob Boze Bell created a portrait of the Kid and Paulita's embrace. Titled *Under the Mistletoe*, the painting is now in the author's collection.

35. Ibid., p. 141.

36. Ibid., p. 143.

37. William A. Keleher, *Violence in Lincoln County 1869–1881* (Albuquerque: University of New Mexico Press, 1957), p. 282.

38. Utley, p. 166.

39. *Santa Fe New Mexican*, December 28, 1880.

40. Keleher, p. 300.

41. Nolan, p. 260.

42. Ibid., p. 258.

43. Ibid., pp. 260–61.

44. Ibid., p. 262.

45. Ibid., p. 264.

46. Ibid.,

47. Keleher, p. 315.

48. Ibid., pp. 317–18.

49. Utley, p. 175.

50. Keleher, p. 318.

51. Bell, p. 152.

52. Cramer, pp. 167–68.

53. Ibid., p. 168.

54. Mary Hudson Brothers, *Billy the Kid* (Farmington, N.M.: Hustler Press, 1949), p. 32.

55. Stephen Tatum, *Inventing Billy the Kid* (Tucson: University of Arizona Press, 1997), pp. 32–33.

56. Ibid., p. 33.

57. Bell, p. 155.

58. Nolan, p. 273.

59. Ibid.

60. Ibid.

61. Bob Boze Bell interview with the author, Cave Creek, Arizona, November 10, 2004.

62. *Las Vegas Daily Optic*, May 4, 1881.

63. Lynda A. Sanchez, "They Loved Billy the Kid," *True West*, vol. 31, no. 1 (January 1984), p. 14.

64. James Sanchez, interview with the author, Lincoln, New Mexico, November 19, 2004.

65. Nolan, p. 277.

66. Bell, p. 160.

67. Ibid.

68. Nolan, p. 280.

69. Ibid.

70. Ibid., pp. 281–82.
71. Utley, p. 192.

Epilogue • Billy's Never-ending Ride

1. Paul Andrew Hutton, "Dreamscape Desperado," *New Mexico Magazine*, vol. 68, no. 6 (June 1990), p. 57.
2. Frederick Nolan, *The West of Billy the Kid* (Norman: University of Oklahoma Press, 1998), p. 287.
3. Ibid., pp. 287–88.
4. *Santa Fe Weekly Democrat*, July 21, 1881.

BIBLIOGRAPHY

PRIVATE COLLECTIONS

Robert McCubbin Collection
Bob Boze Bell Collection
Buckeye Blake Collection

ARCHIVES, MUSEUMS, LIBRARIES, AND HISTORICAL SOCIETIES

Arizona State Library, Archives and Public Records, Phoenix, Arizona
Arizona Department of Corrections, Phoenix, Arizona
The Billy the Kid Outlaw Gang, Inc., Capitan, New Mexico
Casa Malpais Museum, Springerville, Arizona
Colorado Historical Society, Denver, Colorado
Denver Art Museum, Denver, Colorado
Denver Metro Convention and Visitors Bureau, Denver, Colorado
Fort Selden State Monument, Radium Springs, New Mexico
Fort Sumner State Monument, New Mexico State Monuments, Fort Sumner, New Mexico
Historic Preservation Alliance of Wichita and Sedgwick County, Wichita, Kansas
Historical Society of Oak Park and River Forest, Oak Park, Illinois
The Hubbard Museum of the American West, Ruidoso Downs, New Mexico
Kansas State Historical Society, Topeka, Kansas
Library of Congress, Manuscript Division, WPA Federal Writers' Project Collection. Manu-
    scripts from the Federal Writers' Project, "WPA Life Histories from New Mexico," Wash-
    ington, D. C.
The Lincoln County Historical Society, Carrizozo, New Mexico
Lincoln State Monument, Lincoln, New Mexico
Masonic Grand Lodge of New Mexico, Albuquerque, New Mexico
Museum of the Kansas National Guard, Topeka, Kansas
Museum of New Mexico, Santa Fe, New Mexico
National Archives and Records Administration, 1870 Federal Population Census; 1880 Federal
    Population Census, Washington, D.C.

New Mexico Folklore Society, Albuquerque, New Mexico

New Mexico Farm & Ranch Heritage Museum, Las Cruces, New Mexico

New Mexico State Records Center and Archives, Santa Fe, New Mexico

Old Cowtown Museum, Wichita, Kansas

The Panhandle-Plains Historical Museum, Canyon, Texas

Recursos de Santa Fe, Santa Fe, New Mexico

Round Valley Public Library, Springerville, Arizona

Sacramento Mountains Historical Museum, Cloudcroft, New Mexico

Silver City Museum, Silver City, New Mexico

Texas Office of the Governor, Archives and Information Services Division, Texas State Library and Archives Commission, Austin, Texas

Townsend Library, New Mexico State University at Alamogordo, Alamogordo, New Mexico

University of Missouri—Columbia, Columbia, Missouri

Western History/Genealogy Department, Denver Public Library, Denver, Colorado

Western History Photography Collection of Denver Public Library, Denver, Colorado

BOOKS

Ackerman, Kenneth D. *Dark Horse: The Surprise Election and Political Murder of President James A. Garfield.* New York: Carroll & Graf Publishers, 2003.

Adams, Ramon F. *A Fitting Death for Billy the Kid.* Norman: University of Oklahoma Press, 1960.

———. *The Cowboy Dictionary.* Norman: University of Oklahoma Press, 1968; New York: Perigee Books, 1993.

American Guide Series. Compiled by Workers of the Writers' Program of the Works Projects Administration, *New Mexico: A Guide to the Colorful State.* New York: Hastings House, 1940.

Antheam, Robert. *The Coloradans.* Albuquerque: University of New Mexico Press, 1976.

Arms, L. R. *A Short History of the Noncommissioned Officer.* El Paso, Tex.: U.S. Army Museum of the Noncommissioned Officer, Fort Bliss, Texas, 1989.

Asbury, Herbert. *The Gangs of New York: An Informal History of the Underworld.* New York: Alfred A. Knopf, 1927, 1928.

Athearn, Lewis. *The Mythic West in Twentieth Century America.* Lawrence: University of Kansas Press, 1986.

Ball, Eve. *Ma'am Jones of the Pecos.* Tucson: University of Arizona Press, 1969.

Bancroft, Hubert Howe. *History of Arizona and New Mexico, 1530–1888.* San Francisco: History Company, 1889.

Barnes, Will C. *Arizona Place Names.* Tucson: University of Arizona Press, 1988.

Beck, Warren A. *New Mexico: A History of Four Centuries.* Norman: University of Oklahoma Press, 1962.

Bell, Bob Boze. *The Illustrated Life and Times of Billy the Kid.* Phoenix: Tri Star-Boze Publications, 1992, 1996.

Bellesiles, Michael. *Arming America: The Origins of a National Gun Culture*. Brooklyn, N.Y.: Soft Skull Press, 2003.

Berry, Susan, and Sharman Apt Russell. *Built to Last: An Architectural History of Silver City, New Mexico*. Silver City, N.M.: Silver City Museum Society, 1995.

Bird, Isabella. *A Lady's Life in the Rocky Mountains*. Norman: University of Oklahoma Press, 1999.

Blevins, Winfred. *Dictionary of the American West*. New York: Facts on File, 1993.

Boddington, Craig, ed. *America: The Men and Their Guns That Made Her Great*. Los Angeles: Petersen Publishing Co., 1981.

Bourke, John. *On the Border with Crook*. New York: Charles Scribner's Sons, 1891.

Bowman, John S., gen. ed. *The World Almanac of the American West*. New York: World Almanac, imprint of Pharos Books, 1986.

Brothers, Mary Hudson. *Billy the Kid*. Farmington, N.M.: Hustler Press, 1949.

Brown, J. Cabell. *Calabazas or Amusing Recollections of an Arizona City*. San Francisco: Valleau & Peterson, 1892.

Brown, Dee. *The American West*. New York: Simon & Schuster, 1994.

Brown, Richard Maxwell. "Violence," *The Oxford History of the American West*, ed. Clyde A. Milner II, Carol A. O'Connor, and Martha A. Sandweiss. New York and Oxford, U.K.: Oxford University Press, 1994.

Bruns, Roger A. *The Bandit Kings: From Jesse James to Pretty Boy Floyd*. New York: Crown Publishers, 1995.

Bryan, Howard. *Wildest of the Wild West: True Tales of a Frontier Town on the Santa Fe Trail*. Santa Fe: Clear Light Publishers, 1988.

Burns, Walter Noble. *The Saga of Billy the Kid*. Garden City, N.Y.: Doubleday, Page & Co., 1926.

Butler, Anne M. *Daughters of Joy, Sisters of Misery: Prostitutes in the American West, 1865–90*. Urbana and Chicago: University of Illinois Press, 1987.

Campbell, Randolph B. *Gone to Texas: A History of the Lone Star State*. New York and Oxford, U.K.: Oxford University Press, 2003.

Casey, F. R. *The Western Peace Officer: A Legacy of Law and Order*. Norman: University of Oklahoma Press, 1972.

Cather, Willa. *Death Comes for the Archbishop*. New York: Alfred A. Knopf, 1926.

Cawelti, John G. *The Six-Gun Mystique*. Bowling Green, Ohio: Bowling Green University Popular Press, 1971.

Cline, Donald. *Alias Billy the Kid: The Man behind the Legend*. Santa Fe: Sunstone Press, 1986.

———. *Antrim & Billy*. College Station, Tex.: Creative Publishing Company, 1990.

Coe, George C. *Frontier Fighter*. Chicago: Lakeside Press, 1984.

The Columbian History of Education in Kansas. Topeka: Hamilton Printing Company, 1893.

Conklin, E. *Picturesque Arizona*. New York: Continent Stereoscopic Company, 1878.

Connable, Alfred, and Edward Silberfarb. *Tigers of Tammany: Nine Men Who Ran New York*. New York: Holt, Rinehart and Winston, 1967.

Cramer, T. Dudley. *The Pecos Ranchers in the Lincoln County War*. Oakland, Calif.: Branding Iron Press, 1996.

Cutler, William G. *History of the State of Kansas*. Chicago: A. T. Andreas' Western Historical Publishing Co., 1882–1883.

Dean, Eric T., Jr. *Shook over Hell: Post-Traumatic Stress, Vietnam, and the Civil War*. Cambridge, Mass., and London: Harvard University Press, 1997.

Dunlap, Ralph. *Masons in Early Lincoln County prior to 1900*. Lincoln, N.M.: Lincoln Masonic Foundation, 1994.

Dykes, J. C. *Billy the Kid: The Bibliography of a Legend*. Albuquerque: University of New Mexico Press, 1952.

Ellis, Richard N., ed. *New Mexico Historic Documents*. Albuquerque: University of New Mexico Press, 1975.

Erdoes, Richard. *Saloons of the Old West*. Salt Lake City and Chicago: Howe Brothers, 1985.

Farish, Thomas Edwin. *History of Arizona*, volume 2. San Francisco: Filmer Brothers Electrotype Company, 1915.

Foner, Eric, and John A. Garraty, ed. *The Reader's Companion to American History*. Boston: Houghton Mifflin Company, 1991.

Friedman, Lawrence M. *Crime and Punishment in American History*. New York: HarperCollins, 1993.

Fulton, Maurice G. *History of the Lincoln County War*. Tucson: University of Arizona Press, 1968.

Garrett, Pat. *The Authentic Life of Billy, The Kid, The Noted Desperado of the Southwest, Whose Deeds of Daring and Blood Made His Name a Terror in New Mexico, Arizona and Northern Mexico*. Norman: University of Oklahoma Press, 1954.

Gibson, A. M. *The Life and Death of Colonel Albert Jennings Fountain*. Norman: University of Oklahoma Press, 1965.

Giese, Dale F. *Forts of New Mexico*. Silver City, N.M.: Privately printed, 1991.

Goetzmann, William H., and William N. Goetzmann. *The West of the Imagination*. New York and London: W. W. Norton, 1986.

Golway, Terry. *The Irish in America*. New York: Hyperion, 1997.

Haak, W. A. *Copper Bottom Tales: Historic Sketches from Gila County*. Globe, Ariz.: Gila County Historical Society, 1991.

Harris, Richard. *National Trust Guide Santa Fe*. New York: John Wiley & Sons, 1997.

Hart, Herbert M. *Old Forts of the Far West*. New York: Bonanza Books, by arrangement with Superior Publishing Company, Seattle, 1965.

Henn, Walter R. *A Stroll thru Old Lincolntown*. Lincoln, N.M.: Lincoln County Historical Publications, 1996.

Hertzog, Peter. *La Fonda: The Inn of Santa Fe*. Santa Fe: Press of the Territorian, 1962.

———. *Little Known Facts about Billy the Kid*. Santa Fe: Press of the Territorian, 1963.

Hine, Robert V., and John Mack Faragher. *The American West: A New Interpretive History*. New Haven and London: Yale University Press, 2000.

Hobsbawm, Eric J. *Social Bandits and Primitive Rebels*. Glencoe, Ill.: Free Press, 1959.

Hoig, Stan. *Jesse Chisholm: Ambassador of the Plains*. Niwot: University Press of Colorado, 1991.

Hollon, W. Eugene. *Frontier Violence: Another Look*. New York: Oxford University Press, 1974.

Horn, Calvin. *New Mexico's Troubled Years: The Story of the Early Territorial Governors*. Albuquerque: Horn & Wallace, 1963.

Hough, Emerson. *The Story of the Outlaw*. New York: Grosset & Dunlap, 1905.

Hoyt, Henry F. *A Frontier Doctor*. Chicago: R. R. Donnelley & Sons, 1979.

Hunter, J. Marvin. *The Trail Drivers of Texas*. Austin: University of Texas Press, 1985.

Jacobson, Joel. *Such Men as Billy the Kid*. Lincoln and London: University of Nebraska Press, 1994.

Josephson, Matthew. *The Robber Barons: The Great American Capitalists 1861–1901*. New York: Harcourt, Brace and Co., 1934.

Julyan, Robert. *The Place Names of New Mexico*, rev. ed. Albuquerque: University of New Mexico Press, 1998.

Kadlec, Robert F., ed. *They Knew Billy the Kid: Interviews with Old-Time New Mexicans*. Santa Fe: Ancient City Press, 1987.

Kaler, S. P., and R. H. Manning. *History of Whitley County, Indiana*. Indianapolis: B. F. Bowen & Co., 1907.

Keleher, William A. *The Maxwell Land Grant: A New Mexico Item*. Santa Fe: Rydal Press, 1942.

———. *The Fabulous Frontier*. Santa Fe: Rydal Press, 1945.

———. *Turmoil in New Mexico 1846–1868*. Santa Fe: Rydal Press, 1952.

———. *Violence in Lincoln County, 1869–1881*. Albuquerque: University of New Mexico Press, 1957.

Klasner, Lily. *My Girlhood among Outlaws*. Tucson: University of Arizona Press, 1972.

Kooistra, Paul. *Criminals as Heroes: Structure, Power & Identity*. Bowling Green, Ohio: Bowling Green State University Popular Press, 1989.

Koop, Waldo E. *Billy the Kid: The Trail of a Kansas Legend*. Wichita: Kansas City Posse of the Westerners, 1965.

Lamar, Howard Robert. *The Far Southwest 1846–1912: A Territorial History*. New Haven and London: Yale University Press, 1966.

Lavash, Donald R. *William Brady: Tragic Hero of the Lincoln County War*. Santa Fe: Sunstone Press, 1987.

Leckie, William H. *The Buffalo Soldiers: A Narrative of the Negro Cavalry in the West*. Norman: University of Oklahoma Press, 1967.

Libert, Uchill Ida. *Howdy, Sucker! What P. T. Barnum Did in Colorado*. Denver: Pioneer Peddler Press, 2001.

Lupiano, Vincent dePaul, and Ken W. Sayers. *It Was a Very Good Year: A Cultural History of the United States from 1776 to the Present*. Holbrook, Mass.: Bob Adams, Inc., 1994.

Lyon, Thomas J. "The Literary West," *The Oxford History of the American West*, ed. Clyde A. Milner II, Carol A. O'Conner, and Martha A. Sandweiss. New York: Oxford University Press, 1994.

McCarty, John L. *Maverick Town: The Story of Old Tascosa*. Norman: University of Oklahoma Press, 1946.

McKee, John DeWitt. "The Unrelenting Land," *The Spell of New Mexico*, ed. Tony Hillerman. Albuquerque: University of New Mexico Press, 1976.

Melzer, Richard. *When We Were Young in the West: True Stories of Childhood*. Santa Fe: Sunstone Press, 2003.

Metz, Leon G. *Pat Garrett: The Story of a Western Lawman*. Norman: University of Oklahoma Press, 1973.

———. *El Paso Chronicles: A Record of Historical Events in El Paso, Texas*. El Paso: Mangan Books, 1993.

Miller, Nyle H., and Joseph W. Snell. *Why the West Was Wild: A Contemporary Look at the Antics of Some Highly Publicized Kansas Cowtown Personalities*. Norman: University of Oklahoma Press, 1963.

Mooney, Volney P. *History of Butler County*. Lawrence, Kan.: Standard Printing Company, 1916. Transcribed by Carolyn Ward, Columbus, Kansas.

Mullin, Robert N. *The Boyhood of Billy the Kid*. Southwestern Studies, vol. 5, no. 1, Monograph no. 17. El Paso: Texas Western Press, 1967.

Munk, Joseph A. *Arizona Sketches*. New York: Grafton Press, 1905.

Myers, Lee. *Fort Stanton, New Mexico: The Military Years 1855–1896*. Lincoln, N.M.: Lincoln County Historical Society Publications, 1988.

Nolan, Frederick. *The Life & Death of John Henry Tunstall*. Albuquerque: University of New Mexico Press, 1965.

———. *Bad Blood: The Life and Times of the Horrell Brothers*. Stillwater, Okla.: Barbed Wire Press, 1994.

———. *The West of Billy the Kid*. Norman: University of Oklahoma Press, 1998.

Nonte, George C., Jr., *Firearms Encyclopedia*. New York: Harper & Row, 1973.

Nordholt, Jan Willem Schulte. *The Myth of the West: America as the Last Empire*. Grand Rapids, Mich.: William B. Eerdmans Publishing Company, 1995.

Nunn, Joan. *Fashion in Costume, 1200–2000*. Chicago: New Amsterdam Books, A & C Black Ltd., 2000.

Nusbaum, Rosemary. *The City Different and the Palace*. Santa Fe: Sunstone Press, 1978.

Ondaatje, Michael. *The Collected Works of Billy the Kid*. New York: W. W. Norton, 1970.

Otero, Miguel Antonio, Jr. *The Real Billy the Kid: With New Light on the Lincoln County War*. Houston: Arte Público Press, 1998.

Ott, Katherine. *Fevered Lives: Tuberculosis in American Culture since 1870*. Cambridge, Mass.: Harvard University Press, 1996.

Parish, William J. *The Charles Ilfeld Company: A Study of the Rise and Decline of Mercantile Capitalism in New Mexico*. Cambridge, Mass.: Harvard University Press, 1961.

Parker, Lowell. *Arizona Towns and Tales*. Phoenix: Phoenix Newspapers, Inc., 1975.

Pearce, T. M., ed. *New Mexico Place Names*. Albuquerque: University of New Mexico Press, 1965.

Prassel, Frank Richard. *The Great American Outlaw: A Legacy of Fact and Fiction*. Norman: University of Oklahoma Press, 1993.

Priestley, Lee, with Marquita Peterson. *Billy the Kid: The Good Side of a Bad Man*. Las Cruces, N.M.: Yucca Tree Press, 1993.

Pritchard, Russ A., Jr. *Civil War Weapons and Equipment*. Guilford, Conn.: Lyons Press, 2003.

Rasch, Philip J. *Gunsmoke in Lincoln County*. Laramie: National Association for Outlaw and Lawman History, Inc., in affiliation with the University of Wyoming, 1997.

———. *Warriors of Lincoln County*. Laramie: National Association for Outlaw and Lawman History, Inc., in affiliation with the University of Wyoming, 1998.

Rasch, Philip J., with Allan Radbourne. *Trailing Billy the Kid*. Laramie: National Association for Outlaw and Lawman History, Inc., in affiliation with the University of Wyoming, 1995.

Reid, Robert Leonard. *America, New Mexico*. Tucson: University of Arizona Press, 1998.

Ridley, Jasper. *The Freemasons: A History of the World's Most Powerful Secret Society*. New York: Arcade Publishing, 1999.

Roberts, David. *A Newer World: Kit Carson, John C. Frémont, and the Claiming of the American West*. New York: Simon & Schuster, 2000.

Robinson, Pauline Durrett, and R. L. Robertson. *Tascosa: Historic Site in the Texas Panhandle*. Amarillo, Tex.: Paramount Publishing Company, n.d.

Rosa, Joseph G. *The Gunfighter: Man or Myth?* Norman: University of Oklahoma Press, 1969.

Rosenberg, Bruce A. *The Code of the West*. Bloomington: Indiana University Press, 1982.

Russell, Bill, and Delbert Trew. *Twice Told Tales of the Llano Estacado*. Lubbock, Tex.: Hurricane Printing, 2003.

Ryan, John. *Fort Stanton and Its Community, 1855–1896*. Las Cruces, N.M.: Yucca Tree Press, 1998.

Schlereth, Thomas J. *Victorian America: Transformations in Everyday Life*. New York: HarperCollins, 1991.

Shoumatoff, Alex. *Legends of the American Desert*. New York: Alfred A. Knopf, 1997.

Slotkin, Richard. *Gunfighter Nation: The Myth of the Frontier in Twentieth-Century America*. Norman: University of Oklahoma Press, 1998.

Smith, Henry Nash. *Virgin Land: The American West as Symbol and Myth*. Cambridge, Mass., and London: Harvard University Press, 1978.

Southworth, Dave. *Gunfighters of the Old West*. Round Rock, Tex.: Wild Horse Publishing, 1997.

Steiner, Stan. *The Waning of the West*. New York: St. Martin's Press, 1989.

Steckmesser, Kent Ladd. *The Western Hero in History and Legend*. Norman: University of Oklahoma Press, 1965.

Tatum, Stephen. *Inventing Billy the Kid*. Tucson: University of Arizona Press, 1997.

Tefertiller, Casey. *Wyatt Earp: The Life behind the Legend*. New York: John Wiley & Sons, Inc., 1997.

Tobias, Henry J., and Charles E. Woodhouse. *Santa Fe: A Modern History 1880–1990*. Albuquerque: University of New Mexico Press, 2001.

Trimble, Marshall. *Arizona: A Cavalcade of History*. Tucson: Rio Nuevo Publishers, 2003.

Tuska, Jon. *Billy the Kid: A Handbook*. Lincoln and London: University of Nebraska Press, 1983.

Twitchell, Ralph Emerson. *The Leading Facts of New Mexico*, vol. 2. Albuquerque: Horn & Wallace, 1963.

Utley, Robert M. *Four Fighters of Lincoln County*. Albuquerque: University of New Mexico Press, 1986.

———. *High Noon in Lincoln County: Violence on the Western Frontier*. Albuquerque: University of New Mexico Press, 1987.

———. *Billy the Kid: A Short and Violent Life*. Lincoln and London: University of Nebraska Press, 1989.

Wallace, Irving. *The Fabulous Showman: The Life and Times of P. T. Barnum*. New York: Alfred A. Knopf, 1959.

Wallis, Michael. *The Real Wild West: The 101 Ranch and the Making of the American West*. New York: St. Martin's Press, 1999.

———. *Heaven's Window: A Journey through Northern New Mexico*. Portland, Ore.: Graphic Arts Center Publishing, 2001.

———, and Suzanne Fitzgerald Wallis. *Songdog Diary: 66 Stories from the Road*. Tulsa, Okla.: Council Oak Books, 1996.

Ward, Geoffrey, with Ric Burns and Ken Burns. *The Civil War*. New York: Vintage Books, 1994.

Weber, David J., ed. *Foreigners in Their Native Land: Historical Roots of the Mexican Americans*. Albuquerque: University of New Mexico Press, 1973.

Weddle, Jerry. *Antrim Is My Stepfather's Name*. Phoenix: Arizona Historical Society, 1993.

Weigle, Marta, and Peter White. *The Lore of New Mexico*. Albuquerque: University of New Mexico Press, 1988.

Werner, M. R. *Barnum*. New York: Garden City Publishing Co., 1927.

Westphall, Victor. *Thomas Benton Catron and His Era*. Tucson: University of Arizona Press, 1973.

Wheeler, Keith. *The Townsmen*. New York: Time-Life Books, 1975.

Wilson, Chris. *The Myth of Santa Fe: Creating a Modern Regional Tradition*. Albuquerque: University of New Mexico Press, 1997.

Wilson, John P. *Merchants, Guns, and Money: The Story of Lincoln County and Its Wars*. Santa Fe: Museum of New Mexico Press, 1987.

Wills, Garry. *A Necessary Evil: A History of American Distrust of Government*. New York: Simon & Schuster, 2002.

Wood, Edward W., Jr. *Beyond the Weapons of Our Fathers*. Golden, Colo.: Fulcrum Publishing, 2002.

Howard Zinn. *A People's History of the United States: 1492 to Present* Rev. and updated ed. New York: HarperPerennial, 1995.

PERIODICALS, PAPERS, AND JOURNALS

Ackerly, Neal W., Ph.D. "A Navajo Diaspora: The Long Walk to Hwéedi." Silver City, N.M.: Dos Rios Consultants, 1998.

Buchtel, W. H. "A Paradise for Dyspeptics and Consumptives: The Climate of Colorado." February 1873, Western History Photography Collection of Denver Public Library.

Burchard, P. R. "Our Educational Outlook." *Scribner's Monthly*, vol. 4, no. 1 (May 1872).

Colwell-Chanthaphonh, Chip. Center for Desert Archaeology, Tucson, Arizona, "The 'Camp Grant Massacre' in the Historical Imagination," a paper presented April 25–26, 2003, at the Arizona History Convention, Tempe, Arizona.

Forrest, Earle R. "The Fabulous Sierra Bonita." *Journal of Arizona History*, vol. 6, no. 3 (Autumn 1965).

Hill, Gertrude. "Henry Clay Hooker: King of the Sierra Bonita." *Arizoniana: The Journal of Arizona History*, vol. 2, no. 4 (Winter 1961).

Hughes, Matt S., Grand Orator. "A Triad of Masonic Ideals," delivered 1912, California Grand Oration, Grand Lodge, F & A. M. of California.

Hutton, Paul Andrew. "Dreamscape Desperado." *New Mexico Magazine*, vol. 68, no. 6 (June 1990).

Keiger, Dale. "Why Metaphor Matters." *Johns Hopkins Magazine* (February 1998).

Kildare, Maurice. "Saga of the Gallant Sheriff." *The West: True Stories of the Old West*, vol. 9, no. 3 (August 1968).

Lyon, Peter. "The Wild, Wild West." *American Heritage*, vol. 11, no. 5 (August 1960).

McMurtry, Larry. "Inventing the West." *New York Review of Books*, vol. 47, no. 130 (August 10, 2000).

Muske-Dukes, Carol. "Howdy, Pardner," review of *Cowboy*, by Sara Davidson. *Washington Post*, June 14, 1999.

New Mexico Quarterly, vol. 27, no. 3 (Autumn 1957).

O'Toole, Fintan. "The Many Stories of Billy the Kid." *New Yorker* (December 28, 1998–January 4, 1999).

Park, Joseph F. "The 1903 'Mexican Affair' at Clifton." *Journal of Arizona History*, vol. 18 (Summer 1977).

Rasch, Philip J., and R. N. Mullin. "New Light on the Legend of Billy the Kid." *New Mexico Folklore Record*, vol. 7 (1952–1953).

———, and R. N. Mullin. "Dim Trails: The Pursuit of the McCarty Family." *New Mexico Folklore Record*, vol. 8 (1953–1954).

Real West, vol. 28 (August 1985), pp. 22–27.

Rossel, John. "The Chisholm Trail." *Kansas Historical Quarterly* vol. 5, no. 1 (February, 1936).

Root, George A. "Ferries in Kansas, Part IX—Arkansas River: Concluded." *Kansas Historical Quarterly*, vol. 5, no. 2 (May, 1936).

Sanchez, Lynda A. "They Loved Billy the Kid." *True West*, vol. 31, no. 1 (January 1984).

Slatta, Richard. "Eric J. Hobsbawm's Social Bandit: A Critique and Revision." *A Contra Corriente: A Journal on Social History and Literature in Latin America*, vol. 1, no. 1 (Fall 2004).

Tanner, Becky. "Early Wichita Helped Put 'Wild' in the Old West." *Wichita Eagle*, June 19, 2004.

Tennert, Robert A. "A Different Perspective: Victorian Travelers in Arizona, 1860–1900." *Journal of Arizona History*, vol. 29, no. 4 (Winter 1988).

Vogt, William M. Editorial, *Wild West* (February 1995).

Ward, Geoffrey C. "Henry the Kid." *American Heritage*, vol. 41, no. 3 (April 1990).

Weisberg, Robert. "Values, Violence, and the Second Amendment: American Character, Constitutionalism, and Crime." Stanford Law School, Public Law Research Paper No. 37. *Houston Law Review*, http://papers.ssrn.com/sol3/papers.cfm?abstract_id=311082.

Yost, Genevieve. "History of Lynchings in Kansas." *Kansas Historical Quarterly*, vol. 2, no. 2 (May 1933).

ELECTRONIC DOCUMENTS AND SOURCES

Ancestry.com

Ancestry.com, *Irish Immigrants: New York Port Arrival Records, 1846–1851* (database online). Provo, Utah: Ancestry.com, 2001. Original data: *Famine Irish Entry Project, 1845–1851*. Electronic database from the National Archives and Records Administration, Washington, D.C.

Ancestry.com, *1850 United States Federal Census* (database online). Provo, Utah: MyFamily .com, Inc., 2004. Original data: *1850 United States Federal Census*. M432, 1009 rolls. National Archives and Records Administration, Washington, D.C.

Bidstrup, Scott. "A Shameful Legacy: The Shocking Mismanagement of America's Public Lands," 2000, 2002, essay in hypertext, www.bidstrup.com/publiclands.htm.

Billy the Kid Historic Preservation Society (BTKHPS), www.billythekidhistoricpreservation .com.

Girand, Jan, ed. *Roswell Web Magazine*, www.roswellwebmag.com/main.htm, Roswell, New Mexico, April 21, 2004.

Handbook of Texas Online, s.v. "MOODY, ROBERT," www.tsha.utexas.edu/handbook/online/ articles/view/MM/fmo2.html (accessed May 1, 2005).

Handbook of Texas Online, s.v. "SALT WAR OF SAN ELIZARIO," www.tsha.utexas.edu/ handbook/online/articles/SS/jcs1.html.

Handbook of Texas Online, s.v. "NEWMAN, SIMEON HARRISON," www.tsha.utexas.edu/ handbook/online/articles/view/NN/fne41.html.

Hoosiersoldiers.com.

RootsWeb.com.

United States National Archives. *Civil War Compiled Military Service Records* (database online). Provo, Utah: Ancestry.com, 1999.

Voices, KanColl's online magazine, vol. 3, no. 1 (Spring 1999).

www.aboutbillythekid.com

www.denvergov.org.

Government Documents

Library of Congress, Manuscript Division, WPA Federal Writers' Project Collection. Manuscripts from the Federal Writer's Project, "WPA Life Histories from New Mexico."
Report of the Adjutant General of the State of Kansas, 1861–65.
Rothman, Hal K. *Promise Beheld and the Limits of Place: A Historic Resource Study of Carlsbad Caverns and Guadalupe Mountains National Parks and the Surrounding Areas.* Washington D.C.: U.S. Government Printing Office, 1998).
Scurlock, Dan. *From the Rio to the Sierra: An Environmental History of the Middle Rio Grande Basin.* Fort Collins, Colo.: Rocky Mountain Research Station, U.S. Department of Agriculture, May 1998.

Newspapers/Magazines

Alamogordo (New Mexico) *News*
Albuquerque Journal
American Heritage
American West
Arizona Citizen (Tucson)
Arizona Highways
Arizona Weekly Star (Tucson)
B.T.K.O.G. Gazette
Daily Kansas State Record (Topeka)
Daily New Mexican (Santa Fe)
Denver Post
El Defensor Chieftain, Internet edition (Socorro)
El Paso (Texas) *Times*
Ford County (New Mexico) *Globe*
Fort Worth Star-Telegram
Grant County Herald (Silver City, New Mexico)
Grant County Independent (Silver City, New Mexico)
Harper's Weekly
Indianapolis World
Journal of American Folklore
Journal of Popular Culture
Las Cruces (New Mexico) *Borderer*
Las Vegas (New Mexico) *Daily Optic*
Las Vegas (New Mexico) *Gazette*
Lincoln County (New Mexico) *News*
Mesilla (New Mexico) *News*

Mesilla Valley (New Mexico) *Independent*
New Mexico Magazine
New Mexico Quarterly
New York Times
Real West
Silver City (New Mexico) *Enterprise*
Silver City (New Mexico) *Herald*
Silver City (New Mexico) *Independent*
Silver City (New Mexico) *Mining Life*
Santa Fe New Mexican
Tucson (Arizona) *Citizen*
Walnut Valley Times (El Dorado, Kansas)
Wichita (Kansas) *Eagle*
Wichita (Kansas) *Tribune*
Wichita (Kansas) *Vidette*
Wichita (Kansas) *Weekly Eagle*

INTERVIEWS

Bob Boze Bell, interview by author, Cave Creek, Arizona, November 4, 2004.
Jim Blair, 1937, unpublished manuscript in the files of the New Mexico Writers' Project, Museum of New Mexico, Santa Fe, compiled by Frances E. Totty.
Ellen Bradbury-Reid, interview by author, September 26, 2005.
Nora Henn, interview by author, Lincoln, New Mexico, November 20, 2004.
DeAnne Kessler, interview by author, Lincoln, New Mexico, November 19, 2004.
Jack Rigney, interview by author, Lincoln, New Mexico, November 20, 2004.
Gwendolyn Rogers, interview by author, Lincoln, New Mexico, November 19, 2004.
James Sanchez, interview by author, Lincoln, New Mexico, November 19, 2004.
Chauncey O. Truesdell, Phoenix, Arizona, from Silver City Museum files, January 9, 1952.

ACKNOWLEDGMENTS

MANY PEOPLE ARE convinced that the more books one writes, the easier the process of writing a book becomes. In fact, the opposite is true, at least for me. The oft-quoted line attributed to sportswriter Red Smith says it best: "Writing is easy. All you do is sit down at a typewriter and open a vein." I wholeheartedly agree. This biography is my fourteenth published book, and nothing about the act of writing it was in any way easy. Without the help I received from a host of sources, including individuals and institutions, I would have bled to death at my computer keyboard, and this book would not have been written.

First and foremost, my undying gratitude to my wife, best friend, role model, and creative partner, Suzanne Fitzgerald Wallis. Once more, Suzanne stuck by me through the birthing of yet another book. Her encouragement, advice, and constructive criticism helped make this book a reality. Kudos also to our companion Cosmo, a feline son of the Osage prairie and constant muse.

My lasting thanks to my son, John, who not only accompanied me on a key research trek in Arizona but also was always there to act as a sounding board and source of creative wisdom. Whether at John's Arizona desert abode with his loving wife, Tamra, and my granddaughter, sweet Charlotte, or in one of the Kid's old haunts, the time we spent together will stay with me forever.

On the home front, throughout the arduous writing process, my dear friends Steve and Sue Gerkin offered me their constant support at the times I needed it the most. The fine pair of spurs Steve gave me as the writing neared an end will always be one of my revered totems. *Muchas gracias* to you both.

My deepest thanks and praise to my agent and friend forever, James Fitzgerald. Among the luckiest days of my life were those when I first collided with the Fitzgerald clan and when I later earned their embrace. As agent and literary guide none is better than Jim Fitzgerald. The diligent Anne Garrett, Jim's associate at the James Fitzgerald Agency, deserves high praise for her encouragement and assistance.

At W. W. Norton, my longtime friend and editor Robert Weil showed as always his deft hand and critical eye when it comes to the fine art of precision editing. Bob is a caring and astute editor, and my loyalty to him goes back many years to some of my earliest books. Simply put, Bob Weil is the very best at what he does, sculpting the written word. His capable assistant, Tom Mayer, is yet another in a long line of editorial protégés whom Bob has helped mold into some of the leading forces in publishing today. Thanks so much, Tom, for your incredible help with this book.

Robert McCubbin is known for his tasty chile con queso, his remarkable dog, Bear ("cross between a Pomeranian and a stuffed toy"), and his vast library, including an exceptional collection of Old West photographs and library. I have had the pleasure of sampling the chile con queso and playing with Bear (who passed away in May 2006), and some of Bob's finest photograph portraits are found in this book. Thanks to Bob, who always speaks the truth, for making this book complete.

My gratitude also goes to Bob Boze Bell, Cave Creek, Arizona, and Buckeye Blake, Weatherford, Texas, two of my favorite artists and genuine Old West aficionados. Gents, your artistic interpretations of the Kid and the rough-and-tumble times when he lived are remarkable and much appreciated. *Muchas gracias, amigos.*

Many authors long before me have told the story of Billy the Kid. I am indebted to all of them, especially the few that got it right. At the top of the list has to be Frederick Nolan, who early in my writing process offered me encouragement and sage wisdom. Other writers who influenced this book include Robert Utley, Jerry Weddle, Bob Boze Bell, William Keleher, and John Wilson.

In Lincoln County, New Mexico, I owe special thanks to many people, especially Nora Henn, a persistent researcher and careful writer, who opened her home to Suzanne and me. Affectionately known as Mother Henn, she provided historical context and the lasting memory of a cozy afternoon spent sipping strong coffee and digesting the insight of a genuine wisdom keeper.

I am indebted to Karen Mills, historical records clerk for Lincoln County, for introducing me to Mother Henn as well as pointing me toward several other key sources of information. Karen made available invaluable records and relevant documents and also never missed when recommending the best dining spots in Carrizozo and Capitan.

While researching in the historic town of Lincoln, we were smart enough to bunk at Casa de Patrón, in our opinion the best bed-and-breakfast we ever encountered, bar none. After hours spent researching, interviewing, and chasing ghosts, we sat by the fire and dreamed of the ambrosia that awaited us the next day at the breakfast table. Jerry and Cleis Jordan are consummate hosts. They not only made us comfortable but also shared their own passion for the history and culture of New Mexico, the land of little time.

Others I am indebted to for their help and guidance include: DeAnn Kessler, manager, and Gwendolyn Rogers, exhibits, Lincoln State Monument, Lincoln, New Mexico; Jack Rigney, former monument manager, Lincoln, New Mexico; Scott Smith, manager, Fort Sumner State Monument, Fort Sumner, New Mexico; Brian Graney, senior archivist, and Melissa A. Salazar, C.A., archives bureau chief, New Mexico State Records and Archives, Santa Fe, New Mexico; Janean Grissom, Taiban, New Mexico; Tammie Maddox, Lincoln County Clerk, Carrizozo, New Mexico; Michael Romero Taylor, Santa Fe, New Mexico; William B. Boehm, curator, unpublished materials, Rio Grande Historical Collections, University Library, New Mexico State University, Las Cruces, New Mexico; Susan Sutton, Reference Services, Indiana Historical Society Collections & Library, and William Henry Smith Memorial Library, Indianapolis, Indiana; Mary Nelson, Department of Special Collections, Wichita State University Libraries, Wichita, Kansas; Western History and Genealogy Department, Denver Public Library, Denver, Colorado; Susan Berry, director, Jackie Becker, curator of collections/photo archivist, and Pat Bennett, coordinator, Silver City Museum, Silver City, New Mexico; Tomas Jaehn, Fray Angelico Chavez History Library, Palace of the Governors, Santa Fe, New Mexico.

INDEX

Page numbers in *italics* refer to illustrations.

ABOUT THE AUTHOR

A BEST-SELLING AUTHOR and award-winning reporter, Michael Wallis is a historian and biographer of the American West who has gained national prominence for a body of work beginning in 1988 with his biography of Frank Phillips titled *Oil Man*.

His thirteen other books include *Route 66: The Mother Road*, credited with sparking the resurgence of interest in the highway, as well as *The Real Wild West: The 101 Ranch and the Creation of the American West; Mankiller: A Chief and Her People; Way Down Yonder in the Indian Nation;* and *Pretty Boy: The Life and Times of Charles Arthur Floyd.* His work has appeared in hundreds of national and international magazines and newspapers, including *Time, Life, People, Smithsonian, The New Yorker,* and the *New York Times.*

Wallis has won many prestigious awards and honors. They include the Will Rogers Spirit Award, the Western Heritage Award from the National Cowboy Hall & Western Heritage Museum, the Oklahoma Book Award from the Oklahoma Center for the Book, and the Best Western Non-fiction Award from the Western Writers of America.

He was inducted into the Writers Hall of Fame of America and the Oklahoma Professional Writer's Hall of Fame and was the first inductee into the Oklahoma Route 66 Hall of Fame. He received the Arrell Gibson Lifetime Achievement Award from the Oklahoma Center for the Book as well as the Lynn Riggs Award and the first John Steinbeck Award.

A charismatic speaker who has lectured extensively throughout the United States, Wallis was featured as the voice of the Sheriff in *Cars,* an animated feature film from Pixar Studios.

Wallis and his wife, Suzanne Fitzgerald Wallis, make their home in Tulsa, Oklahoma.